LES MURRAY

Collected Poems

Minerva

A Minerva Paperback
COLLECTED POEMS

First published in Great Britain 1991
by Carcanet Press Limited
This Minerva edition published 1992
by Mandarin Paperbacks
Michelin House, 81 Fulham Road, London SW3 6RB

Minerva is an imprint of the Octopus Publishing Group,
a division of Reed International Books Limited

A CIP catalogue record for this title
is available from the British Library
ISBN 0 7493 9859 0

Printed and bound in Great Britain
by Cox & Wyman Ltd, Reading, Berkshire

Contents

from THE ILEX TREE, *1965*

The Burning Truck   3
The Widower in the Country   4
Noonday Axeman   5
The Away-bound Train   7
Spring Hail   9
Driving Through Sawmill Towns   11

from THE WEATHERBOARD CATHEDRAL, *1969*

Evening Alone at Bunyah   13
The Princes' Land   17
Ill Music   19
Troop Train Returning   19
Blood   20
The Abomination   22
Once in a Lifetime, Snow   23
Recourse to the Wilderness   25
The Commercial Hotel   27
The Incendiary Method   28
An Absolutely Ordinary Rainbow   29
Working Men   31
A Walk with O'Connor   31
Senryu   33
The Ballad Trap   33

Hayfork Point 34

The Fire Autumn 34

The Canberra Remnant 37

from POEMS AGAINST ECONOMICS, *1972*

Toward the Imminent Days 38

Lament for the Country Soldiers 44

The Conquest 45

The Ballad of Jimmy Governor 48

SMLE 50

Vindaloo in Merthyr Tydfil 55

A Helicopter View of Terrestrial Stars 55

Incorrigible Grace 58

Walking to the Cattle Place

    1. Sanskrit 59

    2. Birds in Their Title Work Freeholds
       of Straw 59

    3. The Names of the Humble 61

    4. The Artery 63

    5. Death Words 65

    6. The Commonwealth of Manu 65

    7. Stockman Songs 67

    8. The Bush 68

    9. Poley Bullock Couplets 69

    10. The Boeotian Count 69

    11. Novilladas Democráticas 71

    12. Hall's Cattle 72

    13. Boöpis 74

    14. The Pure Food Act 75

    15. Gōlōka 76

from LUNCH AND COUNTER LUNCH, *1974*

József 81

Folklore 83

The Police: Seven Voices

1. *The Knuckle Garden*   84
2. *Plainclothes Park*   85
3. *Discontent, Reading Conan Doyle*   85
4. *Rostered Duty*   87
5. *The Lips Move During Anointing*   88
6. *The Breach*   89
7. *Sergeant Forby Lectures the Cadets*   91

Aqualung Shinto   93

The Canberra Suburbs' Infinite Extension   96

Thinking About Aboriginal Land Rights, I Visit
the Farm I Will Not Inherit   97

Their Cities, Their Universities   97

Kiss of the Whip   101

On the Wreckage of a Hijacked Airliner   102

Escaping Out There   102

Portrait of the Artist as a New World Driver   104

Company   105

Cycling in the Lake Country   106

Sidere Mens Eadem Mutato   111

The Broad Bean Sermon   115

The Action   117

The Edge of the Forest   118

from ETHNIC RADIO, *1977*

Lachlan Macquarie's First Language   120

The Euchre Game   120

The Mitchells   121

The Flying-fox Dreaming   122

Visiting Anzac in the Year of Metrication   123

The Powerline Incarnation   126

Sydney and the Bush   127

The Returnees 128

Spurwing Plover 131

Laconics: The Forty Acres 132

Creeper Habit 133

Tanka: The Coffee Shops 134

The Gallery 134

Employment for the Castes in Abeyance 137

The Cardiff Commonwealth Arts Festival Poetry
Conference 1965, Recalled 139

Driving to the Adelaide Festival 1976 via the
Murray Valley Highway 140

The Buladelah-Taree Holiday Song Cycle 141

The Swarm 151

Four Gaelic Poems

   1. *Free Kirk Cemetery, Northern
     New South Wales* *151*

   2. *A Skirl for Outsets* *152*

   3. *The Gum Forest* *153*

   4. *Elegy for Angus Macdonald of Cnoclinn* *155*

Rainwater Tank 157

The Future 158

Cowyard Gates 159

Immigrant Voyage 160

The Craze Field 164

from THE PEOPLE'S OTHERWORLD, *1983*

For a Jacobite Lady 166

The Grassfire Stanzas 167

Homage to the Launching-place 168

First Essay on Interest 169

The Fishermen at South Head 171

The Doorman 172

Anthropomorphics   173

The New Moreton Bay   173

The Sydney Highrise Variations
    1. Fuel Stoppage on Gladesville Road Bridge
      in the Year 1980   174
    2. View of Sydney, Australia, from Gladesville
      Road Bridge   175
    3. The Flight from Manhattan   176
    4. The C19–20   177
    5. The Recession of the Joneses   178

Quintets for Robert Morley   179

Bent Water in the Tasmanian Highlands   180

Equanimity   182

The Forest Hit by Modern Use   184

Shower   185

The Quality of Sprawl   186

Three Poems in Memory of My Mother,
Miriam Murray née Arnall
    Weights   188
    Midsummer Ice   188
    The Steel   189

Machine Portraits with Pendant Spaceman   195

The International Poetry Festivals Thing   199

Little Boy Impelling a Scooter   201

Self-portrait from a Photograph   202

The Hypogeum   203

An Immortal   204

Second Essay on Interest: the Emu   205

A Retrospect of Humidity   207

Flowering Eucalypt in Autumn   208

The Chimes of Neverwhere   209

The Smell of Coal Smoke   211

The Mouthless Image of God in the Hunter-Colo Mountains   212

Time Travel   214

Three Interiors   215

Morse   217

Late Snow in Edinburgh   218

Art History: the Suburb of Surrealls   219

The Dialectic of Dreams   220

Satis Passio   222

from THE DAYLIGHT MOON, 1987

Flood Plains on the Coast Facing Asia   224

Cumulus   228

Federation Style on the Northern Rivers   229

Easter 1984   232

Physiognomy on the Savage Manning River   233

The Dream of Wearing Shorts Forever   237

At the Aquatic Carnival   240

The Sleepout   242

Tropical Window   242

Louvres   243

The Edgeless   245

The Drugs of War   246

Letters to the Winner   247

The China Pear Trees   248

The Vol Sprung from Heraldry   250

The Megaethon: 1850, 1906–29   251

Fastness   254

1980 in a Street of Federation Houses   256

The Milk Lorry   258

The Butter Factory 259

Bats' Ultrasound 260

Roman Cage-cups 260

The Lake Surnames 262

Nocturne 263

Lotus Dam 264

At Min-Min Camp 265

Hearing Impairment 267

At Thunderbolt's Grave in Uralla 268

Infra Red 271

Poetry and Religion 272

Inverse Ballad 273

Relics of Sandy 274

Joker as Told 275

Writer in Residence 276

A Public Figure 277

The Young Woman Visitor 277

The Grandmother's Story 277

The Line 279

Extract from a Verse Letter to Dennis Haskell 280

Max Fabre's Yachts 281

The Man with the Hoe 282

Aspects of Language and War on the
Gloucester Road 284

The Idyll Wheel: Cycle of a Year at Bunyah,
New South Wales, April 1986–April 1987

    Preface 290

    APRIL
    Leaf Spring 291

    MAY
    When Bounty Is Down to Persimmons and Lemons 292

JUNE
The Kitchens   294

JULY
Midwinter Haircut   297

AUGUST
Forty Acre Ethno   298

SEPTEMBER
Mercurial   299

OCTOBER
Freshwater and Salt   300

NOVEMBER
The Misery Cord   302

DECEMBER
Infant Among Cattle   303

JANUARY
Variations on a Measure of Burns   304

FEBRUARY
Feb   305

MARCH
Masculeene, Cried the Bulls   307

APRIL
The Idyll Wheel   308

INDEX OF TITLES   311

INDEX OF FIRST LINES   315

Collected Poems

The Burning Truck

FOR MRS. MARGARET WELTON

It began at dawn with fighter planes:
they came in off the sea and didn't rise,
they leaped the sandbar one and one and one
coming so fast the crockery they shook down
off my kitchen shelves was spinning in the air
when they were gone.

They came in off the sea and drew a wave
of lagging cannon-shells across our roofs.
Windows spat glass, a truck took sudden fire,
out leaped the driver, but the truck ran on,
growing enormous, shambling by our street-doors,
coming and coming . . .

By every right in town, by every average
we knew of in the world, it had to stop,
fetch up against a building, fall to rubble
from pure force of burning, for its whole
body and substance were consumed with heat
but it would not stop.

And all of us who knew our place and prayers
clutched our verandah-rails and window-sills,
begging that truck between our teeth to halt,

3

keep going, vanish, strike . . . but set us free.
And then we saw the wild boys of the street
go running after it.

And as they followed, cheering, on it crept,
windshield melting now, canopy-frame a cage
torn by gorillas of flame, and it kept on
over the tramlines, past the church, on past
the last lit windows, and then out of the world
with its disciples.

The Widower in the Country

I'll get up soon, and leave my bed unmade.
I'll go outside and split off kindling wood
from the yellow-box log that lies beside the gate,
and the sun will be high, for I get up late now.

I'll drive my axe in the log and come back in
with my armful of wood, and pause to look across
the Christmas paddocks aching in the heat,
the windless trees, the nettles in the yard . . .
and then I'll go in, boil water and make tea.

This afternoon, I'll stand out on the hill
and watch my house away below, and how
the roof reflects the sun and makes my eyes
water and close on bright webbed visions smeared
on the dark of my thoughts to dance and fade away.
Then the sun will move on, and I will simply watch,
or work, or sleep. And evening will come on.

Getting near dark, I'll go home, light the lamp
and eat my corned-beef supper, sitting there
at the head of the table. Then I'll go to bed.
Last night I thought I dreamed—but when I woke
the screaming was only a possum ski-ing down
the iron roof on little moonlit claws.

Noonday Axeman

Axe-fall, echo and silence. Noonday silence.
Two miles from here, it is the twentieth century:
cars on the bitumen, powerlines vaulting the farms.
Here, with my axe, I am chopping into the stillness.

Axe-fall, echo and silence. I pause, roll tobacco,
twist a cigarette, lick it. All is still.
I lean on my axe. A cloud of fragrant leaves
hangs over me moveless, pierced everywhere by sky.

Here, I remember all of a hundred years:
candleflame, still night, frost and cattle bells,
the draywheels' silence final in our ears,
and the first red cattle spreading through the hills

and my great-great-grandfather here with his first sons,
who would grow old, still speaking with his Scots accent,
having never seen those highlands that they sang of.
A hundred years. I stand and smoke in the silence.

A hundred years of clearing, splitting, sawing,
a hundred years of timbermen, ringbarkers, fencers
and women in kitchens, stoking loud iron stoves
year in, year out, and singing old songs to their children

have made this silence human and familiar
no farther than where the farms rise into foothills,
and, in that time, how many have sought their graves
or fled to the cities, maddened by this stillness?

Things are so wordless. These two opposing scarves
I have cut in my red-gum squeeze out jewels of sap
and stare. And soon, with a few more axe-strokes,
the tree will grow troubled, tremble, shift its crown

and, leaning slowly, gather speed and colossally
crash down and lie between the standing trunks.
And then, I know, of the knowledge that led my forebears
to drink and black rage and wordlessness, there will be silence.

After the tree falls, there will reign the same silence
as stuns and spurs us, enraptures and defeats us,
as seems to some a challenge, and seems to others
to be waiting here for something beyond imagining.

Axe-fall, echo and silence. Unhuman silence.
A stone cracks in the heat. Through the still twigs, radiance
stings at my eyes. I rub a damp brow with a handkerchief
and chop on into the stillness. Axe-fall and echo.

The great mast murmurs now. The scarves in its trunk
crackle and squeak now, crack and increase as the hushing
weight of high branches heels outward, and commences
tearing and falling, and the collapse is tremendous.

Twigs fly, leaves puff and subside. The severed trunk
slips off its stump and drops along its shadow.
And then there is no more. The stillness is there
as ever. And I fall to lopping branches.

Axe-fall, echo and silence. It will be centuries
before many men are truly at home in this country,
and yet, there have always been some, in each generation,
there have always been some who could live in the presence of
    silence.

And some, I have known them, men with gentle broad hands,
who would die if removed from these unpeopled places,
some again I have seen, bemused and shy in the cities,
you have built against silence, dumbly trudging through noise

past the railway stations, looking up through the traffic
at the smoky halls, dreaming of journeys, of stepping
down from the train at some upland stop to recover
the crush of dry grass underfoot, the silence of trees.

Axe-fall, echo and silence. Dreaming silence.
Though I myself run to the cities, I will forever
be coming back here to walk, knee-deep in ferns,
up and away from this metropolitan century,

to remember my ancestors, axemen, dairymen, horse-breakers,
now coffined in silence, down with their beards and dreams,
who, unwilling or rapt, despairing or very patient,
made what amounts to a human breach in the silence,

made of their lives the rough foundation of legends—
men must have legends, else they will die of strangeness—
then died in their turn, each, after his own fashion,
resigned or agonized, from silence into great silence.

Axe-fall, echo and axe-fall. Noonday silence.
Though I go to the cities, turning my back on these hills,
for the talk and dazzle of cities, for the sake of belonging
for months and years at a time to the twentieth century,

the city will never quite hold me. I will be always
coming back here on the up-train, peering, leaning
out of the window to see, on far-off ridges,
the sky between the trees, and over the racket
of the rails to hear the echo and the silence.

I shoulder my axe and set off home through the stillness.

The Away-bound Train

FOR CON KIRILOFF

I stand in a house of trees, and it is evening:
at the foot of the stairs, a creek runs grey with sand.

A rocking, unending dim sound,
a racket as if of a train,
wears through my sleep, and I wake
to find it late afternoon

at which I sit up, rub my eyes—
beneath us, the carriage-wheels moan
on their winter-wet, wind-polished rails,
but the train hurries on, hurries on. .

The loco horn beams out its admonition
at a weatherboard village standing on the fields.

The near hills rise steeply and fall,
the hills farther off settle down:
I light up a cigarette, wipe
my breath from the cold window-pane.

The upland farms are all bare,
except where dark, storm-matted fern
has found its way down from the heights,
or landslides have brought down raw stone

for, outside, it's silent July,
when wet rocks stare from the hills
and thistles grow, and the rain
walks with the wind through the fields—

and this is my country, passing by me forever:
beyond these hills and paddocks lies the world.

Outside, it is timeless July,
when horses' hoofs puncture the chill
green ground, mud dogging their steps,
and summer's plough sleeps in the barn,

when rabbits camp up in the mouths
of flooded burrows, and dogs
under creekbanks wince at the thump
of a gun fired close to the earth.

The cold time, the season of clouds
beyond the end of the year,
when boxwood chunks glare in the stove—
but that is the past. I am here.

I look across the clear, receding landscape:
from a distant ridge, a horseman eyes the train.

The train never slackens its speed:
an iron bridge echoes, is gone,
on the far bank, twilit and tall,
the green timber gathers us in.

And we dash through the forest, my face,
reflected, wanders and sways
on the glass of the windowpane, and
I press my nose to my nose ...

the loco horn sounds far across the uplands:
a man with no past has all too many futures.

I take out a book, read a phrase
five times—and put the book down.
The window-sash chatters. My mind
trails far in the wake of the train

where, away in the left-behind hills,
through paddock and cattlecamp I
go drifting down valleys towards
the peopled country of sleep ...

I wait in the house. It is raining in the forest.
If I move or speak, the house will not be there.

Spring Hail

This is for spring and hail, that you may remember:
for a boy long ago, and a pony that could fly.

We had huddled together a long time in the shed
in the scent of vanished corn and wild bush birds,
and then the hammering faltered, and the torn
cobwebs ceased their quivering and hung still
from the nested rafters. We became uneasy
at the silence that grew about us, and came out.

The beaded violence had ceased. Fresh-minted hills
smoked, and the heavens swirled and blew away.
The paddocks were endless again, and all around
leaves lay beneath their trees, and cakes of moss.
Sheep trotted and propped, and shook out ice from their wool.
The hard blue highway that had carried us there
fumed as we crossed it, and the hail I scooped
from underfoot still bore the taste of sky
and hurt my teeth, and crackled as we walked.

This is for spring and hail, that you may remember
a boy long ago, and a pony that could fly.

With the creak and stop of a gate, we started to trespass:
my pony bent his head and drank up grass
while I ate ice, and wandered, and ate ice.
There was a peach tree growing wild by a bank
and under it and round, sweet dented fruit
weeping pale juice amongst hail-shotten leaves,
and this I picked up and ate till I was filled.

I sat on a log then, listening with my skin
to the secret feast of the sun, to the long wet worms
at work in the earth, and, deeper down, the stones
beneath the earth, uneasy that their sleep
should be troubled by dreams of water soaking down,
and I heard with my ears the creek on its bed of mould
moving and passing with a mothering sound.

This is for spring and hail, that you may remember
a boy long ago on a pony that could fly.

My pony came up then and stood by me,
waiting to be gone. The sky was now
spotless from dome to earth, and balanced there
on the cutting-edge of mountains. It was time
to leap to the saddle and go, a thunderbolt whirling
sheep and saplings behind, and the rearing fence
that we took at a bound, and the old, abandoned shed

forgotten behind, and the paddock forgotten behind.
Time to shatter peace and lean into spring
as into a battering wind, and be rapidly gone.

It was time, high time, the highest and only time
to stand in the stirrups and shout out, blind with wind
for the height and clatter of ridges to be topped
and the racing downward after through the lands
of floating green and bridges and flickering trees.
It was time, as never again it was time
to pull the bridle up, so the racketing hooves
fell silent as we ascended from the hill
above the farms, far up to where the hail
formed and hung weightless in the upper air,
charting the birdless winds with silver roads
for us to follow and be utterly gone.

This is for spring and hail, that you may remember
a boy and a pony long ago who could fly.

Driving Through Sawmill Towns

I

In the high cool country,
having come from the clouds,
down a tilting road
into a distant valley,
you drive without haste. Your windscreen parts the forest,
swaying and glancing, and jammed midday brilliance
crouches in clearings . . .
then you come across them,
the sawmill towns, bare hamlets built of boards
with perhaps a store,
perhaps a bridge beyond
and a little sidelong creek alive with pebbles.

2

The mills are roofed with iron, have no walls:
you look straight in as you pass, see lithe men working,

the swerve of a winch,
dim dazzling blades advancing
through a trolley-borne trunk
till it sags apart
in a manifold sprawl of weatherboards and battens.

The men watch you pass:
when you stop your car and ask them for directions,
tall youths look away—
it is the older men who
come out in blue singlets and talk softly to you.

Beside each mill, smoke trickles out of mounds
of ash and sawdust.

3

You glide on through town,
your mudguards damp with cloud.
The houses there wear verandahs out of shyness,
all day in calendared kitchens, women listen
for cars on the road,
lost children in the bush,
a cry from the mill, a footstep—
nothing happens.

The half-heard radio sings
its song of sidewalks.

Sometimes a woman, sweeping her front step,
or a plain young wife at a tankstand fetching water
in a metal bucket will turn round and gaze
at the mountains in wonderment,
looking for a city.

4

Evenings are very quiet. All around
the forest is there.
As night comes down, the houses watch each other:
a light going out in a window here has meaning.

You speed away through the upland,
glare through towns
and are gone in the forest, glowing on far hills.

On summer nights
ground-crickets sing and pause.
In the dark of winter, tin roofs sough with rain,
downpipes chafe in the wind, agog with water.
Men sit after tea
by the stove while their wives talk, rolling a dead match
between their fingers,
thinking of the future.

Evening Alone at Bunyah

I

My father, widowed, fifty-six years old,
sits washing his feet.
The innocent sly charm
is back in his eye of late years, and tonight
he's going dancing.

I wouldn't go tonight, he says to me
by way of apology. *You sure you won't come?*
What for? I ask. *You know I only dance
on bits of paper.* He nods and says, *Well, if
any ghosts come calling, don't let 'em eat my cake.*

I bring him a towel and study his feet afresh:
they make my own feel coarse. They are so small,

so delicate he can scarcely bear to walk
barefoot to his room to find his dancing shoes
and yet all day he works in hobnailed boots
out in the forest, clearing New South Wales.

No ghosts will come, Dad. I know you dote on cake.
I know how some women who bake it dote on you.
It gets them nowhere.
You are married still.

2

Home again from the cities of the world.
Cool night, and the valley relaxes after heat,
the earth contracts, the planks of the old house creak,
making one more adjustment, joist to nail,
nail to roof, roof to the touch of dew.

Smoke stains, rafters, whitewash rubbed off planks . . .
yet this is one house that Jerry built to last:
when windstorms came, and other houses lost
roofs and verandahs, this gave just enough
and went unscathed, for all the little rain
that sifted through cracks, the lamps puffed out by wind
sucked over the wallplate, and the occasional bat
silly with fear at having misplaced the dark.

When I was a child, my father was ashamed
of this shabby house. It signified for him
hard work and unjust poverty. There would come
a day when he'd tear it down and build afresh.
The day never came. But that's another poem.

No shame I felt in those days was my own.
It can be enough to read books and camp in a house.
Enough, at fourteen, to watch your father sit
at the breakfast table nursing his twelve-gauge
shotgun, awaiting the doubtful reappearance
of a snake's head at a crack in the cement
of the skillion fireplace floor.

The blood's been sluiced
away, and the long wrecked body of the snake
dug out and gone to ash these thirteen years,
but the crack's still there,
and the scores the buckshot ripped beside the stove.

3

There is a glow in the kitchen window now
that was not there in the old days. They have set
three streetlights up along the Gloucester road
for cows to stray by, and night birds to shun,
for the road itself's not paved, and there's no town
in the valley yet at all.
It is hoped there will be.

Today, out walking, I considered stones.
It used to be said that I must know each one
on the road by its first name, I was such a dawdler,
such a head-down starer.
I picked up
a chunk of milk-seamed quartz, thumbed off the clay,
let the dry light pervade it and collect,
eliciting shifting gleams, revealing how
the specific strength of a stone fits utterly
into its form and yet reflects the grain
and tendency of the mother-lode, the mass
of a vanished rock-sill tipping one small stone
slightly askew as it weighs upon your palm,
and then I threw it back towards the sun
to thump down on a knoll
where it may move a foot in a thousand years.

Today, having come back, summer was all mirror
tormenting me. I fled down cattle tracks
chest-deep in the earth, and pushed in under twigs
to sit by cool water speeding over rims
of blackened basalt, the tall light reaching me.

Since those moth-grimed streetlamps came,
my dark is threatened.

4

I stand, and turn, and wander through the house,
avoiding those floorboards that I know would creak,
to the other verandah. Here is where I slept,
and here is where, one staring day, I felt
a presence at my back, and whirled in fright
to face my father's suit, hung out to air.

This country is my mind. I lift my face
and count my hills, and linger over one:
Deer's, steep, bare-topped, where eagles nest below
the summit in scrub oaks, and where I take
my city friends to tempt them with my past.

Across the creek and the paddocks of the moon
four perfect firs stand dark beside a field
lost long ago, which holds a map of rooms.
This was the plot from which we transplants sprang.
The trees grew straight. We burgeoned and spread far.
I think of doors and rooms beneath the ground,
deep rabbit rooms, thin candlelight of days . . .
and, turning quickly, walk back through the house.

5

Night, and I watch the moonrise through the door.
Sitting alone's a habit of mind with me . . .
for which I'll pay in full. That has begun.
But meanwhile I will sit and watch the moon.

My father will be there now, at a hall
in the dark of the country, shining at the waltz,
spry and stately, twirling at formal speeds
on a roaring waxed-plank floor.
The petrol lamps
sizzle and glare now the clapping has died down.
They announce some modern dance. He steps outside
to where cigarettes glow sparsely in the dark,
joins some old friends and yarns about his son.

Beneath this moon, an ancient radiance comes
back from far hillsides where the tall pale trunks
of ringbarked trees haphazardly define
the edge of dark country I could not afford
to walk in at night alone
lest I should hear
the barking of dogs from a clearing where no house
has ever stood, and, walking down a road
in the wilderness, meet a man who waited there
beside a creek to tell me what I sought.

Father, come home soon.
Come home alive.

The Princes' Land

FOR VALERIE, ON HER BIRTHDAY

Leaves from the ancient forest gleam
in the meadow brook, and dip, and pass.
Six maidens dance on the level green,
a seventh toys with an hourglass,

letting fine hours sink away,
turning to sift them back again.
An idle prince, with a cembalo,
sings to the golden afternoon.

Two silver knights, met in a wood,
tilt at each other, clash and bow.
Upon a field semé of birds
Tom Bread-and-Cheese sleeps by his plough.

But now a deadly stillness comes
upon the brook, upon the green,
upon the seven dancing maids,
the dented knights are dulled to stone.

The hours in the hourglass
are stilled to fine fear, and the wood
to empty burning. Tom the hind
walks in his sleep in pools of blood.

The page we've reached is grey with pain.
Some will not hear, some run away,
some go to write books of their own,
some few, as the tale grows cruel, sing Hey

but we who have no other book
spell out the gloomy, blazing text,
page by slow page, wild year by year,
our hope refined to what comes next,

and yet attentive to each child
who says he's looked ahead and seen
how the tale will go, or spied
a silver page two pages on,

for, as the themes knit and unfold,
somewhere far on, where all is changed,
beyond all twists of grief and fear,
we look to glimpse that land again:

the brook descends in music through
the meadows of that figured land,
nine maidens from the ageless wood
move in their circles, hand in hand.

Two noble figures, counterchanged,
fence with swift passion, pause and bow.
All in a field impaled with sun
the Prince of Cheese snores by his plough.

Watching bright hours file away,
turning to sift them back again,
the Prince of Bread, with a cembalo
hums to the golden afternoon.

Ill Music

My cousin loved the violin
and played it gracefully in tune
except when, touching certain chords,
he fell down, shrieked and bit at boards
till blood and froth stood on his chin.

Some talked of Providence, or sin,
or feared the rot had now got in
to a family tree once pruned with swords—
but these are words.

And Jim said little when his kin
found a place to place him in,
nor did he ever tell his guards
how notes may run, and catch, and veer towards
that pitch where shrieks and suns begin—
for these are words.

Troop Train Returning

Beyond the Divide
the days become immense,
beyond our war
in the level lands of wheat,
the things that we defended are still here,
the willow-trees pruned neatly cattle-high,
the summer roads where far-back bullock drays
foundered in earth and mouldered into yarns.
From a ringbarked tree, as we go cheering by
a tower and a whirlwind of white birds,
as we speed by
with a whistle for the plains.

On kitbags in the aisle, old terrors doze,
clumsy as rifles in a peacetime train.

Stopped at a siding
under miles of sun,
I watch a friend I mightn't see again
shyly shake hands, becoming a civilian,
and an old Ford truck
receding to the sky.

I walk about. The silo, tall as Time,
casts on bright straws its coldly southward shade.

All things are spaced out here
each in its value.
The pepper-trees beside the crossroads pub
are dim with peace,
pumpkins are stones
in fields so loosely green.

In a little while, I'll be afraid to look
out for my house and the people that I love,
they have been buried in the moon so long.

Beyond all wars
in the noonday lands of wheat,
the whistle summons shouters from the bar,
refills the train with jokes and window noise.
This perfect plain
casts out the things we've done
as we jostle here, relaxed as farmers, smoking,
held at this siding
till the red clicks green.

Blood

Pig-crowds in successive, screaming pens
we still to greedy drinking, trough by trough,
tusk-heavy boars, fat mud-beslabbered sows:
Gahn, let him drink, you slut, you've had enough!

Laughing and grave by turns, in milky boots,
we stand and yarn, and whet our butcher's knife,
sling cobs of corn—Hey, careful of his nuts!
It's made you cruel, all that smart city life.

In paper spills, we roll coarse, sweet tobacco.
That's him down there, the one we'll have to catch,
that little Berkshire with the pointy ears.
I call him Georgie. Here, you got a match?

The shadow of a cloud moves down the ridge,
on summer hills, a patch of autumn light.
My cousin sheathes in dirt his priestly knife.
They say pigs see the wind. You think that's right?

I couldn't say. It sounds like a fair motto.
There are some poets—Right, he's finished now.
Melon-sized and muscular, with shrieks
the pig is seized and bundled anyhow

his twisting strength permits, then sternly held.
My cousin tests his knife, sights for the heart
and sinks the blade with one long, even push.
A wild scream bursts as knife and victim part

and hits the showering heavens as our beast
flees straight downfield, choked in his pumping gush
that feeds the earth, and drags him to his knees—
Bleed, Georgie, pump! And with a long-legged rush

my cousin is beside the thing he killed
and pommels it, and lifts it to the sun:
I should have knocked him out, poor little bloke.
It gets the blood out if you let them run.

We hold the dangling meat. Wet on its chest
the narrow cut, the tulip of slow blood.
We better go. We've got to scald him next.
Looking at me, my cousin shakes his head:

What's up, old son? You butchered things before . . .
it's made you squeamish, all that city life.
Sly gentleness regards me, and I smile:
You're wrong, you know. I'll go and fetch the knife.

I walk back up the trail of crowding flies,
back to the knife which pours deep blood, and frees
sun, fence and hill, each to its holy place.
Strong in my valleys, I may walk at ease.

A world I thought sky-lost by leaning ships
in the depth of our life—I'm in that world once more.
Looking down, we praise for its firm flesh
the creature killed according to the Law.

The Abomination

Long before dawn, I rose by Paddy's Lantern,
lit up my own and walked through miles of dew
with my striding shadow, adze and burlap bag
to check my traps. The woods were cold and deep,
the fence on the ridgeline tingled, wet with stars.

Away below, in a gully facing in
towards the dark, a stumphole fire glowed
but I looked away and went on with my round,
killing each rabbit with a practised chop
and dropping it, still straining, in my bag.

A winding course of unhurried killings led
me down the dark to my farthest track, which lay
a short walk from the fire. Here I killed
one final time, and slung my heavy bag
to approach the blaze—as I had known I would.

Behind the black terrazzo of old heat
light glared from crumbling pits. Old roots are tough
but when they catch, their blinding rings inch deep
and rage for months and suck your breath away
if you kneel before them too long, peering in . . .

as I knew I had by the pallor of the sky.
Scrambling up to go, I told myself
no harm in this. I was just looking down
to see how far back the earth might be unsafe.
It wouldn't do to break through on such heat.

Budded with light on light, the butts of glare
in their fire-burrows were a deeper fact
that stared down my evasions, and I found
a rabbit in my hands and, in my mind,
an ancient thing. And it was quickly done.

Afterwards, I tramped the smoking crust
heavily in on fire, stench and beast
to seal them darkly under with my fear
and all the things my sacrifice might mean,
so hastily performed past all repair.

Once in a Lifetime, Snow

FOR CHRIS AND MARY SHARAH

Winters at home brought wind,
black frost and raw
grey rain in barbed-wire fields,
but never more

until the day my uncle
rose at dawn
and stepped outside—to find
his paddocks gone,

his cattle to their hocks
in ghostly ground
and unaccustomed light
for miles around.

And he stopped short, and gazed
lit from below,
and half his wrinkles vanished
murmuring *Snow*.

A man of farm and fact
he stared to see
the facts of weather raised
to a mystery

white on the world he knew
and all he owned.
Snow? Here? he mused. I see.
High time I learned.

Here, guessing what he meant
had much to do
with that black earth dread old men
are given to,

he stooped to break the sheer
crust with delight
at finding the cold unknown
so deeply bright,

at feeling it take his prints
so softly deep,
as if it thought he knew
enough to sleep,

or else so little he
might seek to shift
its weight of wintry light
by a single drift,

perceiving this much, he scuffed
his slippered feet
and scooped a handful up
to taste, and eat

in memory of the fact
that even he
might not have seen the end
of reality ...

Then, turning, he tiptoed in
to a bedroom, smiled,
and wakened a murmuring child
and another child.

Recourse to the Wilderness

FOR PETER BARDEN

Towards the end of the long Australian peace
when I was a twenty-two-year-old with failings,
ostentatious, untravelled, with a gift for dependence,
penury had grown stale; my childhood was in danger,
so I preceded you, in all but spirit,
to the Outside country
where the sealed roads end,
the far, still Centre.

Today, a sequence from that equivocal season
danced in my memory:
I saw myself away in South Australia,
still a novice, but learning,
having already felt frost through my blanket,
learned how to dig a hip-hole, to sleep quickly,
how to camp in good cover, especially in cities.
A month from home, barely,
and I'd even made a beginning

in the more advanced, more fruitful major subjects:
jettisoning weight, non-planning, avoidance of thought
in favour of landscape, stones and the travelling sky.

All that day, I had traversed the German country
—vast fields of September, distant adobe houses—
hungry, such was my mood, for the exotic,
I'd listened for German in casual talk overheard
in winecellar towns at peace with their horizons.

Now it was night. Damp furrows smelt of spring,
cool iron and thistle-stems. Far-off windows shone
approaching, receding. Cars dipped below the world's edge
on unknown roads.

And I walked on and on
upbraiding myself with melancholy pleasure
for past insufficiencies, future humiliations:
You are always at fault. Nor will this ever change,
etcetera, etcetera.

Later that night
the horror of Hell stared down at me for a great time,
silent, with horns,
till I reared awake, and found
myself bedded down on hay in a dawn-wet paddock
with twenty curious rams forgathered round me.

Under that augury, I hitchhiked on all that day
out of the fenced and fertile south-east districts
and, just on sundown, entered the waterless kingdom.

In the silent lands
time broadens into space.
Approaching Port Augusta, going on,
iron-brown and limitless, the plains
were before me all day. Burnt mountains fell behind
in the glittering sky.

At dawn, the sun would roll up from his lair
in the kiln-dry lake country, fire his heat straight through
the blind grey scrub, awaken me beside wheeltracks
and someone's car, and I would travel on.

At noon, far out in a mirage, I would brew
tea with strangers, yarn about jobs in the North
which I meant not to get
and, chewing quietly, watch maybe an upstart
dust-devil forming miles off, going high
to totter, darken
and, quite suddenly, vanish,
leaving a formless, thinning stain on the heavens.

Where the spirits of sea-cliffs
hovered on the plain
I would remember routines we had invented
for putting spine into shapeless days: the time
we passed at a crouching trot down Wynyard Concourse
telling each other in loud mock-Aranda and gestures
what game we were tracking down what haunted gorge,
frivolous games
but they sustained me like water,

they, and the is-ful ah!-nesses of things.

The Commercial Hotel

Days of asphalt-blue and gold
murmurous with stout and flies,
lorries bought, allotments sold,

and recent heroes, newly old,
stare at their beer with bloating eyes.
Days of asphalt-blue and gold

dim to saloon bars, where unfold
subtleties of enterprise,
lorries bought, allotments sold,

where, with fingers burnt, the bold
learn to be indirect, and wise.
Days of asphalt-blue and gold

confirm the nation in its mould
of wages, contract and supplies,
lorries bought, allotments sold,

and the brave, their stories told,
age and regard, without surmise,
days of asphalt-blue and gold
lorries bought, allotments sold.

The Incendiary Method

Hungry that year
for a quick resolution
a blasting reply
to clean out the mind
of the years' slow piling
of question on question
I fumbled a match
and lit the grey, tattered
fuse of a paperbark
tree in the swamps
and watched it howl up
a tower of flame,
sweet oil and smuts
for my summer banner
over the pools
and startled beasts
feeding on rushes.

The fire swarmed
and then petered out
in a trickle of remnant
sparks and small candles
and I said to myself
in the guilt of my gleeful
search for more tea-trees
with tarpaper trunks,
there are more ways than one
of cleansing the spirit
and while I may know
this way can burn cities
it won't burn them here
in the dark of this swamp
a sixty-foot blaze
in the dark of this poem
with only beasts watching
over the pools
and smoking rushes.

An Absolutely Ordinary Rainbow

The word goes round Repins,
the murmur goes round Lorenzinis,
at Tattersalls, men look up from sheets of numbers,
the Stock Exchange scribblers forget the chalk in their hands
and men with bread in their pockets leave the Greek Club:
There's a fellow crying in Martin Place. They can't stop him.

The traffic in George Street is banked up for half a mile
and drained of motion. The crowds are edgy with talk
and more crowds come hurrying. Many run in the back streets
which minutes ago were busy main streets, pointing:
There's a fellow weeping down there. No one can stop him.

The man we surround, the man no one approaches
simply weeps, and does not cover it, weeps
not like a child, not like the wind, like a man
and does not declaim it, nor beat his breast, nor even
sob very loudly—yet the dignity of his weeping

holds us back from his space, the hollow he makes about him
in the midday light, in his pentagram of sorrow,
and uniforms back in the crowd who tried to seize him
stare out at him, and feel, with amazement, their minds
longing for tears as children for a rainbow.

Some will say, in the years to come, a halo
or force stood around him. There is no such thing.
Some will say they were shocked and would have stopped him
but they will not have been there. The fiercest manhood,
the toughest reserve, the slickest wit amongst us

trembles with silence, and burns with unexpected
judgements of peace. Some in the concourse scream
who thought themselves happy. Only the smallest children
and such as look out of Paradise come near him
and sit at his feet, with dogs and dusty pigeons.

Ridiculous, says a man near me, and stops
his mouth with his hands, as if it uttered vomit—
and I see a woman, shining, stretch her hand
and shake as she receives the gift of weeping;
as many as follow her also receive it

and many weep for sheer acceptance, and more
refuse to weep for fear of all acceptance,
but the weeping man, like the earth, requires nothing,
the man who weeps ignores us, and cries out
of his writhen face and ordinary body

not words, but grief, not messages, but sorrow,
hard as the earth, sheer, present as the sea—
and when he stops, he simply walks between us

mopping his face with the dignity of one
man who has wept, and now has finished weeping.

Evading believers, he hurries off down Pitt Street.

Working Men

Seeing the telegram go limp
and their foreman's face go grey and stark,
the fettlers, in their singlets, led him
out, and were gentle in the dark.

A Walk with O'Connor

A winter's day of wind, and no horizon.
Out of the vagueness, breakers on cold grey sand.
Leaving Bondi behind, we followed the dim coast south
over tongues of land
between the Pacific and the red-tiled homes,
exulted our way over heights with talk of heroes,
disputed down through scrub to famous coves
and scaled low cliffs, position by quotation,
hand over hand.

At Waverley, where the gravestones stop at the brink,
murmuring words, to the rebel's tomb we went,
an exile's barrow of Erin-go-bragh and pride
in grey-green cement:
we examined the harps, the hounds, the lists of the brave
and, reading the Gaelic, constrained and shamefaced, we tried
to guess what it meant
then, drifting away,
translated Italian off opulent tombstones nearby
in our discontent.

On a farther beach, though,
where mile-long water, folding, crashed on sand
with a shudder of glee
we caught up drift battens, invoking Cuchulain sent mad,
and fought with the sea,
persuading each other that, in our own lives, this
was how it might be,
how, in the nature of purpose and of men,
it might well be.

But farther again
in a place of thorn and cliff
discussing ways
with nightfall closing in
we came to the old forts with their low tomb doors,
ladders of rust, gaunt casemates loud with wind
and the stench of man
and we spoke of the gun crews and the great oiled guns
that all the heydays of our childhood war
had never once engaged an enemy
or made much more than urgent spouts of boil
far out on the shining grid
of a fire-plan . . .

I looked at O'Connor
and he spoke to me,
but these were as many aspects of our quest,
I mean the Quest that summons all true men,
as that evening's light
permitted us to see.

Senryu

Just two hours after
Eternal Life pills came out
someone took thirty.

The Ballad Trap

In the hanging gorges
the daring compact wears thin,
picking meat from small skeletons,
counting damp notes in a tin,

the rifle birds ringing at noon
in the steep woods,
hard-riding boys dazed at the brink
of their attitudes,

the youngest wheedling for songs,
his back to the night,
dark mountains the very English
for souring delight:

Remember the Escort? Remember
lamps long ago
and manhood filched from the horse police
and a name from Cobb and Co.

Their metre hobbled, the horses
hump their dark life,
longing for marriage, the tall man
sharpens his knife—

Yes, let us sing! cries the Captain
while we have breath.
Better, God knows, than this thinking.
The ballad ends with their death.

Hayfork Point

Dazzling blue eyes
of winter stare from the box-trees
the shadows of barns are thin with frosted straw.

All over the country
the dented light of milk cans.

Cold proteins cling
to the wet-lipped cane-knife blocking
swedes by the sty for a tumult of fat squealers.
For the mouths of following cattle, boys on tractors
bayonet green stacks and hoy them down the sky
green spinning in air.
The bull, looking up,
is drenched in flying meadow.

Pinched hours pass
and farmers lug dull cans
but magpies, dismissing weight, lift over stones now
alighting on wires ever farther off
to balance at behests
of song, and spring

for something has turned
and from the heavens, gently
invisibly, gently
grass goes on falling.

The Fire Autumn

The walls of the country this year, the forest escarpments,
the seacoast stump-mountains are fired with amber and buff
like autumn in the Jura, October legends of fall,
some hilltops are sailing the storm-rains with almost bare poles
and the logs that still smoulder in gullies are not far from mist.
Up the steep timber roads, though, in under the heights
you are too close for charm. The fire-killed leaves stick unmoved
like the scales of monsters that lived at too blinding a pitch
to stay in existence. The ruins of bullock-bell trails

are bared to midsummer. The froth of rain rots on black bark.
We have heard that the smoke from this coast was seen far
    out over
the curve of the earth, on the open Pacific, on islands.
We know certain colours and cooling nuances are gone,
much birdsong, too, some millions of wealth, a few persons
baked in sheet iron. The word *sylvan* cracks in the sun.

But this is order. This is the fire autumn
in the ancient of rocks, the paradise of lost eons.
We have been to see autumn in Europe. It is beautiful but
humanized to despair in those poor remnant woods
with tourist paths leading to every clump of Waldeinsamkeit.
The great year of man has entered a burning season:
the chainsaw, junked beercans, newsprint, the torrents of birth
are one fire with that great autumn the North world conducts
through her nation-states, through the unuttered minds of
    officials
with every fuel from oil to musicians to fields.
In the year of the moon-shot, the column of Trajan at Rome,
kept prisoner by the Italian government, as Greece
holds the Parthenon (they are not of our world, these
    monuments)
murmured to us, *Your masters are burning the earth
to keep it in flight round not even the Sun any more
but that sheer point that even the Daystar (mostly) obeys
at the heart of their gravities. The point is smaller than Man
and they're desperate with joy. They have overcome dignity.*
The spiralling captives continued their motionless climb.

Since mankind went critical, time is a fiery screen
on which all the scenes we may call the world play at once,
housewives in the sky, jets over bullock-carts, music,
the updraft of real things drawn spinning into the act
rattles our brains. Reentering calm, some burn up.
Murder forms out of nothing in streets unspeakably adult.
The clatter of fallout scares soldiers from under your clothes.
Of the wealthy, so many are living now in the future
that wombs become wardrobes. Only the poor need be born.

And yet, in clothes that come boxed from that whirlwind
we have walked out among the great aircraft that bend the
 horizon,
growing ever more beautiful for ever more prodigious flight.
We have handled the taut, racked machine-guns that shot war
 to shreds
and, circling their complex near-absolute fitness of form
over the mass mud-graves, some have felt themselves leap
clean over the apple-bough wheels of the great star factory.

The cesspools of maturity are heaving with those who leap
 short.
Some are citing as Europe's last knowledge (Oh burning Israel)
that nothing not founded upon the irrational can stand,
but some land in good country at a venture of kindness
and such is the humour, the grace of the Infinite Man,
that in towns grown at ease with their landscapes, strolling,
 they find
old cars, weatherboards, dumb oildrums standing in grass
have come into truth as firmly almost as mountains.
Things lacking this radiance not wholly of light, this silence
of momentous containment, the Unrevealed Torah of objects,
spin with the world. They are deadly. On girls bored to sleep
they beget fibro children who wither youth into days.

But some who come to our country as being the farthest
out on earth towards the country they sought
are waiting to hear, where they lie in their deckchairs and
 graves,
that, with distance, the serious laws of the universe change,
and more, growing native, still find the limitless country
too near for speech. The dignity growing on trees
in the drystick forests, the mines in the waste land, the stones,
is not solar, nor deeply mortal. In dour shirtsleeve joy
they answer the Sun of a universe where it is clear
that this earth is continuous with nothing but the unknown.

Like a distant coast beyond shimmer, too still for cloud,
the trees of my forests and breakaway mountains are feathering
with gold of emergence, with claret, cerise, liquid green,

faint blues fat with powder, new leaves clustered thick down
    the length
of charcoal-stiff bark. Brush water is licking stones clean.
The tracks of birds glitter. Blunt mountains steer towards noon
and all down December, black thaw will be riding the streams.
For this also is order. This is a farther season
in the ancient of rocks, the paradise of far eons,
and I am asking the dead to wait, with forgiveness,
the innocent planets are grinding their keepers to gold.

The Canberra Remnant

Eavesdropping rain
a quiet car
a sense of mountains
in the air,

dark houses sleeping
beneath the freez-
ing drip of Europ-
ean trees,

lost paddock and stone
under the lake
and only a few
souls still awake

to polish a bead,
to turn a page,
to label a fly
or a golden age

in a thousand redeeming
projects they
keep safe from the Government
of the Day.

Toward the Imminent Days

FOR GEOFF AND SALLY LEHMANN

I

Midmorning, September, and red tractors climb
on a landscape wide as all forgiveness. Clouds
in the west horizon, parrots twinkling down
on Leary's oats, on Stewarts' upturned field—

good friends are blood relations that you choose.
The phrase discovers me in the heart of farmland
harpstringing fences, coming back into my life.
A thick coin flips out of my mouth, I leap over thistles

and I think of your wedding, I make it shine among trees
in a vast evening cattlecamp lit by jewelled pendants, by plates,
by brass lamps suspended on trace chains at great height.
The beams of carlights conjure our bustling assembly.

Now the minister comes, with rapid changes of car,
and all of us, painters, centurions in mufti, horses,
lawyers discoursing on sheepback, all drink up quickly,
the hush of Queensland falling on sculptress and ghost.

As the words begin, your pledges rising, whole branches
of blossom appear on the tree your lives have reached,
from out of sight of land, an incredibly high
hymeneal piping makes my wineglass sing—

or so I choose to remember it in the country
and from that glass I'll drink your health always,
recalling your abundant house, the dancing,
your shovelled cake rich as the history of Calabria.

2

Topping ridges, considering some poor late gift
(my gifts this year are so very nearly ineffable)
I think of a day too great for the calendar numbers

that, faintest in winter, grows like a buried moon,

a radiant season swelling through the horizons
beyond September, mortality crumbling down
till on summer mornings, a farm boy can see through the hills
the roots of pumpkin-vines knotting clean under New England.

With Advent so near beneath a man's pitchfork,
the wild and paddocks rising into each other
in the whole green crescent of the tented air,
to keep the dead at peace, wise farmers talk drought,

Hanrahan's comfort—but wheat is crowding through cities.
Cabinet ministers pace in the light of Canowindra
as cattle cross on the stockroutes, a commonwealth walking,
young men leap rivers and, lounging in grasses that threaten

the smaller brick towns, they long for a splendid alert.
Only marriage will save them. The hills are so riddled with fun
that timber dance-halls hide out in the ruins of whisky
and Holdens surging from under barns at midday

are buffed by almost uncontainable winds
for the woman of seed who is the landscape is seizing
all things in her gift. Verandahs sail home on the hills
till the imminent day is burned remote by the sun.

3

Singing, All living are wild in the imminent days,
I walk into furrows end-on and they rise through my flesh
burying worlds of me. It is the clumsiest dancing,
this walking skewways over worn-ocean that heaps

between skid and crumble with lumped stones in ambush
    for feet
but it marches with seed and steadiness, knowing the land.
As the dogs set out from the house, minute, black, running,
I am striding on over the fact that it is the earth

that holds our mark longest, that soil dug never returns
to primal coherence. Dead men in the fathoms of fields
sustain without effort millennial dark columns
and to their suspension, the crystal centuries come—

But now I am deep in butter-thick native broom
wading, sky-happy, a cotton-bright drover of bees.
As I break out of flowers, the dogs who have only
chaos for language, and territory dense in their fur,

mob me, leaping, and I am too merry with farms
not to run with them, to trample my shadow on sticks:
outpacing dignity, I collide with sheer landscapes
dancing with dogs in the rain of information.

4

In my aunt's house, the milk jug's beaded crochet cover
tickles the ear. We've eaten boiled things with butter.
Pie spiced like islands, dissolving in cream, is now
dissolving in us. We've reached the teapot of calm.

The table we sit at is fashioned of three immense
beech boards out of England. The minute widths of the years
have been refined in the wood by daughters' daughters.
In the year of Nelson, I notice, the winter was mild.

But our talk is cattle and cricket. My quiet uncle
has spent the whole forenoon sailing a stump-ridden field
of blady-grass and Pleistocene clay never ploughed
since the world's beginning. The Georgic furrow lengthens

in ever more intimate country. But we're talking bails,
stray cattle, brands. In the village of Merchandise Creek
there's a post in a ruined blacksmith shop that bears
a charred-in black-letter script of iron characters,

hooks, bars, conjoined letters, a weird bush syllabary.
It is the language of property seared into skin
but descends beyond speech into the muscles of cattle,
the world of feed as it shimmers in cattle minds.

My uncle, nodding, identifies the owners
(I gather M-bar was mourned by thousands of head).
It has its roots in meadows deeper than Gaelic,
my uncle's knowledge. Farmers longest in Heaven

share slyly with him in my aunt's grave mischievous smile
that shines out of every object in my sight
in these loved timber rooms at the threshold of grass.
The depth in this marriage will heal the twentieth century.

5

Broad afternoon. The hired boy and I
stack saccaline in the hammer-mill by the sheds
till the air is coarse with silage. Clouds of fowls
and black, shape-shifting turkeys frisk our output

but we are watching how my cousins flare
around the cowbails, yarding up fresh milkers,
knee-gripping buckets (strophe, antistrophe);
no primitive bush pumpkin eaters here,

these are prosperous, well-mannered children;
gentle with cows. Even the youngest's a dairyman
concerned with his poddy-calves. No one here will be
a visitor gnawed by lifelong celebration.

We look at them. Even the hired boy knows,
at his age, that freedom is memory. He sees hope
in asking me about cities. How can I tell him
the cities are debris driven by explosions

whose regulation takes a merciless cunning?
I love my cities too well not to start at least there.
I turn his question away, out into the hills
where the bold rabbit-shooter may learn his life from a pool

or consider the turkeys (their splendour coherent with filth)
if they mistake your toes for corn, look out!
my grandfather vomited once and our fowls got blind drunk—
I rack my past for a health the boy can use.

6

In the land of cows-to-milk
there was once a wobbly calf
and he grew to be a bull
scraping up armorial dirt
with a pedigree to bellow
in the bullness of his season
and we used to chase him home—
whoa back bull!
through our neighbours' flagrant fences
till my father linked a chain
round his horns to catch and lead:
You will save your herd-improvements
for our own herd, mister bull!
He was docile for a time
till he found he was the strong one
and began to trot—whoa bull!

Whoa bull—and the running started
as depicted in the friezes.
Loop his chain around a sapling
(wrench of splinters) try a tree!

Block him, yard 'him, bloody bull,
I'll sell you for dogmeat, screamed
my short-legged father, clinging, swinging
on the chain and prancing faster
than the sons of man can run
skipping on the ringbarked hills
stumbling, leaping on the mountains.
Jersey farmer, Jersey bull
raging under the horizons
until, sometime after dark,
soaked with tropic and Antarctic
spray and dust of Innamincka
in murderous mutual respect
man and bull would stagger home
linked, supporting one another

wheezing Corn, moaning Supper
shedding forests from their chain.

When you see him, ask my father.

7

Dog roses, wild clematis, indigo
crossing the creek on my mind's feet, though,
I walk on home where the stars are thinnest, glancing
back at the village with one human house

that is my uncle's farm. Nightjars fly through me,
snipping winged ants. Into the brimming hills
cattle graze beyond the human marriages,
and the one-globe kitchen windows, miles apart,

approach the quiet of boats far out on the year
whose wake is all that will persist of them.
What lasts is the voyage of families down their name.
Houses pass into Paradise continually,

voices, loved fields, all wearing away into Heaven.
As the cornplanter sings out to the rising month
bush-hidden creeks in the rabbit country wash
like a clear stone in my mind, the heavenly faculty.

Hiles' paddock leans on its three-strand fence in the dark
bending the road a little with its history.
Our lives are refined by remotest generations.
Months late, I catch up with your wedding once again,

the candles laughter chicken-legs speeches champagne
I pass with a wave (lifting a friend from the wheeltracks)
and full of a lasting complicity, old henchmen,
about the life of this world, strike home over grass.

For your wedding, I wish you the frequent image of farms.

Lament for the Country Soldiers

The king of honour, louder than of England,
cried on the young men to a gallant day
and ate the hearts of those who would not go

for the gathering ranks were the Chosen Company
that each man in his lifetime seeks, and finds,
some for an hour, some beyond recall.

When to prove their life, they set their lives at risk
and in the ruins of horizons died
one out of four, in the spreading rose of their honour

they didn't see the badge upon their hat
was the ancient sword that points in all directions.
The symbol hacked the homesteads even so.

The static farms withstood it to the end,
the galloping telegrams ceasing, the exchanges
ringing no more in the night of the stunned violin,

and in the morning of insult, the equal remember
ribaldry, madness, the wire jerking with friends,
ironic salutes for the claimants of the fox-hunt

as, camped under tin like rabbiters in death's gully,
they stemmed the endless weather of grey men and steel
and, first of all armies, stormed into great fields.

But it was a weight beyond speech, the proven nation,
on beasts and boys. Newborn experiment withered.
Dull horror rotting miles wide in the memory of green.

Touching money, the white feather crumpled to ash,
cold lies grew quickly in the rank decades
as, far away, the ascendant conquered courage,

and we debauched the faith we were to keep
with the childless singing on the morning track,
the Sportsmen's Thousand leaping on the mountains,

now growing remote, beneath their crumbling farms,
in the district light, their fading companies
with the king of honour, deeper than of England

though the stones of increase glitter with their names.

The Conquest

Phillip was a kindly, rational man:
Friendship and Trust will win the natives, Sir.
Such was the deck the Governor walked upon.

One deck below, lieutenants hawked and spat.
One level lower, and dank nightmares grew.
Small floating Englands where our world began.

•

And what was trust when the harsh dead swarmed ashore
and warriors, trembling, watched the utterly strange
hard clouds, dawn beings, down there where time began,

so alien the eye could barely fix
blue parrot-figures wrecking the light with change,
man-shapes digging where no yam roots were?

•

The Governor proffers cloth and English words,
the tribesmen defy him in good Dhuruwal.
Marines stand firm, known warriors bite their beards.

Glass beads are scattered in that gulf of style
but pickpockets squeal, clubbed in imagination,
as naked Indians circle them like birds.

•

They won't Respond. They threaten us. Drive them off.
In genuine grief, the Governor turns away.
Blowflies form trinkets for a harsher grief.

As the sickness of the earth bites into flesh
trees moan like women, striplings collapse like trees—
fever of Portsmouth hulks, the Deptford cough.

      •

It makes dogs furtive, what they find to eat
but the noonday forest will not feed white men.
Capture some Natives, quick. Much may be learned

indeed, on both Sides. Sir! And Phillip smiles.
Two live to tell the back lanes of his smile
and the food ships come, and the barracks rise as planned.

      •

And once again the Governor goes around
with his Amity. The yeasts of reason work,
triangle screams confirm the widening ground.

No one records what month the first striped men
mounted a clawing child, then slit her throat
but the spear hits Phillip with a desperate sound.

      •

The thoughtful savage with Athenian flanks
fades from the old books here. The sketchers draw
pipe-smoking cretins jigging on thin shanks

poor for the first time, learning the Crown Lands tune.
The age of unnoticed languages begins
and Phillip, recovering, gives a nodded thanks.

      •

McEntire speared! My personal Huntsman, speared!
Ten Heads for this, and two alive to hang!
A brave lieutenant cools it, bid by bid,

to a decent six. The punitive squads march off
without result, but this quandong of wrath
ferments in slaughters for a hundred years.

•

They couldn't tell us how to farm their skin.
They camped with dogs in the rift glens of our mind
till their old men mumbled who the stars had been.

They had the noon trees' spiritual walk.
Pathetic with sores, they could be suddenly not,
the low horizon strangely concealing them.

•

A few still hunt way out beyond philosophy
where nothing is sacred till it is your flesh
and the leaves, the creeks shine through their poverty

or so we hope. We make our conquests, too.
The ruins at our feet are hard to see.
For all the generous Governor tried to do

the planet he had touched began to melt
though he used much Reason, and foreshadowed more
before he recoiled into his century.

The Ballad of Jimmy Governor

H. M. PRISON, DARLINGHURST, 18TH JANUARY 1901

You can send for my breakfast now, Governor.
The colt from Black Velvet's awake
and the ladies all down from the country
are gathered outside for my sake.

Soon be all finished, the running.
No tracks of mine lead out of here.
Today, I take that big step
on the bottom rung of the air
and be in Heaven for dinner.
Might be the first jimbera there.

The Old People don't go to Heaven,
good thing. My mother might meet
that stockman feller my father
and him cut her dead in the street.
Mother, today I'll be dancing
your way and his way on numb feet.

But a man's not a rag to wipe snot on,
I got that much into their heads,
them hard white sunbonnet ladies
that turned up their short lips and said
my wife had a slut's eye for colour.
I got that into their head

and the cow-cockies' kids plant up chimneys
they got horse soldiers out with the Law
after Joe and lame Jack and tan Jimmy—
but who learnt us how to make war
on women, old men, babies?
It ain't all one way any more.

The papers, they call us bushrangers:
that would be our style, I daresay,
bushrangers on foot with our axes.
It sweetens the truth, anyway.

They don't like us killing their women.
Their women kill us every day.

And the squatters are peeing their moleskins,
that's more than a calf in the wheat,
it's Jimmy the fencer, running
along the top rail in the night,
it's the Breelong mob crossing the ranges
with rabbitskins soft on their feet.

But now Jack in his Empire brickyard
has already give back his shoes
and entered the cleanliness kingdom,
the Commonwealth drums through the walls
and I'm weary of news.

I'm sorry, old Jack, I discharged you,
you might have enjoyed running free
of plonk and wet cornbags and colour
with us pair of outlaws. But see,
you can't trust even half a whitefeller.
You died of White Lady through me.

They tried me once running, once standing:
one time ought to do for the drop.
It's more trial than you got, I hear, Joe,
your tommyhawk's chipped her last chop.
I hope you don't mind I got lazy
when the leaks in my back made me stop.

If any gin stands in my print
I'll give her womb sorrow and dread,
if a buck finds our shape in the tussocks
I'll whiten the hair in his head,
but a man's not a rag to wipe boots on
and I got that wrote up, bright red,

where even fine ladies can read it
who never look at the ground
for a man that ain't fit to breed from

may make a terrible bound
before the knacker's knife gets him.
Good night to you, father. Sleep sound.

Fetch in my breakfast, Governor,
I have my journey to make
and the ladies all down from the country
are howling outside for my sake.

SMLE

I

January, heat. Raw saplings stand like cattle
in the distance of farms. Cornfields out there decaying
to slatternly paper in the blacksnake days . . .
Perched in this tree against the eastern sun

I am watching the shallows where my cousins toss
slow-sinking bait, small things that try to swim.
The river burns my face. Islands of wind—
my shot surrounds me, flooding upward, knocking

birds by the hundreds from the swamp-oak fringe
to cry and escape the wave that fades and fades.
Yelling Three! my cousins, wading out, Four!
and I skither down barefeet-first where flung-out mullet

almost move. The utter weight that annulled them
will not stop. It burns them hugely with grass
in the numb dimension, gill-furrows ravaged by specks
their fins fibrillate. They are swimming away in their muscles

but what has remained of the universe won't give—
we strip a swamp-oak branch to thread them on
and revert to farmers. I eject a spent shell,
a tang of brass, a seed that will not grow

2

except in solitude. My Lee Enfield goes home
slung athwart my shoulder, heavy as talent.
Neither a musket, the weapon of masses by rank,
nor a machine-gun, guardian of statistics,

it points at country where it is roughly at home
in obsolescence. Pity the road-signs that lead
into that legend of billy tea, post-and-rail fence
and jackaroo, pulped in the wired slough at Pozières,

the acceptable shillings. Bayonet-lug to butt-plate,
impassive as the true touchstone, you gleam, old rifle,
tall as my hip. I almost followed you once.
I have new masters now, though. They are rewriting the world.

They make me homesick for honour, that terrible country
the poor still believe in. But let's evade the modernities,
mechanical recoil, furious cycle of gas.
Much that you taught me I have slowly learned,

the way you could contain insupportable pressure
just long enough is still germane to my shoulder
like the line of your sights on a plane above your stock
and the burned steel light in your barrel, a rational abyss—

3

I think it is under the Pyrenees, that city.
A gunsmith is shaping a spiral tube from flat steel;
Homage, murmur the killed, to Catalonia
and the Prussian needles are witching the peasants to clay

but Copernicus' wheel is cutting the grooves that expelled us
to whistle up nations in deep glades of the world.
Not by the plough alone did the grain cities come.
Landtaker's title I sing, and its fulminate seal.

At Bunker Hill, though, on a bright day, the wind in the lanes
is freezing squire and scullion clean through their jack.

The men on the hillside are enjoying their skill
as much as their principles. But all servility reels

from the shock of that day. There is almost a moment,
a longbow time of voices speaking equality
and candid with weapons. Oh where will the poor gibbet hide?
They'll sentence me next time, growls Ben Hall. So I'll earn it.

The man with the rifle reversed and black-powder beard
has the air of one looking farther into republics.
Thanks for the arms, Colonel. We'll know when to salute
and the delegates saying We'll have no earlier gods.

These things were the New World. It lasted as long as the wilds.
Now the addicts of wheels, dug in out of sight beneath
    boredom,
are hiding their children for safety among the ascendancies.
The New World erodes through plastic and joins the dark
    stream.

The children are way ahead with their mullet emblem.
Forward, the Murrays! In the mountain country
above the farms, I could hold out, eat birds—
I smile away the small madness of preparation,

replacing the bolt. Less easy to smile away man-sized
kangaroos spurting, downed statesmen kicking like deer
in the poisonous ruin of courage we have achieved.
The moon-shot loose in my pocket, I walk among trees.

    4

Unlocking, they rise in me, the deep-stacked rifles,
Mauser, Garand, Carcano, Dreyse, Lebel,
straight pull and falling block, Mannlicher's clip . . .
rifles, at such attention all their days,

what else could come out of them but death?
And there is no machine unquestioned by their oiled

and summary grace. Your rod and staff, old Cain,
have battered us human. How few can stand even that.

Only boys argue, or cheer, hearing weapons condemned:
the invocation shines clearly enough between cries.
How many are there could bear the vision of history,
let alone Nature? Grooved turn-bolt receiver, tongued sear.

For many boys, it is the first pressure of history,
not to say power, a rifle slapped in their hands
whose steel eye calibrates the windage of politics
as that other eye is said to measure love

by wise adolescents in a belt-fed epoch.
The aimed jets whining, the boys facing front on new grass
glory in the green vortex that whirls them away.
The spirit of ultimate ground on the wreckage of green

is metal and wood, as ever, in two bloody hands.
Of those who shoot, some few are riflemen.
Cold claimants mine their Versailles from the fat of the rest.
I would pay many gold teeth for a softer conviction.

5

There are humans truly unwarlike. They live well guarded.
They are protected by everything on earth.
It is the far rim of things their chimneys sustain
from the warrior pent among soldiers, the corporal suddenly

leading his company, the naked youth trap-shooting Turks.
There are also wolves in sheep country who recommend grass
and salvations so avid that blood squeezes out between verbs.
The nation-states examine their entrails in fear.

War is wasted, the General cries, on civilians
but I saw a black angel dancing in war-surplus
shouting Let wars break out of the circle of war!
The man of foresight, quiet beneath bricks, rewarding

human exposure, smiles. His fingers select
a mint brass clip, the nails of Christ and two spares.
So honour's abolished—and we are still in the world.
There will be cover for him in the leafless centuries.

I part the grass very gently, I hide among towns
and Browning, Tokarev, Vetterli, Mondragón
consider the works of their fingers. One checks an alignment,
one fits a return-spring. Absorbed as the stainers of glass.

6

Rolling straight over my Enfield's human dimensions
under the farmer's barbed wire into the road
where tractors are passing, I scale a ripe scree of melons
and wave to the driver good-day! My rifle lies down,

a sudden lurch half-buries it under rotundities.
And perhaps indeed it will be as easy as that,
perhaps the mountains will strip off their rocks and cry Kiss me!
or the grocer turned spirit unravel his gut without pain.

If not, the rocket will have to lie down with the lamb.
I wave at the wings to the right and left of mankind:
only the politics come out either end, boys!
The farmer smiles, imagines I'm swatting something.

I choose for my rising to be a son of that place
where rifle and sword are stars of our evolution,
steel of our own sphere. You have to be almost a person
to use either rightly according to its nature

and ever use a rifle as less than it is,
as truncheon, quarterstaff, musket, symbol, display,
belongs to tyranny. There's a scale closer to peace
on my rear sight than any tout's elevation.

January, heat. In the circle of live and dead farms
I stack the wholly obedient person of death
up high in the house out of child-reach
and go to eat fish with my remaining compatriots.

Vindaloo in Merthyr Tydfil

The first night of my second voyage to Wales,
tired as rag from ascending the left cheek of Earth,
I nevertheless went to Merthyr in good company
and warm in neckclothing and speech in the Butcher's Arms
till Time struck us pintless, and Eddie Rees steamed in brick
    lanes
and under the dark of the White Tip we repaired shouting

to I think the Bengal. I called for curry, the hottest,
vain of my nation, proud of my hard mouth from childhood,
the kindly brown waiter wringing the hands of dissuasion
O vindaloo, sir! You sure you want vindaloo, sir?
But I cried Yes please, being too far in to go back,
the bright bells of Rhymney moreover sang in my brains.

Fair play, it was frightful. I spooned the chicken of Hell
in a sauce of rich yellow brimstone. The valley boys with me
tasting it, croaked to white Jesus. And only pride drove me,
forkful by forkful, observed by hot mangosteen eyes,
by all the carnivorous castes and gurus from Cardiff
my brilliant tears washing the unbelief of the Welsh.

Oh it was a ride on Watneys plunging red barrel
through all the burning ghats of most carnal ambition
and never again will I want such illumination
for three days on end concerning my own mortal coil
but I signed my plate in the end with a licked knife and fork
and green-and-gold spotted, I sang for my pains like the free
before I passed out among all the stars of Cilfynydd.

A Helicopter View of Terrestrial Stars

Turn slowly in fields
and there is a star all around you.
Even out in wide country, the bush gone back miles,
in the angle of paddock and fence-line, the embayments of light,

it is the old star of settlement
that will dilate, or contract perhaps, in your time.
Back just at the edge of memory, it was not there.

And rising up
in our forward posture
under a palm-tree of blades above stelliform cities
memory is strengthened regarding the human task, seeing Asia below
the river-plains throned with the tenant constellations
that fall back from gravel, from height
like Saxons from heather
till each middle kingdom appears in the light of cleared space
a tissue worthy of language,
a pulse among stems.

Beside some of these
the shield of David is young.
Only the hunters' frail meteor descends
from more ancient darkness. That may flicker out in our lifetime.
The star of work will go nova, maybe. But not cold
for it is time
and every true human clearing is where time began
and has been kept open.

And these are the stars for our journey in this revelation,
the galaxy earth we have built.
In every azimuth we are thinking of our country,
oh, not the triple-cross canton, that tick-gate of caste
on the Shareholder Plains,
we think of the lonely stars of our consent
to what is done far down in smoking fields
and rotors and engine
throb too loud for speech.

Vietnam, Viet Nam,
green ladder of the ruthless,
what classes scale your struts of print and flesh.
It is very low down,
perhaps not crop-high now beneath the chopper-blades
that the rays of effort keep their ancient core.

Flames swivel from food
as the abstractions hit.
Among the impact-shapes, pit here, corpse there,
the scar of a house looks strangely well-positioned,
its faint, unhurried reasons
surrounding it still.

By the tailed rockets' crux and criss-cross
who will be enemy in the crowded man's war?
The last creatures? The hills?
Soldiers and earthmovers here are so hugely equipped.

Our hovering metal containment
is steadily pierced.
What we contain, we brought. It is loose in the world.
Discharged through us
it flows back redoubled
into our country that wanted to doze until greatness.

And sent to buy safety
from the conjured wind
we are dismissed from the stars of long contemplation
to fight in a running-dog war
or a running-dog peace,
two aerolites that wake no cattle-duffers.

It saps the mind's tree
it dulls the iron roof's candour
and the emulous spirit who wants these forgotten rejoices,
crying abroad *A third of all fields must be struck
by the star called politics*
and such longed-for estoiles of terror
as light the unloved—

South, south in our conquered home island
turn slowly in fields
and there is a star all around you.
Only on featureless plain or flat-calm sea
are you always mid-point.

There wind the furrows' old Gaelic
and smoke in cleared days.
You can never be whole there again, having entered Time's spiral,
it's so often proclaimed,
but what have we loved better since?
Timekeeping, perhaps? Our scab of dependence the Crown?
The zodiac Money?

Look from Kurnell. The houses
are aching with tedious light.
Hard to say whether the subtle sky-rim of our tenure
or the home-paddock heart is more unexplored,
which faith more benumbed in memory
or cluttered with lines.

Is it too harsh to hope this hamburger consummation,
this speeded-up print of our riches,
may drive some to faith,
to thinking of futures that have concurrence of trees?

To look, with some failure of reticence, on into home country
where the dogger runs barefoot through the whole fire-season
to dance with storekeepers' children and long-legged cranes,
and the lady is honoured young
at last, and the holy ground
and every man is finely employed as a species.

Incorrigible Grace

Saint Vincent de Paul, old friend,
my sometime tailor,
I daresay by now you are feeding
the rich in Heaven.

Walking to the Cattle Place

A MEDITATION

At once I came into a world wherein I recovered my full being.
                                                    —*Tagore*

1. Sanskrit

Upasara, the heifer after first mating,
adyaśvīnā, the cow about to calve, strīvatsā
the cow who has borne a heifer calf (atrināda
the calf newly born). I will smuggle this sūtra.

Around the sleeping house, dark cattle rubbing
off on stiff corner joists their innocent felt
and the house is nudged by a most ancient flow.
I will wake up in a world that hooves have led to.

To be of Europe also is a horn-dance,
cattle-knowledge. Even here, where Europa,
dumped rusty in her disgrace, gathered childhood afresh
by the draywheels' mercy, on creeks of the far selections.

Before the moon, away out, a rogue heifer dings
her bell on strained wire. A wrangling dry tintinnation
tells me she's through, and struggling on to her hooves.
She will never pierce the greater grid she has conjured.

But, a vulgar fruit of the Disruption, to talk
as if salvation were the soul's one food.
Today for no sin much, neither killing a brahmin
nor directly a cow, I will follow cattle.

2. Birds in Their Title Work Freeholds of Straw

At the hour I slept
kitchen lamps were sending out barefoot children
muzzy with stars and milk thistles
stoning up cows.
They will never forget their quick-fade cow-piss slippers
nor chasing such warmth over white frost, saffron to steam.
It will make them sad bankers.

It may subtly ruin them for clerks
this deeply involved unpickable knot of feeling
for the furred, smeared flesh of creation, the hate, the concern.
Viciously, out of sight, they pelt cows with stove-lengths
and hit them with pipes,
and older brothers sometimes, in more frenzied guilt,
have rancid, cracked eyes.
The city man's joke doesn't stretch to small minotaur bones.

But strange to think, as the dairy universe
reels from a Wall Street tremor, a London red-shift
on the flesh-eating graphs
and no longer only the bright and surplus children
get out of these hills,
how ghostly cows must be crowding the factory floors now
and licking black turbines
for the spectral salt
till the circuit-breaker's stunning greenhide crack
sears all but wages.

·

In the marginal dialect of this valley
(Agen my son grows up, tourists won't hear it)
udders are *elders*.

It was very bad news for the Kirk:
old men of the hard grey cloth, their freckled faces
distended, squeezing grace through the Four Last Things
in a Sabbath bucket.
I can tell you sparetime childhoods force-fed this
make solid cheese, but often strangely veined.
I'm thinking of aunts who had telescopes to spot
pregnancies, inside wedlock or out
(there is no life more global than a village)
and my father's uncles, monsters of hospitality.

Perhaps we should forget the seven-day-week tinned bucket
and the little children dead beat at their desks—

Caesar got up and Milked then he Got his soldiers—
but birds in their title work freeholds of straw
and the eagle his of sky.

Dripstone for Caesar.

3. The Names of the Humble

Fence beyond fence from breakfast
I climb through into my thought
and watch the slowing of herds into natural measures.

Nose down for hours, ingesting grass, they breathe grass,
trefoil, particles, out of the soft-focus earth
dampened by nose-damp. They have breathed great plateaux
    to dust.

But a cow's mouth circling on feed, the steady radius
shifting (dry sun) as she shifts,
subsumes, say, two-thirds of mankind. Our cities, our circles.

They concede me a wide berth at first. I go on being harmless
and some graze closer, gradually. It is like watching
an emergence. Persons.

Where cattletrucks mount
boustrophedon to the hills
I want to discern the names of all the humble.

     •

A meaningful lack in the mother-tongue of factories:
how do you say *one* cattle? Cow, bull, steer
but nothing like *bos*. *Cattle is chattel*, is owned

by man the castrator,
body and innocence, cud and death-bellow and beef.
Bush people say *beast*, and mean no more fabulous creature

and indeed, from the moon to the alphabet, there aren't many.
Surely the most precious Phoenician cargo
was that trussed rough-breathing ox turned dawnward to lead
all Europe's journey.

●

Far back as I can glimpse with descendant sight,
beyond roads or the stave-plough, there is a boy on cold upland,
gentle tapper of veins, a blood-porridge eater,
his ringlets new-dressed with dung, a spear in his fist,

it is thousands of moons to the cattle-raid of Cooley

but we could still find common knowledge, verb-roots
and noun-bark enough for an evening fire of sharing
cattle-wisdom,

though it is a great year yet
till Prithu will milk from the goddess *(O rich in cheer, come!)*
and down through his fingers into the rimmed vessel earth

grain and food-gardens.
We are entirely before
the seed-eater towns.

●

A sherry-eyed Jersey looks at me. Fragments of thoughts
that will not ripple together worry her head

it is sophistication trying to happen

there's been betrayal enough, and eons enough.
Or no more than focus, then,
trying to come up as far as her pupils.

Her calm gifts all central,
her forehead a spiked shield to wolves
she bobs in her hull-down affinities.

The knotted sway pole along which her big organs hang
(it will offer them ruthlessly downward when knob joints cave in)
rests unafraid in enzyme courtesies, though,

steadier than cognitions speckling brains.

Since I've sunk my presence into the law
that every beast shall be apportioned space
according to display, I unfurl a hand.

She dribbles, informing
her own weighted antique success,
and stays to pump the simpler, infinite herbage.

●

Her Normandy bones
the nap of her Charolais colour

the ticks on her elder are such
muscatels of good blood.

If I envy her one thing
it is her ease with this epoch.
A wagtail switching left-right, left-right on her rump.

Where cattletracks climb
rice-terrace-wise to the hills
I want to speak the names of all the humble.

4. The Artery

It is patience and stalks in the wide house of cattle
the zenith warming to unswallow stowage
and quietly chew. It is uttermost custom,
the day of these beings who licked the glimmering ice
from the north returning world, from the still man-figures.

But mouths stop suddenly. Heads turn. A roan bullock sound—
thin leather sniping them, the driven beef mob, oncoming,
is filling the road, dog-harried, fence-deflected
up shallow cuttings, down them, their elegant squeeze-shaped
hoofs swirl up a sky bath stockman, wheeling, don't venerate

and, indecisive, the cows run, stopping. A freshet
that will not carry these with it is going down-country
to the slowing saleyard pools, the bare holding lakes
and then in great spurts to the ocean without limits.
Come back, mother cows. Plates flower for these children.

They are going to the plains of cash and the captive bolt,
to the clotted panic, the eunuch mounting in crushes, écoutez
mugir ces atroces abats: see, brains, where man's hunger
whirrs in the firmament. They are taken up flying
stately in the feathers of the knives, they are shown dominion

before, to the last lymph tear, they are chilled from dripping
and marbled in their fat they are pillars of the city
till out of cool rooms they crowd into our veins
through the sawdust gate. Soutine was mad three days
painting a bull suspended in loud strange honour,

till the police smashed in, and the huge meat gagged down
    landings.
It is near the bone, it is black as the Angus studbook
the thought of this comedy feeding our muscles. The dead
upright are buffoons, they nudge their own tragedy. Meet
it probably isn't, to prod a dance from hung haunches

in metres invented for reasons of bouphonia,
but I wouldn't chop prose for it, facing it. My stature.
More than cattle are pent in the long crush of the roads
but a whistling butcher may slice through the tears in things
and a poor man savour them. It was this horror,
beyond the great ice, that launched us. Luscious bone-fruit.
What silk will tie this artery of knowledge?

5. Death Words

Beasts, cattle, have words, neither minor nor many.
The most frightening comes with a sudden stilt jump: the
    blood-moan
straight out of earth's marrow, that *clameur*, huge-mouthed,
raised when they nose death at one of their own

and only then. The whole milking herd at that cry
will come galloping, curveting, fish-leaping in furious play-steps
on the thunderstruck paddock, horning one another. A hock
    dance.
A puddle of blood will trigger it, even afterbirth.

They make the shield-wall over it, the foreheads jam down
on where death has stuck, as if to horn to death Death
(dumb rising numerous straw-trace). They pour out strength
enormously on the place, heap lungs' heat on the dead one.

It is one word they enact in the horn-gate there
and the neighbour herds all running to join in it
hit the near fences, creaking. We've unpicked many million
variants from our own like wake. This is a sample.

Roughly all at once, though, from the last-comers inward
the bunched rite breaks up. They grow aimless, calm down
in straggling completion. You might say Eat, missa est.
It is uttered just once for each charnel. They will feed

a tongue's nub away from then on. Their word of power
is formal, terrible, but, for an age now, stops there.
At best, ours ramify still. Perhaps God is inevitable.
He will not necessarily come, though, again, in our species.

6. The Commonwealth of Manu
AFTER A DISCUSSION WITH WALTER DAVIS

Just for a moment
it seemed true of our country equally:

Brahmin, Kshatriya,
Vaishya, Shudra,
the four castes in our country, too, plus such as myself
and the genuine black men.

Brahmins? Yes, certainly.
Warriors, too, faintly honoured. (In April, their feast.)
Then merchants and drudges. A vast majority drudges
to tighten one bolt all day, and remember equality.

Vaishya, though, merchant, lowest of the twice-born,
consider his dominance:
the whole nation turning on him,
his the government, his the laws, his the profits,

his systems the System.
All his, the glory of goods
to make silent the rivers, to level the untidy hills,
a dispensation not found in the laws of Manu.

Who, in the old country, stands as god to those merchants?
Ganesha mainly, isn't it, the elephant-headed,
he whose steed is a rat, Ganesha the greedy one,
overcomer of obstacles?

Consider the elephant,
thick-skinned, intelligent, vast,
the beast of long affection, long revenge,
capable of absorbing a whole pond.
Unable to jump. And very private at love.

Ganesha the god, provider of unearned good luck,
has a lovable tusk, and a cobra for a belt.
His other face is failure,
insanity, death.
Men dream they are swimming the wind.
Under this aspect, called Ganapati, he can
sometimes be appeased by a sacrifice of morals.

Just for a moment, it seemed so patently true,
considered without charity,
that this thread of Krishna I am spinning faltered,

this thread, these cattle.

7. Stockman Songs

Going to Rubuntja, the cattle-train. Banging two trailers.
Going empty to Urubuntja. Whipping like a duelling spear, but
    noisy.

    •

The artesian bore, that iron waterhole, that flowering water-
    bush;
thirsty calves come around. It dances on, stamping up steam.

    •

Cattle trailing to Rubuntja. Dotted on the sand-plain, tja:na:

    •

My wife's uncle Blue-tongue Lizard. He tastes of spinifex.
I chased him under the flat rocks there near Anakota.

    •

The clumsy bull, see! He's written a cheque on that cow's flank,
in the dust of her flank, on the fur, a long water cheque.

    •

My sad big horse. Men noticed his testicles. Horse.

    •

Look out, kangaroos! Jimmy Kulnma is casting lead fingers
in the sand, for his brown gun. Look out, kangaroos!

•

The iron waterhole, the iron gnamma-hole,
like a fat pigeon fluffing up, preening all day long.

•

How they howl, burning, how they fly, the cone-haired
     initiands;
falling, they are grass-trees on Tnorula, they are palms in
     Pmolangkinja.

•

Cattle walking to Rubuntja, roan among the leopardwood trees.

8. The Bush

"The boss at home, Missus?" A man couldn't tell suitors from
     buyers—
I could. They were shyer—Then you put your saddles in store—
And you kissed me once and started naming the sires
you'd give the boys home from agistment at Grammar and
     Shore—

The moon dipper, poured, is rising out of late rain,
the wind also rising confirms the bed of the house.
Old fencers sleep straight. The feeding dams ripple and blur.
The white bull of Wagga goes into the mountains again.

—And that was your father. The second time I dared call
he frogmarched me into the library, gnawed his moustache:
See you were wounded. He poured out two Haigs. I hope
you're still in a state to show our young filly the bush?

Fifty years' blue ribbons dimming the hall
—And are we weary of showing each other the bush?

9. Poley Bullock Couplets

Old Poley, pin bullock. The round one has left me slack here.
It is a kind of rest, this waiting, at pasture.

●

The first stones that Wheel broke, setting out, were my sex—
to think before me he was he was no more than a paradox.

●

Horses? Weak-boned screamers, all farting and zest.
When I followed war, it was the long stay: conquest.

●

I was most kin to humans when we trudged bedraggled,
one hide to the common rain, neither leading nor led.

●

The keenest whip-hands were those with stripes to pass on
but their yarn was right: a bull's breath will kill oxen.

●

I feed with man's foster mother. Dim company for her,
I wait for my one child, the wheel, to roll free of power.

10. The Boeotian Count

         Maudie
                  Maisie
         Shit-in-the bail
     Quince
             Blossom   Daisy
                  shy Abigail
      Primavera
                Strawberry   Doris
    one with a twostroke udd-

                    ah   Marrabel   Arabelle
            Horace   huge Onnanolia
                        dear
            Kayleen   little
    Glory   flies
            Calico   please
                    Chloreen   spare Anatolia
    Ambidextra
    IRON for creatures who   Portia
    slobber at extra   Persia
        teats
        on the sly   swish!
                                    in my eye
                full of KNOTS   bastard!
        if the milk's ropy   incontinent Sadie
    stone an old lady
    (quiet, you filth
                        how come you crossed water?)
        Oh   be kind, then, to Rose
                                        Gopi
                and Rose's   daughter
                    lame
                                            Utopie
        slavename
        brandname   earnotch   ring

                                    the far crows
                                        are
    Bottla   boys who knew horsewords
                    all died for the King   sleepy
            Corka
                                        Nugget
            Biddy
                Sheila   Jerusalem
                        Boxy
                    Janet
    Hafod   Joanie Walker
                boys who scorn cowtalk
                gladden the bayonet
            Hendre   Silkie
                    PetuniaPecuniaRegynaMahalia
            Godsend   li

70

                              Lily   Meg
                              li
            sundry   Bulleero
                         (lay glossolalia)
                                        Brindle-
                    -down-from-the-moon
      Hool 'em up, Nipper
                                   more milkers than Brown
                                   more points than the warriors
                                   this infinite muster
                              the Cape   Ungundhlovu
                              the royal kraal of Ulster
                         nurses of Camembert
                         King of Franks
                    and that staunch spreidh of
                                   cantons,
                         I give you thanks
      Moocher
                              and Dopey   old Cornucopie
                              and Honeycomb   rainbeaded
                                                       and warm
                         I pray that Hughie
                              will send you
                              safe home
                         where ploughing is playing
                    where Karma is Līlā.

11. Novilladas Democráticas

The fancy rider sent his Texan boots
to the showground fence to warn off polished wood.

Hearing talk of a princely purse, the bullock
was riddling trucks with his sad Mongol bow.

Filtering through the chrome and rust horizon
came boys and bark and shirts of landless red.

When the rider nocked the quarrel of his skill
the first leap slipped the dust of all his driving

moons travelled beneath him. His sex hit mountains and
    threads.
The bullock tried to explode in burgundy spittle

the state borders looping over him flourished their wheels
the sun in a frenzy was rhythmically tearing its clothes

his rapid brim cooled Brunette Downs. A moleskin pigeon
was trying to fly five ways from the roof of the sea

and the watchers strangled gnarled and woollen beasts
yelling Huge! The monster was jumping a jack-knife

and a number of hands into the wall of the country.
Burlesque sounds out of horses, men running like grass.

For a while, one human burned to be extinct
as longhorns. But a clown persuaded him.

The Skuthorpe rider, next up, picked his words
with a match. Beauty! Give him the wild cow's milk!

A derelict spirit begged to drink from swords
but was dismissed to futures of glazed paper.

12. Hall's Cattle

> Returning in chagrin from that defeat, Sir Frederick (Pottinger)
> consoled himself by ordering his men to burn down Sandy Creek
> homestead and to shut Hall's and McGuire's cattle in the mustering
> paddock to starve . . . Hall went back to the smoking ruins of his
> home and the stinking corpses of his cattle: "There's no evidence to try
> you on, my man, but in the meantime this will teach you a lesson."

> J. S. Manifold, WHO WROTE THE BALLADS

Upwind on Sandy Creek, cooking
not meat in a three-legged pot,
the future's oldest vessel,
sit McGuire and Hall.

Rails mortised in ironbark,
no special engine,
summoned this ruin within scent of water.
Rails regular as caste

in a tidy mind.
The homestead of course ash.
If he lacked hide before
he has a huge start now, Hall, home from acquittal.

For little enough, for a phrase of Kerry grammar
those English bailiff's bastards triced up Father
and learnt him how to sing his hundred lines
of the Hanover anthem . . .

So they did mine
but he was Devon.
Flies, humming, trinket blue and poison green—
I know little of Ireland.

Yes, police-baronet Pottinger
the drafting paddock poles
knock, splinter and rebound.
Poor starving heads.

They'll sentence me next time.
They have sentenced our sort
and all I know is this life.
I know nothing of America.

The water trough chamois'd smooth
with the last saliva, flies' foretaste.
When the dingoes hit
there is gargling for tongues.

Bushrangering isn't my work
but work is in prison
and the volunteer warders
have disgraced all reason.

When crows scatter down,
black fence sitters, meaning to stay,
they hack the bulbed eyes out first—
a day comes a man stops saying luck.

I'm thinking of a caper
to get them laughed out of the world,
a little war without deaths—
they are not worth lives.

Upwind of Cubbin Bin, slamming
the lid back on steam
in a three-legged vessel, Ben Hall
sits by his farm

and, rising, shakes mountains and watches
blue sergeants rage in their chains
the straight man's out on the moonlight side
and holidays shake from his reins.

It is a day for the poor,
their own saddle on a blood horse,
as the bush flies breed
to feed on noble brains.

13. Boöpis

Coming out of reflections
I find myself in the earth.
               My cow going on
into the creek from this paspalum-thatched tunnel-track
divides her hoofs among the water's impediments,
clastic and ungulate stones.
               She is just deep
enough to be suckling the stream when she drinks from it.

Wetted hooves, like hers,
incised in the alluvium
this grave's-width ramp up through the shoulder of the bank
but cattle paunches with their tongue-mapped girths also
brushed in glazes,

easements and ample places
at the far side of things from subtractive plating of spades
or the vertical slivers a coffin will score, sinking.

North, the heaped districts, and south
there'd be at least a Pharaoh's destruction of water
suspended above me in this chthonic section.
Seeds fall in here from the poise
of ploughland, grass land.
                         I could be easily
foreclosed to a motionless size in the ruins of gloss.

The old dead, though, are absorbed, becoming strata.
The crystals, too, of glaze or matt, who have
not much say in a slump
seem coolly balanced toward me.
                          At this depth among roots
I thank God's own sacrifice
that I am not here with seeds and a weighty request
from the upper fields,
my own words constrained with a cord.
Not being that way, if I met the lady of summer,
the beautiful cow-eyed one, I would be saying:

Madam, the children of the overworld
cannot lay down their instruments at will.
Babel in orbit maps the hasty parks,
missile and daisy scorn the steady husbands
and my countrymen mix green with foreign fruit.

14. The Pure Food Act

Night, as I go into the place of cattle.

Night over the dairy
the strainers sleeping in their fractions,
vats
and the mixing plunger, that dwarf ski-stock, hung.

On the creekstone cement
water driven hard through the Pure Food Act

dries slowest round tree-segment stools,
each buffed
to a still bum-shine,
sides calcified with froth.

Country disc-jocks
have the idea. Their listeners aren't all human.
Cows like, or let their milk for, a firm beat
nothing too plangent (diesel bass is good).
Sinatra, though, could calm a yardful of horns
and the Water Music
has never yet corrupted honest milkers
in their pure food act.

The quiet dismissal switching it off, though,
and carrying the last bucket, saline-sickly
still undrinkable raw milk to pour in high
for its herringbone and cooling pipe-grid
fall
to the muscle-building cans.

His wedding, or a war,
might excuse a man from milking
but milk-steeped hands are good for a violin
and a cow in rain time is
a stout wall of tears.

But I'm britching back.

I let myself out through the bail gate.
Night, as I say.
Night, as I go out to the place of cattle.

15. Gōlōka

Their speech is a sense of place
night makes remote
lucerne fields in the dark hills are renamed
Moorea, Euboea.

That bull invoking Mundubbera, Karuah
and Speewah, now, Speewah
is trying his sultanate out on infinite space.

Sleepy, lingually liquescent.
It is a delectation, the matter of rock-salt,
a drawn, sparkling mouth

squaremouth, though, for the mother
mourning at the five-bar
gate for her tongue-sculpted, milky one
manhandled to the mad chute, steel-barred,
gone above gears.

No. Calling back the lost ones
is long, but not weak.
Older than crying, and less for yourself.

When heifers processing
the planet's uncountable crop
butt, or show horns, glower, jump fur-marred aside
and afterwards lick
they are establishing
the order of precedence of the Sun King's court
a needed concern
the risen will have cast off.

Effacing the cave-clay hand
from the shoulders of cattle, and the pet cattle-names
from the souls of slaves,
will be night work for us before that wide enablement.

What I know, says the man
who has come out of his house,
is nothing recent. An old song and an ancient one.

The ancient tune is faint (fainter still, the kings in her)
but it keeps me farming
rather than raping, or embalming, the land.
The other's the New World. We won't be peasants again.

Children are leaping
and wives are setting out cakes on trestle tables
(cuisine is class, but cookery is cake)
Camerons with Schultzes Breens married Crowhursts Joy
turned Catholic
the meaning of lists a weave we are cruellest maintaining it
a tissue wider than countries it carries all blood
it must only change slowly. Disorder is drawn to the gaps
the more we expect it we would love to be honest
but we know when to be.
This is community. Courage had better be real.

A black woman murmurs:
The Son of God, he said all hidden things would come out
he wasn't nervous.

A cornbag quilt and an aeroplane to sow clover
suit my breed of jokes
says the strong man facing the moon.
We'll suffer culture for some of our devilry yet
as Athens comes for our hide, or sends Arcadia.
Consequences hurt worse, but they impoverish less
being Nature.

I stand to one side of this night work
wishing it ease
for the minuscule stitch of baptismal clothes to tip through it
and five-course breakfasts eaten with great knives.

Through fences mended
with bedsprings, for intransigence,
and out between tussocks come all the tame and wild cattle
with their boat-prow briskets and brow-whorls and
prehuman gifts:
rank loyalty ritual
curiosity, frenzy, affection, remembrance of ambush
and their farther own: ear-focus, digestion of hard sugar,
a nose for oestrus.

The moon rides herd on a tide of fertile crescents.
Right among the tables people are touching the cattle
not mastering. Meeting.
They mingle and they take steps
humans laugh cattle nuzzle fur shifts over joints and no voice
pretends a transaction.
Humped decorum, cows pee. Charlie's Wain in the sky full of grass
sprinkles the creatures
all here are flesh of heaven as roughly as stones.

When Cloven Hoof and Wheel made war on a chair
the Hoof was burned to hide the holes in his back
that was indeed war
good people resigned from dancing and lived in the air
much wearing of black
then madness was easy. That day crumbles here. More future
in a little girl feeding the clean beasts rainbow cake.

•

Scattered, at the nub of things,
over that blood-and-dung mirror-floor, the leaf-giving
earth, men and bulls,
they of Murcia, they of Nîmes, the Nandi bull, the white bull
of Washpool, and he of the Cassidys, and they of the
drinkers of *bikavér*
they are single beyond counting; the people and the horned
people stand
in the sad forbearance
of those inescapably armed.

I am looking at the place where the names well out of field stone,
at the feared successor of plenty, the place like curved water.
In the fullness of work, it is health to see this,
the cattle-sphere fitting the green
and hard yellow worlds.

I am looking at equality where it seeks no victories.

•

The delivered stampede
continuing around me in feasting, the herds graze among us
in planetary dispersions. A Xhosa herdkeeper
salutes me, with his spoon:
Xho, eater from tins!

Xhe! I wholly agree,
sitting on cram-full bags.
There's also drinking from a jar. The depôt pleasures.
What better in Carthage or Rome
when they became cover?

The king of justice (human)
would not enter Paradise without the lost, or his dog
—living and work are one thing, or the rivers die,
my neighbour's wife's saying,
a blackfellow told me tonight, and I knew. I knew.
Dozens of us clasp hands with her, for courage.

Laughter, away down the creek
gradually less competitive:
the literal disports.

Nearer sit poncho-wrapped figures
sipping through silver tubes. Antique, polite,
they would insult you first.
They are sizing up ringers (whose weapons would be improvised)
and the ringers themselves are praising this inside country.
Yes. Nice patch of storm.

Hard men, talking places
on a night-watch track:
Camooweal. Caaguazú.
Rectangular grind of cattle jaws all around them.

The houses of humans walking home in dew-dark
are hillsides apart.

As I enter my own, the moon is coming weather
and the sun dry honey
in every cell of the wood.

I have travelled one day.

József
M.J.K. 1883–1974 IN PIAM MEMORIAM

You ride on the world-horse once
no matter how brave your seat
or polished your boots, it may gallop you
into undreamed-of fields

but this field's outlandish: Australia!
To end in this burnt-smelling, blue-hearted
metropolis of sore feet and trains
(though the laughing bird's a good fellow).

Outlandish not to have died
in king-and-kaiserly service,
dismounted, beneath the smashed guns
or later, with barons and credit

after cognac, a clean pistol death.
Alas, a small target, this heart.
Both holes were in front, though, entry
and exit. I learned to relish that.

Strange not to have died with the Kingdom
when Horthy's fleet sank, and the betting
grew feverish, on black and on red,
to have outlived even my Friday club

and our joke: *senilis senili*
gaudet. I bring home coffee now.
Dear God, not one café in this place,
no Andrássy-street, no Margaret's Island . . .

no law worth the name: they are British
and hangmen and precedent-quibblers
make rough jurisprudence at best.
Fairness, of course; that was their word.

I don't think Nature speaks English.
I used to believe I knew enough
with *gentleman, whisky, handicap*
and perhaps *tweed*. French lacked all those.

I learned the fine detail at seventy
out here. Ghosts in many casinos
must have smiled as I hawked playing cards
to shady clubs up long stairways

and was naturalized by a Lord Mayor
and many bookmakers, becoming a
New Australian. My son claims he always
was one. We had baptized him Gino

in Hungary. His children are natives
remote as next century. My eyes
are losing all faces, all letters,
the colours go, red, white, now green

into Hungary, Hungary of the poplar trees
and the wide summers where I am young
in uniform, riding with Nelly,
the horseshoes' noise cupping our speeches.

I, Mórelli József Károly,
once attorney, twice gunshot, thrice rich,
my cigarettes, monogrammed, from Kyriazi,
once married (dear girl!) to a Jew

(gaining little from that but good memories
though my son's uniforms fitted her son
until it was next year in Cape Town)
am no longer easy to soften.

I will eat stuffed peppers and birds' milk,
avoid nuns, who are monstrous bad luck,
write letters from memory, smoke Winstons
and flex my right elbow at death

and, more gently, at living.

Folklore

What are the sights of our town?

Well, there is that skeleton they hang
some nights in the bar of the Rest
and everyone laughing in whispers
the barmaid broke down one time, laughing.
The cord goes up through the ceiling
to the undersprings of the big
white bed in the Honeymoon Suite
and when those bones even jiggle
there's cheers (and a donnybrook once)
and when they joggle, there's whooping
and folk stalking out in emotions
and when they dance—hoo, when they dance!
he knows every tune on the honeymoon
flute, does the hollow-hipped fellow.
There are a few, mind, who drink on
straight through it all. Steady drinkers.
Up over the pub there's the sky
full of stars, as I have reflected
outside, while guiding the course of my
thoughts. Some say there's a larger

cord goes up there, but I doubt it
I mean
but then I'm no dancer.

Besides that, there's meatworks and mines.

The Police: Seven Voices

1. The Knuckle Garden

In the city of Cargo
at the very centre of it
is the Knuckle Garden

Alibis melt off like grease
names, causes, soak into the tiles
in the Knuckle Garden

This garden is kept by blue serge
men with thick pocketknife nails
and impatient fellows

Their opinions are petrol, and steel,
blurred elastic, and knowing the time,
they are wholly practical

With strong lights to shine through hard men
and hoses—men have died fighting those,
Laocoöns, distending

Men have died of falling downstairs
have ruptured their spleen eating pies
have confessed to God's death

And women have bled from soul-searching
but let us, however altered
the shape of our smiles, be content

For factory whistles would choke
and the flag catch afire from its stars
without these ministers

Nor would the great Cargo come
or keep on its shelves, without
the Knuckle Garden.

2. Plainclothes Park

Thinking my old thought in the eye-stinging dark:
the Motive Revealer. People are so undeclared.
A button, now, on a unit in your pocket—
I was wiring that airy device in the mid-city park.

There'd be luminous face colours. Visible only to you.
Green for lying, yellow when you had them scared.
Violence? Red. When a man reached intense pink, you'd hit him
first. Or change tack. I've had various meanings for blue . . .

The man sitting next to me thought his kink out loud:
*The body—you know? There are design flaws God left
hanging. Too many non-overridable programmes.
Why shouldn't we will new teeth, new hair, new organs?*

*Will-overrides, friend. We need to start working on these,
and shielding. Good God! All that soft rippable belly
without a bone casque. And non-retractable genitals!*
My trouble, I muttered, is with doubt, not knees.

His face was no colour that betokens guilt
but I questioned him (and I think he questioned me).
No result. He left the park shortly after
and vanished from sight in the city we had built.

3. Discontent, Reading Conan Doyle

CI: the detectives. After the age of belief
we're what happened to mystery. Our model explainaway trade
brings complex relief.

Not quite your suave Sherlocks, we know
fences, sperm, payoffs, the squalor of minds, and where
the husbands go.

The gentlemen Sherlocks
trail their gentlemen quarry, one case at a time.
Let us touch our forelocks.

From cars, under glass
we watch the citizens: Touchables and Not
is our theory of class.

The uniform branch have their mystery, the Peace:
shall meaning be slow, at home, at the factory, at church
or loose in the streets?

We still defend logic—
try bringing a fat man down off a love-death pact
and you learn about magic—

but our mystery's the Score
that is, knowing it. Which is the Upper Hand.
That's to say, the Law.

Not of course for some.
Say the Law's a regent till the King comes back
if he does come.

Reading modern stuff at times
you'd think all crime was protest, or illusion—
we should charge the victims.

Doubts, then, and changes:
don't ever book on them. The old sleuths dealt, like us,
only with strangers

so if we're sent
to interview you, in especially the poorer suburbs,
don't run. Don't quote the law. If you're a man

be in employment.

4. Rostered Duty

This is the hour the Crucified Bludger is fed
a tin dish held to his mouth and his night's stain hosed down
before he is driven slow-slow through the fibro-tile streets
and the message gets through to moaners, to oversleepers,
to migrants who dream dark police, to blokes thinking Sickie.

This is the hour the hurrying frowners at railway
stations don't look but all read his placard: WORK-SHY.
Soon, outside factory and depot, flies supping his wounds,
he will be ignored by staff, by management, by unions,
all too mature to look. Very few people focus,

not the realists, nor the long planners, not the fellows
with trades in demand, nor the ones proud they can shovel
as much as God's truck can dump; self-provers and winners
never see him at all, and talk about him constantly.
But everyone knows the form: on a quiet day

passing Hey Folks PLANETWIDE Pow! Discounts / Trade Ins!
I've been known to say to the salesfolk there not looking
Gooday, how's the carrot? Yes, I've had my turn,
served my tour with the Bludger. Every policeman does one.
I've picked airgun slugs out of him, tuned his trannie on race days,

heard him howl in the truck bay, echoing the oil drums.
I've supervised him and his wife on a visiting day—
No madam we can't let him down—and had her scream
into my face *ME! crucify ME, God damn you!*
At least it's intense. Jail is drearier employment.

When he'd get randy we'd turn him face to the van.
I think of him often, spread-Andrewed on four bolts
parked facing the sea for a treat of a summer evening
(when he bit my hand to the bone he saw more sunsets).
I remember him watching the big ships loading bales

and unloading bales, as the radio quacked Production.
This is a shop, boys, not a nation, a man said,
making a gesture. A poet growled *Misemployment*

87

but poets are kids. A thousand fellows in ties
picking flyspecks from pepper with fine Government needles

or that's what it looked like said *No time to be choosy.*
Unless he's got a job, smiled the chief clerk, *he can't have one.*
It was interesting duty, travelling with the Bludger,
more to the point than backing up wives and collectors
and once you've done it, you're never, like they say, off duty.

5. *The Lips Move During Anointing*
FOR FR EDMUND CAMPION

Stopped
     tilted
           watching a ditch
digger's family eat, in a window,
                   miles on—
blue metal gums my draining reasons
wait
    there'll be time for doubling my tongue
back, in,
         and the bucket and the raincoat
I'm trying to say
on-the-spot dignity Walther speed
                docked
my imaginary body
streaming hurt at the sky like headlights
I'm trying to SAY
         that shame, rolling, boot-walloping
into the sniggers of gambling men tankwater
drinkers pill burners
           I'll be with long gone
horse police in their own steel, made dance
or wire stretched between trees,
that story
I was the scorer you didn't call sport
to blunt men up against the numbers
poor is still
      Christ
        and not money-poor now

I was a copper, not ever a policeman
a john served right on a lorry's tray
I was the joker who made numbers win
I'm learning pity
                    rougher than shear
watching those ones
                    my glazing angle.
I would feed them from my own plate
set aside even fact, with good losing, not
doing my job with a score for a vision
which makes a cop of any fellow
                                unfix me, but, then
from my slewed skidding. I
will, bare-eyed, see them
                            anyway, a long time
happy with lamp pickles worn faces, no one
stacking on the realities
chipped star of black tea
I was a toddler under sad calendars
there, before winning
                        walk, don't spill
this, in my chinstrap cup under the oilskins, this
decency, shape
                there'll be no columns
in justice.
            No setup.

6. The Breach

I am a policeman
it is easier to make me seem an oaf
than to handle the truth

I came from a coaldust town
when I was seventeen, because there was nothing
for a young fellow there

the Force drew me because of a sense I had
and have grown out of

I said to Ware once, Harry, you're the best
cop of the lot: you only arrest falls
he was amused

I seem to be making an inventory of my life
but in that house opposite, first floor
there is a breach
and me, in this body I am careful with,
I'm going to have to enter that house soon

and stop that breach

it is a bad one people could fall through
we know that three have
and he's got a child poised

I have struck men in back rooms late at night
with faces you could fall a thousand feet down
and I've seen things in bowls

the trick is not to be a breach yourself
and to stop your side from being one
I suppose

the sniper Spiteri, when I was just out of cadets—
some far-west cockies' boys straight off the sheep train
came up with their .303s and offered to help
they were sixteen years old

we chased them away, not doubting for a minute
they could do what they said
bury your silver the day we let that start

now I've said my ideals

Snowy cut, snow he cut . . .
A razor-gang hood my uncle claims he met
is running through my mind
in Woolloomooloo, wet streets, the nineteen twenties
dear kind Snowy Cutmore

Snowy cuts no more
he was a real breach

also, in our town, I
remember the old hand bowsers, that gentle apop-
poplexy of benzine in the big glass heads
twenty years since I saw them

There's a moment with every man who has started a stir

when he tires of it, wants to put it aside
and be back, unguilty, that morning, pouring the milk

that is the time to separate him from it
if I am very good I'll judge that time
just about right

the ideal is to keep the man and stop
the breach
that's the high standard

but the breach must close

if later goes all right
I am going to paint the roof of our house
on my day off.

7. Sergeant Forby Lectures the Cadets

Old Warwick, the husband, scratched his head:
they'd run off together, was all he knew.
He didn't know where.
Most would have said where.
He had no theories about the horse.

We stood round it,
the trackers drowsing.

*Our witnesses reckon they told the boarder
you knew, and would shoot him.*

He had no views on that.
They went off together. *I told them Get,*
her and him.

Then some fool poked the horse with a stick.
It bowled us, gagging, clean off the hill.

Country people aren't keen on decay
too many midsummer funerals, I guess,
of beasts, and men. Too many feeds
of ptomaine mutton in the heat

sweets from the handy home botulin kit.
No market for jugged hare or ripe cheese
among that sort.

We had some sort of case:
opportunity, motive, shot horse
but Warwick's counsel made mince of it.
Without bodies, the onus was on us
(I hope the Onus comes on him
some dark night)
but he was right.

And Warwick got off.
He was ten minutes gone
when the answer hit me like a brick:
country people aren't keen on decay
of course!

And we dug under the horse.

The secret of our profession, this:
we dig under the horse.
Dismiss.

Aqualung Shinto

FOR CHRIS KOCH

All day above the Japanese fleet,
the zenith sun between the islands
unmoving. We were after the flagship

and kept diving, finding tackle
jettisoned in her agony. My
shadow over the sand floor curved

on chain, on wavering metal forms,
Don saying *Be careful of any ammo,
it could still give us the instant bends.*

We were following the logic
of a dying ship among islands: here
he would have considered beaching her, here
the sub may have come for the admiral. We dived

in lucid water, tracing down
the death-hours of an Imperial captain
thirty years wiser than we were

in settling steel, in shouting men
in—reached after final avalanche cruising—
a peaceful Sun, that shapelessness.

We would come up from the dreamlight plane
and eat meals aboard the boat
Where we want her to lie, I guess,

*is a place neither dry nor drowned
where we could drift in Dante-style
and observe grotesques of courage*

*performed by knights of bushido in
tight black jackets. Quintessence movies.*
I finished my can. *I would go up*

to Yamada and address him: Captain
I was born in 'thirty-eight
please give me what you own of me.

Those days, below in the sharks' kingdom,
I kept remembering the iron ore ports
the black ships feeding at all times

and ore dust the colour of dried blood
on every object. Baseball Maru,
have you jettisoned anything

but the sword-wearers? That direct style?
(OVERACHIEVERS ARE JAPANESE
I wrote in pentel ink on the bulkhead.)

The water was layered like a pearl
clear-opaque-clear as I swam down
thinking of Marines twenty years in hiding
in dugouts, eating tadpole mush,
waiting to fight, treasuring a mortar

young men approaching fifty still
begging pardon, not having flown winged bombs

NIHON, the ultimate taut ship . . .
It shamed our carefully dazzle-painted
sanity. Don below me bubbled.
We were close to the flagship now
by the debris. Her presence was
longing for form. Her own. Again.
Aloud in my head I told myself
she would rise if I clapped my hands:

towering superstructure, respectable
maritime-power lines—all just
askew by a fraction from machine history

in the copyist's deadness which betrays
cherishment of carp flags and tea brushes

design like poems in a culture-language.

At night, weighing the heart of it:
We are as easy to recruit
as ever, Don said,
but harder to command.

We are almost free of the State
almost clear, again, of armies.
It is time to oppress the State.

I think that is the history
of the rest of this century: cavaliers.
Were you romantic about cavaliers?

In the end it may be safer.
Defaming the high words—honour, courage—
has not stopped us. It has made us mad

we are maddened by a dumb spirit.
I lay there also musing. Waves.
Mishima died. Screams from Lod airport . . .

In the one entirely native
and wisest Japanese faith, I said,
a mirror hangs before sanctuaries.

Oh Zen makes colonials of a few
but each people has its proper Shinto
distinctive as verandah beams

hard to join as a stranger's childhood.
What withers us is that Australia
is a land of shamefaced shrines.

Perhaps, I went on, *the history coming*
is just more peoples passing for white,
fronting for themselves in English

and preserving their life in a closing fraction

from which leap unbelievably savage
flames. Which was your major point.

Imminent below us those nights, big
as an undersea ridge between the islands
a battleship of the Kongo class

was sending out her crew like waves:
Your fathers killed us, their minds aloof
from us in war as in any peace

and we were bringing pine-needle cakes, fox stories.

The Canberra Suburbs' Infinite Extension

Citizens live in peace and honour
in Pearce and Higgins and O'Connor,
Campbellites drive Mercedes-Benzes,
lobbyists shall multiply in Menzies—
but why not name suburbs for ideas
which equally have shaped our years?

I shall play a set of tennis
in the gardens of Red Menace

Shall I scorn to plant a dahlia
in the soil of White Australia?

Who will call down Lewis Mumford
on the streets of Frugal Comfort?

Oh live in Fadden and be content:
everywhere's Environment.

Thinking About Aboriginal Land Rights,
I Visit the Farm I Will Not Inherit

Watching from the barn the seedlight and nearly-all-down
currents of a spring day, I see the only lines bearing
consistent strain are the straight ones: fence, house corner,
outermost furrows. The drifts of grass coming and canes
are whorled and sod-bunching, are issuant, with dusts.
The wind-lap outlines of lagoons are pollen-concurred
and the light rising out of them stretches in figments and wings.
The ambient day-tides contain every mouldering and oil
that the bush would need to come back right this day,
not suddenly, but all down the farm slopes, the polished shell
    barks
flaking, leaves noon-thin, with shale stones and orchids at foot
and the creek a hung gallery again, and the bee trees unrobbed.
By sundown it is dense dusk, all the tracks closing in.
I go into the earth near the feed shed for thousands of years.

Their Cities, Their Universities

The men of my family danced a reel with sugar
    for two generations.
Robbie Burns was involved, that barley spirit
and history, and their fathers' voyage out
    but that is a novel.
The past explains us and it gets our flesh.

You would find most older Murray houses
    girt in some glitter
of bottle-glass in the paddocks, rum necks and whisky ghosts,
Wolfe's dark Aromatic Schnapps mostly grassroots-under now
    and insulin, insulin
as if to help the earth digest such crystals,
the thousand year jag, the gullies of downtrodden light.

It was in these spirits
that Veitch rode the frisky stick horse: *Go in, Mrs Maurer!*
   he's shying at ye!
and Sam towed Reggie-Boy shrieking behind his big Dodge
   in the splintering sulky.

It was through these that Hughie tumbled off his mare
   on the heirloom fiddle
and uncle Jock Clark danced Whee! in the shopping-day street
   prick burst from his trousers
asperging the people, a boneless arm limber as Jock
   and Burns got misquoted.

      ●

From the photograph, they look at me. Intelligent book-shy
   faces.
The scrolls of their fiddles curl at me, the pipe smoke goes up
fuzzy as the toddler who moved, or the man who shook his
   head at a fly
and smeared his last chance at history. The day is a bright one,

the golden wedding of Bella and John Allan,
old Bunyah Johnnie, seated here past the end
of his fabulous hospitality: *small table at Murrays*
today. Only twenty-six, not counting family—
That homestead is long gone—*man should hae led trumps—*
and the times are flattening down. The ringbarked Twenties.

   My great-grandfather John
is remembering what it is to conquer country:
   brush soil upturned,
thin-legged black people who would show you fruit,
a house set fair to a track to capture company.

Isabella, shrunken in silks, is holding minds with him
   (they are first cousins)
Gey strange it is, my hands free all day long now
of flour, milk, feathers. We never had to stint.
   Thank God for that, John.

John Murray of Bunyah, born in a Biscay storm,
    my offshore Basque
    and thriftless as Montrose.

                ●

The drinking Murrays. They were rarely brutal.
It wasn't Murrays who rode the policeman with spurs
or gelded the half-witted youth to spare him problems
    but trotting through town
whips coiled and pipes alight, drawing revellers to them
and holding forth on music and seeds and the wurrld
    in their fathers' accent
and going home after for three nights, cooeeing abstemious
settlers from bed to hooting strathspey contests
and holding Saturday dances from Thursday night on
with their children milking a hundred cows in jig time
and schottische time, as the fiddlers raised the sun,
    that was the notion.

    After the heights
Grandfather, crossed, would upend the breakfast table
    and then his breakfast:
Father's sick. Walk quiet. He'll draw the whip on you.
He has been out of Sense and Worth in timber rooms
where men make bets and spittle beads, whooping their Lallans,
and night-sugar world where Burns is an evil spirit
    and self a form of anger.

                ●

Aunts with a nose for sin, young chaps with haircuts
combed like an open ginger book, pretty girls like a leafed one
relax from their poses, stroll off into marriages, deaths.

    Here at the focus
the sun goes under the paddocks, though, and pipers
are bulging the house with their summoned howling tune
and the drinkers, the brothers, candles in their hands,
are kneeling on the floor to judge the tramping beat

and the style of it:
The big bloke's stepping fine!

And Veitch is confiding the hard drink to get into
a man is the second one. He means, for subversion.
　Veitch's shield against
inspectors, collectors, police is a happy day
that leaves them sitting about, hiccuping and ashamed
or lurching from their cars miles off, ashamed, hiccuping.

Wives and sisters are forbidden the shamanism of glass;
　they go busy, or proud
or brandish the Word, that soured woman's weapon
cold-hammered by Knox, fresh-honed by the Wee Free Kirk,
　hard splinter of that Faith
　which overcame religion,

but the patriarchs are keeping their own time
like a door in the farm-dull days, and separate as logic.
　Boys nodding in cars outside
the pubs work promised ground they will not inherit.
It distils too sweet. Though it is all their wages.
They hear their lives going wheedle-and-away
on the four strained wires of a fiddle, in a spent tradition
Good on ye, Allan! and singing with no terms.
Scotland is a place Dad goes when he drinks rum
　but their feet are tapping.

They wasted their lands for that (and for all that)
　the redhaired Murrays.
The reasons are a novel, incomplete as cultures
now everywhere become. It is almost overt now:

　　we are going to the cause
　　not coming from it.

Kiss of the Whip

In Cardiff, off Saint Mary's Street,
there in the porn shops you could get
a magazine called Kiss of the Whip.
I used to pretend I'd had poems in it.

Kiss of the Whip. I never saw it.
I might have encountered familiar skills
having been raised in a stockwhip culture.
Grandfather could dock a black snake's head,

Stanley would crack the snake for preference
leap from his horse grab whirl and jolt!
the popped head hummed from his one-shot slingshot.
The whips themselves were black, fine-braided,

arm-coiling beasts that could suddenly flourish
and cut a cannibal strip from a bull
(millisecond returns) or idly behead an
ant on the track. My father did that.

A knot in the lash would kill a rabbit.
There were decencies: good dogs and children
were flogged with the same lash doubled back.
A horsehair plait on the tip for a cracker

sharpened the note. For ten or twelve thousand
years this was the sonic barrier's
one human fracture. Whip-cracking is that:
thonged lightning making the leanest thunder.

When black snakes go to Hell they are
affixed by their fangs to carved whip-handles
and fed on nothing but noonday heat,
sweat and flowing rumps and language.

They writhe up dust-storms for revenge
and send them roaring where creature comfort's
got with a touch of the lash. And that
is a temple yard that will bear more cleansing

before, through droughts and barracks, those
lax, quiet-speaking, sudden fellows
emerge where skill unbraids from death
and mastering, in Saint Mary's Street.

On the Wreckage
of a Hijacked Airliner

How did the Oriental
curse go, again? May you live
in literary times?

Escaping Out There

With clutch-slip and tappet-noise
we rotate the Shell station
a Royal Mail Reo
bus gathering speed through the last
sleeve-pluck of motels.
I was right to turn inland from here.

Dressed by two clotheslines
by noon I'll be famous throughout
the birthday-call networks.
Police bikes will leap headlands for me
and feel under paddocks
but I will be away out.

The people around me
restore me like colours. Their heads
are full of quiet electrified porridge and blood
I almost can't bear how delicate the webbings
of their lives are in there, the cattle and front yards and psalms.
The men wear the old war haircuts of this century
and the women's waves are no longer the newest idea.

The driver is practising grips
for his wrestle with ranges
we are leaving the parts where Please and Excuse Me are said
the man up front of me
hands his wife to one side as gently as crockery
getting down their bags.

The hills are coming around us like calves
to a rattled milk bucket
the plovers and waves step away at the crossings we reach.
The offsider can hit drum letterboxes and dogs
with papers and the mail.
He discusses his family, using racehorse names:
Prince Rajah's his eldest, I think. Dickie's Pride is his wife.

The windscreen is filled half the time with nothing but sky
we are getting well out.
Farm people step down
at Howards and Scobies and Where the Old School Got Burnt.
At All the Bloodwoods
and at the Flying-Fox Cooking-Place
timber people step down.
There are no people now at Praising White Moth Larvae
and no one gets off Where the Big Red Bull Went Over.
I wouldn't either.

But crossing that crest, the second sight comes upon us:
You would never again, the rabbiter's wife says to me,
you've grew out of it.
They should be thumped, but in hot blood, says the fencer,
none of this ten-years-cold-steel stuff
you young bastard

I am over the crest
and going on where unadmitted grandmothers
make farms easy-going
and cornbag quilts cover more than kids of a three-dog
winter's night.
I will go on from there to where the west wind rises
further east, the gorge is so far back
and take a job out there with a lazy man.

When strangers come, I'll slope steeply down and grow trees.
My name will rub off out there on the lips of the watershed
and when I am fine as cloud-webbing, I will drift
vaguely down valleys,
me, or my water, if it comes to that,
into further lives

I will make good ancestors.

Portrait of the Artist
as a New World Driver

A car is also
a high-speed hermitage. Here
only the souls of policemen can get at you.
Who would put in a telephone,
that merciless foot-in-the-door
of realities, realties?

Delight of a stick-shift—
farms were abandoned for these pleasures. Second
to third in this Mazda is a stepped inflection
third back to first at the lights
a concessive
V of junction.

Under the overcoming
undiminishing sky you are scarcely supervised:
you can let out language
to exercise, to romp in the grass beyond Greek.
You can rejoice in tongues,
orotate parafundities.

They simplify
who say the Artist's a child
they miss the point closely: an artist
even if he has brothers, sisters, spouse
is an only child.

Among the self-taught
the loners, chart-freaks, bush encyclopedists
there are protocols, too: we meet
gravely as stiff princes, and swap fact:
Did you know some bats can climb side on?

Mind you, Hitler was one of us.
He had a theory. We also count stern scholars
in whose disputes you almost hear the teenage
hobbyist still disputing proof and mint
and wheelmen who murmur *Suffering is bourgeois.*

But swapping cogs to pass a
mountainous rig and its prime mover, I
reflect that driving's a mastery the mastered
are holding on to.
It has gone down among the ancient crafts
to hide in our muscles.

Indeed, if you asked
where the New World is, I'd have to answer
he is in his car
he is booming down the highways
in that funnel of blue-green-gold, tree-flecked and streaming
light that a car is always breaking out of—

We didn't come of
the New World, but we've owned it.
From a steady bang, ever more globes, flying outward;
strange tunings are between us.
Of course we love our shells: they make the anthill
bearable. Of course the price is blood.

Company

Where two or three
are gathered together, that
is about enough.

Cycling in the Lake Country

Dried phlegm of lakes
that die of thirst. Burnt umber
dust, wind-smoothed, on glue.
Miles across, cattle-coloured
are the plains of Ryoanji.

Lakes of craze-brick. The salt
detailing around mallee islands
is two brush-hairs thick
(the galvanized salt farther out
sustains mirage islands).

No ruins in Australia?
Here are the ruins of seas
and ruins in the mouth:
the place-names here are now
pronounced in English.

Choking beasts to kill time
the particulate, millionfold
lake basins, wind-topped,
are eon-strength ocean paste
awaiting pole-melt and rains.

●

This angelic free walking:
is a long meditation of shores
far-reachingly stepping
I cross the immense north stations
ahead of blown grass.

Passing smoke-coloured emus:
the Army, with Lewis guns,
once fought that lot in the wheat country.
Throat-talking sandgropers, they rise
dangling medals of clay.

No man ever composed
a sacred song. The honey ant,
euro and wagtail fathers brought them forth
thigh-slapping in showers of selves,
lying down, being outcrops.

When the humans reeled
under violence, they gave boys'
foreskins to the hawk men
on the whirlwind ground.
Age-long, it sufficed us.

        •

The free-leaping spirit
hunters and white men with wheels
have one fact in common:
heat, flies and self-doubt
fall away from a man dressed in speed.

Roused by the full moon
I ride on along
the wire coasts of the outstation paddocks,
those seas of tranquillity,
in daylight, dry land.

The hull-down homestead passes me, miles off
"I knew you were missing the sea,
love, that first year."
They lie, embraced, their backs to history
she listens to the sea in his chapped ear.

        •

The war is farmers and miners. Both sides own me.
Big wheels revolve, and my mother's Cornish dad
comes into mind: he coughs up red and black,
dying, before my day,
on the Hunter fields.

The gold rushes conquered the world
most work, most love
most art is mining now.
The mullock is still
literal in Kalgoorlie.

Hearing the word *gentleman*
in a public bar there
I recognize a line of evolution
we thought to secure with a distant crown
lest it outgrew privilege.

In Kalgoorlie, though, I meet
a blind gem cutter. She
can put any stone to her cheek
name it and grade it.
She has no fear of cold stones at her cheek.

•

The light-wheeled VeeJays of
Kambalda Yacht Club
set spinnakers and career off
ages into the blue.
There is, naturally, a Commodore.

The day I reach Kambalda
some revenant waters still lie
thumbnail-deep, off the causeway
the sky floating there vast as Huron
but flesh shows between waves.

In sheltered, warm plasma
I dive to ring-finger depth,
no unwelcome settler.
A span deeper, and gravity's
calf begins sucking my hand.

•

Lionel Brockman hides his wife
and children in several stones
and watches from a finch as I camp.
I don't understand the world,
I confess, to coax them.

They are wise to fight shy.
Trees withdrew from my kind
when we said Tactics.
Nor is our takeover smell lessened, now that art
is not culture, but a culture.

I have been drunk in towns
built out of defiance of taste
which is to say, Europe.
I have rolled in the fact
and made a jingling sound.

Who am I to throw clay
at a Valiant abandoned in glare
stripped raw and daubed CONSTIPATED—CAN'T PASS
    A THING
we are a colloquial nation
most colonial when serious.

I am drawn to the noble mad, but
they betray evolution:
they do not lie, or joke.
One I met on the Goldfields would have it honour was sperm
and sadism a preference.

At birth, each Australian
receives a stout bullshit gauge
made of mulga from here
double-edged, emblematic
it is his to break.

Country the forceful can
wreck but not reach

shall welcome the calm man
with nothing to teach,
I sing to Brockman in the mulga forest.

•

Out here, the trees
grow coolly under the earth
and the bush is branches.
Something crashes away
in a dream of tall woods.

Going south all day
I think about the Republic.
I will improve my silence and listen to lives.
Those who would listen
have always been the Republic.

I rest, and my two wheels
continue as if the plains sloped
south, as the map falls.
Sunrise and sunset ride over me,
unending wheels.

•

The Tuareg say
God made the desert last
as his most spacious great hall
to withdraw in from creation.
He is receding north now.

Limestone plain. The round lakes
clutch bulrushes at their deep point
bayonet-stiff between rains
the bottoms shelve in months and days of chalk
white circling rings. Impenetrable hollows.

Riding at noon
the great paddocks swimming with heat

I come to a stone hut. It is hard to think there,
the walls drip with laughter,
the tank, the yards, the downed fence cower with laughter.

•

Young man in a ute:
I'm from over in New South. I bought this block.
A lifetime of work stares at him off the leaves.
In Sydney they keep a black stump with a share
and handles. The first plough on this continent.

In Esperance, I reached a final lake
cupped in rough talcum.
Soft facepowder bloom made all the hanging country
faintly peach. Downward among cloud-wools
I had for long moments
a more-than-perfect self
refined by the lands
in mourning for the sea.
We bobbed at each other as the coast wind passed
the drive-in, and found us.

Sidere Mens Eadem Mutato
A SPIRAL OF SONNETS FOR ROBERT ELLIS

Out of the Fifties, a time of picking your nose
while standing at attention in civilian clothes,
we travelled luxury class in our drift to the city
not having a war, we went to university.
We learned to drink wine, to watch Swedish movies, and pass
as members, or members-in-law, of the middle class
but not in those first days when, stodge-fed, repressed,
curfewed and resented, we were the landladies' harvest.
I had meant to write a stiff poem about that, to be
entitled NOTES FROM THE HOUSE OF MRS HARVEY

it might have been unkind, in part—but then, to be honest
one did evict me for eating my dessert first
and even from the kindliest, we were
estranged, as from parents, in a green Verona,

•

a nail-biting fiefdom of suede boots, concupiscence, tea,
a garden pruned by the *Herald* angels yearly.
In that supermarket of styles, with many a setback
we tried everything on, from Law School Augustan to rat pack
and though in Chinese my progress was smooth up to *K'ung*
and in German I mastered the words that follow *Achtung*
in my slow-cycling mind an eloquence not yet articulate
was trying to say Youth. This. I will take it straight.
And you were losing your bush millenarian faith—I
remember your dread of the Wrath on first tasting coffee.
We were reading Fisher Library, addressing gargoyles on the
        stair,
drafting self after self on Spir-O-Bind notepaper
as the tidal freshers poured in, with hard things to learn
in increasing droves they were getting off at Redfern.

•

Literate Australia was British, or babu at least,
before Vietnam and the American conquest
career had overwhelmed learning most deeply back then:
a major in English made one a minor Englishman
and woe betide those who stepped off the duckboards of that.
Slacking and depth were a single morass. But a spirit
of unresolved life caught more and more in its powerful
field. It slowed their life to bulk wine and pool.
Signals had to be found. The day you gave up fornication
we took your WetChex and, by insufflation,
made fat balloons of them, to glisten aloft in the sun
above the Quad, the Great Hall, the Carillon—
and that was Day One in the decade of chickens-come-home
that day kids began smoking the armpit hairs of wisdom.

•

It is some while since we roomed at Bondi Beach
and heard the beltmen crying each to each.
Good friends were made while snatching culture between
the cogs of the System (they turned slower then)
reemerge, and improve as their outlines grow more clear
(but where's Lesley now? and Jacqueline, what of her?).
Academe has grown edgier. Many still drowse in the sun
but *intellect* sounds like the cocking of a sten gun.
Remember urbanity, by which our time meant
allusion to little-known Names in a special accent?
It persists—but war's grown; war, snarling out of that trip
in which Freud and Marx are left and right thongs in a
    goosestep.
Mind you, Jane Fonda plays in it too. It's fairly thin war.
The tiger is real, and in pain. He is fed on paper.

•

When the decorous towers were shaken by screams and bare
    hands
they deserved to be shaken. They had sought to classify humans.
The kids were constructing a poem of feathers and pain,
a prayer, a list, a shriek, it reached no resolution
except to stay crucial. Their prophets said different things:
Pour wax on the earth. Beat spirals into rings.
But though they shamed Magog their father and crippled
    his war
their own gnawed at them. They colonized one another.
With the cameras running, somehow the beat had to go on
(in times of trend, death comes by relegation)
but selfhood kept claiming the best people hand over fist
in a few months a third of mankind had been called fascist—
as the music slowed, the big track proved to be
"Fantasia of the World as a Softened University".

•

Some things did change. Middle-class girls learned to swear,
men walked on the face of the moon once the Pill had tamed her
and we entered our thirties. No protest avails against that,
The horror of Time is, people don't snap out of it.

Now student politicoes well known in our day
have grown their hair two inches and are running the country.
Revolution's established. There will soon be degrees
conferred, with fistshake and speech, by the Dean of Eumenides.
The degree we attained was that brilliant refraction of will
that leaves one in several minds when facing evil.
It's still being offered. The Church of Jesus and Newman
did keep some of us balanced concerning the meanings of
    human
that greased golden term (all the rage in the new demiurgy)
though each new Jerusalem tempts the weaker clergy.

    •

Academe has gained ground. She is the great house of our age,
replacing Society, granting the entree to privilege
likewise a museum, of peoples, of scholars, of writing—
vampires at times may tend an iron lung.
Her study is fashion, successive lock-gates leaking Time
she loves this new goddess for whom abortion is orgasm,
the talkative one. Nothing, now, less intense
could thrill an elite above unwilled experience.
When our elders, the castes who live by delegation,
turned in, like unlicensed guns, imagination,
thought, spirit, ideals to the all-wise University
there were aspects of learning they did not foresee
like being called the Masses, Funny Little Men
who live in the Suburbs and resemble Eichmann.

    •

Academe is the class struggle, and whatever side
prevails will be hers. But I'm no alma-matricide
her task's also central: not making chemists and lawyers
but getting the passionate through their mating-and-war-years
to compromise. Remember? These shibboleths seem very real
in the light of a burning green stick. But where death's not
    literal
grace must be discerning. We have seen noble minds become
    rabid

and, as democrats, treat the Union stewards like dirt—
doctrine takes such a long view, especially in colonies,
that I'm grateful, like you, for downtown and country-town eyes
that glint and stay subtle while knowledge is power and foreign
through these, and some clowning, we master generalization
that blade of Caesarean rebirth which, day after day,
freed words in us. And cut our homes away.

●

That's the nub and the cork of it. Most rhymes in -ism and
   -ation
are nothing but cabals, though, out to take over the nation
compared with true persons: with Peter who sought gallant war,
with Herr Doktor Kurt H., who was a Siegfried-figure
by his own admission, with Vanessa Max Lawrence Penny
of *Honi Soit* then—they were our peerless company—
with Duncan the Sydney historian, who in an Aust-
ralian course might send off the First Fleet by August:
and Dave Croll who died of a train, having seen much reality
these dine with my uncles and hills in the restaurant of memory
(which is also a starship, a marriage, a crystal of heaven)
with the droll men of Physics who one day would capture the
   Quark
with Germaine a few tables off winning a hard conversation
and Lex who cried *Poetry is not the wine but the cognac* ...

The Broad Bean Sermon

Beanstalks, in any breeze, are a slack church parade
without belief, saying *trespass against us* in unison,
recruits in mint Air Force dacron, with unbuttoned leaves.

Upright with water like men, square in stem-section
they grow to great lengths, drink rain, keel over all ways,
kink down and grow up afresh, with proffered new greenstuff.

Above the cat-and-mouse floor of a thin bean forest
snails hang rapt in their food, ants hurry through several
    dimensions:
spiders tense and sag like little black flags in their cordage.

Going out to pick beans with the sun high as fence-tops,
    you find
plenty, and fetch them. An hour or a cloud later
you find shirtfulls more. At every hour of daylight

appear more than you missed: ripe, knobbly ones, fleshy-sided,
thin-straight, thin-crescent, frown-shaped, bird-shouldered,
    boat-keeled ones,
beans knuckled and single-bulged, minute green dolphins
    at suck,

beans upright like lecturing, outstretched like blessing fingers
in the incident light, and more still, oblique to your notice
that the noon glare or cloud-light or afternoon slants will
    uncover

till you ask yourself Could I have overlooked so many, or
do they form in an hour? unfolding into reality
like templates for subtly broad grins, like unique caught
    expressions,

like edible meanings, each sealed around with a string
and affixed to its moment, an unceasing colloquial assembly,
the portly, the stiff, and those lolling in pointed green slippers . . .

Wondering who'll take the spare bagfulls, you grin with
    happiness
—it is your health—you vow to pick them all
even the last few, weeks off yet, misshapen as toes.

The Action

We have spoken of the Action,
the believer-in-death, maker of tests and failures.
It is through the Action
that the quiet homes empty, and barrack beds fill up, and cities
that are cover from God.
The Action, continual breakthrough,
cannot abide slow speech. It invented Yokels,
it invented the Proles, who are difficult/noble/raffish,
it invented, in short, brave Us and the awful Others.
The smiling Action
makes all things new: its rites are father-killing,
sketching of pyramid plans, and the dance of Circles.

Turning slowly under trees, footing off the river's linen
to come into shade—some waterhens were subtly
edging away to their kampongs of chomped reeds—
eel-thoughts unwound through me. At a little distance
I heard New Year children slap the causeway.
                                                    Floating
in Coolongolook River, there below the junction
of Curreeki Creek,
                    water of the farms upheld me.

We were made by the Action:
the apes who agreed to speech ate those who didn't,
Action people tell us.
Rome of the waterpipes came of the Action, lost it,
and Louis' Versailles, in memory of which we mow grass.
Napoleon and Stalin were, mightily, the Action.
All the Civilizations, so good at royal arts and war
and postal networks—
it is the myriad Action
keeps them successive, prevents the achievement for good
of civilization.

Wash water, cattle water, irrigation-pipe-tang water
and water of the Kyle,
                        the chainsaw forests up there
where the cedar getter walks at night with dangling pockets,

water of the fern-tree gushers' heaping iron,
water of the bloodwoods, water of the Curreeki gold rush,
water of the underbrush sleeping shifts of birds
all sustained me,
                    thankful for great dinners
that had made me a lazy swimmer, marvellous floater,
looking up through the oaks
                            to the mountain Coolongolook,
the increase-place of flying-fox people, dancers—

Now talk is around of a loosening in republics,
retrievals of subtle water: all the peoples
who call themselves The People,
all the unnoticed cultures,
remnants defined by a tilt in their speech, traditions
that call the stars, say, Great Bluff, Five Hounds of Oscar,
the High and Low Lazies,
spells, moon-phase farming—all these are being canvassed.
The time has come round for republics of the cultures
and for rituals, with sound: the painful washings-clean
of smallpox blankets.
It may save the world,
or be the new Action.
                                        Leaves
were coming to my lips, and the picnic on the bank
made delicious smoke.
                    Soon, perhaps, I'd be ready
to go and eat steak amongst Grandmother's people,
talk even to children,
                        dipping my face again
I kneaded my muscles, softening the Action.

The Edge of the Forest

The edge of the forest, hard smoke beyond the paddocks
frays back and is there. Cutters go out through it,
come in again on the ringbarked slopes, down the fence lines.

—You have to send flooded gum quick. It don't stay flooded—
ironbark's a bugger to bark if it comes dry weather—
the man sitting next to me knows inside the forest.

He has his praise out there. Two taps on a trunk
and he can tell you its life. Steering the chainsaw
he can drop a tree on a cigarette paper. His billets

bumped, loading, ring like gongs; they win prizes.
Tallowwood's lovely: it has a deep like fat.
He has raised trucks out of swamp with his quick chain-cunning.

He loves praise, hoards it. The tic's become hereditary.
His arts are the waltz, cards, company, ripostes:
Easy seen you're not two-faced. You wouldn't wear that one.

But at sixty-five, they take your life away.
If work has been shelter, they let in the winter
if work has been drudgery, night mocks the late-freed man
if work has been proof they take the glass away.

At four years old, he was milking easy cows
and was put to the plough at fourteen, the day after school.
Hauling timber with the teams, trusted in cattle dealing

he worked, then and always—long in lieu of pay—
for a sign of love from his irritable father,
the planter of flasks. His nightmare, strawed with praise.

The years hurry by. He was facing the bad birthday.
Neighbours talked heart. They tell you when to die
in a community. Thus when the Company, in person,

told him *Stay on: you're our best man,* some custom
and cliché were bent. It was a commutation.
Life. Life given back. Almost a father speaking.

He will come and go for years yet through the edge of the forest.

Lachlan Macquarie's First Language

The Governor and the seer are talking at night in a room
beyond formality. They are not speaking English.
What like were Australians, then, in the time to come?
They had lost the Gaelic in them. It had become

like a tendon a man has no knowledge of in his body
but which puzzles his bending, at whiles, with a flexing impulse.
They'd wide cities, dram-shops, carriages with wings—
all the visions of Dun Kenneth. The singing at a ceilidh

lacked unison, though: each man there bellowing out of him
and his eyes undirected. Had they become a nation?
They had, and a people. A verandah was their capitol
though they spoke of a town where they kept the English
        seasons.

I heard different things: a farmer was telling his son
trap rabbits and sell the skins, then you can buy your
Bugs Bunny comics!—I didn't understand this. All folk there,
except the child-hating ones, were ladies and gentlemen.

The Euchre Game

So drunk he kept it at tens—and the bloody thing lost!
he bought a farm out of it. Round the battered formica
table the talk is luck more than justice, justice
being the politics of a small child's outcry.

The subtlest eyes in the Southern Hemisphere look at
the cards in front of them. *Well I'll go alone.*
Outside the window, passionfruit flowers are blooming
singly together. Many are not in the sun.

Men lose a trick, deal a fresh hand. Intelligence here
is interest and the refusal of relegation;
those who conceive it chance-fixed to their benefit also
believe in justice. Some of them are what remains of

the Revolution. *Hey, was that for us?* Footsteps
recede down the hall. One looks at the window, three smile:
Europeans! you're all suffering-snobs. Who's away?
The game's loosely sacred: luck is being worked at.

The Mitchells

I am seeing this: two men are sitting on a pole
they have dug a hole for and will, after dinner, raise
I think for wires. Water boils in a prune tin.
Bees hum their shift in unthinning mists of white

bursaria blossom, under the noon of wattles.
The men eat big meat sandwiches out of a styrofoam
box with a handle. One is overheard saying:
drought that year. Yes. Like trying to farm the road.

The first man, if asked, would say *I'm one of the Mitchells.*
The other would gaze for a while, dried leaves in his palm,
and looking up, with pain and subtle amusement,

say *I'm one of the Mitchells.* Of the pair, one has been rich
but never stopped wearing his oil-stained felt hat. Nearly
      everything
they say is ritual. Sometimes the scene is an avenue.

The Flying-fox Dreaming

Now that the west
is lighting in under leaves
and Hookfoot the eagle
has gone from over the forest
there is no sound except the
tree-foxes, unwrapping from rest:

finger-winged night workers
who will soon beat up in tens
and thousands out of this daylong head-down city;
in the offing of scents above earth, they will cast for grown
and native fruit, and home in down-country for miles
on the ripe tree beacons.

Upside down all their days
Antipodean,
night wardrobes their singleness for them. Each bat, alone,
puts off crowding and chatter, once above the perches
he becomes the unfolded, far-speeding, upward-sidestepping,
nightowl-outflying one.

Here, one, his fur ballast
dropped among weeds in its tightening parchment, also
disproves a bush story: they don't excrete through the mouth
to satisfy gravity. All down the valley of fig
and flying-fox men, the lights now of towns are beginning
to gleam. They will burn late. It goes on being appropriate,

even the dead one becoming a clenched oval stone
now clear of all twig-arrest, free of clambering dinners,
free at last of dawns' dazzling comedowns. Windrowing east
over the farms, adroit
at wingshrink turns
he is topping the nectar time, and the pollen harvest,
going on out continually over horizons.

Visiting Anzac in the Year
of Metrication

Gelibolu, Chanakkale—
there's no place called *Gallipoli*
down there, where the summer fires strip
the hills of scrub and rosemary.

Old wire snags the steeps like thorn
and human bones come out of the clay
where squatters' and selectors' boys
and the aghas' sons and their peasant boys

met in a raked boot-scrambling roar
and the *sooling* prints turned black with names
when currents drifted the landing buoys
to the heights of thyme and rosemary.

•

Things sticking out jag at the mind,
Tooths' bottles, messtins, vertebrae
laid down in the bonzer *stoushing* days
the *spirited* and *clean-cut* days

up where the laddering trenches clung
and gravel flew in hobnailed sprays
where ripped and screaming chaps found out
that fellow humans really would,

where crimson-tidemarked puttees bore
histories of crowding in the sea
below the chirrup-haunted thyme,
burst entrails, shell-brass, rosemary.

•

When hard-case jokes and frantic help
poured content into noble sieves
that human lives cannot keep filled
it was the day of *turning round,*

when, firing, wags might turn around
and yell *How's that?* and in a push
a hundred jokers might turn round
and sprawl, and leap. Towns died of that

and the bush went underground:
the nation stalled in elegy
with a Day for massing through the streets
in pub time, wearing rosemary.

       •

At Lone Pine and the Nek, the spinner
has scattered his cranial shilling bets
the king-and-country stones up there
mark no one's grave (Islam burns crosses).

Bowled Walers and stumped Victorians lie
in those broken hills inextricably
with their adversary, who was no less brave.
The misemployed, undone by courage,

have become the Unsaluting Army
and buttoned boys, for all their trades,
are country again, and that funny Missus
Porter's not yet changed poetry.

       •

White bones, inconsolable proof
high scree, incomparable test—
on both points, class warfare has raged
but the war-pipes sail through jam-packed streets

where everyone is turning round:
old men and the ageing wear bright coins
and plain men and battlers' sons are proud
and the *flash* still trust extremity.

Our continent is uncrowded space,
a subtler thing than history.
The Day of our peace will need a native
herb that out-savours rosemary.

•

Down in the flatlands, coming away,
torn cotton bloomed in the few scratch fields
and conscripts on bivouac jogged by,
the Hittite face, the Turan face—

down there, in a day of rabid peace
and wartime love, one thought of how,
to farm blokes, war is Sudden City.
The newchums learned the tram-routes well

but disaster is all our brotherhood,
starved height, incomparable friends,
this is the reign of the measuring god,
this is the pit of rosemary.

•

High, near-Port Lincoln light. Harsh places.
This is the day of Freedom, too—
like the sardine tin lid tied
to the hawk's tail, life presents new faces.

Those shelterless hardscrabble cols
where even the Heads get *knocked* were best
assaulted in youth: we were handiest,
the climbing was overt and in vogue

and done with friends, in company.
Pioneering there, building with planks,
we showed the *battler* style to Death
amongst hoarse screams and rosemary.

The Powerline Incarnation

When I ran to snatch the wires off our roof
hands bloomed teeth shouted I was almost seized
held back from this life
                    O flumes   O chariot reins
you cover me with lurids deck me with gaudies feed
my coronal   a scream sings in the air
above our dance   you slam it to me with farms
that you dark on and off numb hideous strong friend
Tooma and Geehi freak and burr through me
rocks fire-trails damwalls mountain-ash trees slew
to darkness through me   I zap them underfoot
with the swords of my shoes
                         I am receiving mountains
piloting around me   Crackenback   Anembo
the Fiery Walls   I make a hit in towns
I've never visited: smoke curls lightbulbs pop grey
discs hitch and slow   I plough the face of Mozart
and Johnny Cash   I bury and smooth their song
I crack it for copper links and fusebox spiders
I call my Friend from the circuitry of mixers
whipping cream for a birthday   I distract the immortal
Inhuman from hospitals
                    to sustain my jazz
and here is Rigel in a glove of flesh
my starry hand discloses smoke, cold Angel.

Vehicles that run on death come howling into
our street with lights a thousandth of my blue
arms keep my wife from my beauty   from my species
the jewels in my tips
                 I would accept her in
blind white remarriage   cover her with wealth
to arrest the heart   we'd share Apache leaps
crying out *Disyzygy!*
               shield her from me, humans
from this happiness I burn to share   this touch
sheet car   live ladder   wildfire garden shrub—

away off I hear the bombshell breakers thrown
diminishing me   a meaninglessness coming
over the circuits
                    the god's deserting me
but I have dived in the mainstream   jumped the graphs
I have transited the dreams of crew-cut boys named Buzz
and the hardening music
                            to the big bare place
where the strapped-down seekers, staining white clothes, come
to be shown the Zeitgeist
                            passion and death my skin
my heart all logic   I am starring there
and must soon flame out
                            having seen the present god
It who feels nothing   It who answers prayers.

Sydney and the Bush

When Sydney and the Bush first met
there was no open ground
and men and girls, in chains and not,
all made an urgent sound.

Then convicts bled and warders bred,
the Bush went back and back,
the men of Fire and of Earth
became White men and Black.

When Sydney ordered lavish books
and warmed her feet with coal
the Bush came skylarking to town
and gave poor folk a soul.

Then bushmen sank and factories rose
and warders set the tone—
the Bush in quarter-acre blocks
helped families hold their own.

When Sydney and the Bush meet now
there is antipathy
and fashionable suburbs float
at night, far out to sea.

When Sydney rules without the Bush
she is a warders' shop
with heavy dancing overhead
the music will not stop

and when the drummers want a laugh
Australians are sent up.
When Sydney and the Bush meet now
there is no common ground.

The Returnees

As we were rowing to the lakes
our oars were blunt and steady wings

the tanbark-coloured water was
a gruel of pollen: more coming down
hinted strange futures to our cells

the far hills ancient under it
the corn flats black-green under heat
were cut in an antique grainy gold

it was the light of Boeotian art.

•

Bestowing tourbillons that drowned
the dusty light we had used up
pulling the distance to us, we
were conscious of a lifelong sound

on everything, that low fly-humming
melismatic untedious endless
note that a drone-pipe-plus-chants or

(shielding our eyes, rocking the river)

a ballad—some ballads—catch, the one
some paintings and many yarners summon
the ground-note here of unsnubbing art

cicadas were in it, and that Gothic
towering of crystals in the trees
Jock Neilson cutting a distant log

•

still hearing, we saw a snake ahead
winding, being his own schnorkel

aslant in the swimming highlights, only
his head betrayed him, leading two
ripples and a scaled-down swirl. We edged

closer, were defied and breathed at.
A migrant, perhaps? a pioneer?
or had a kookaburra dropped
him, missing the organ-busting ground
and even the flat of the drinking-ground?

•

Touching the oars and riding, we
kept up with the blunt, heat-tasting head
debating its life, and sparing it

which is the good of Athens. Where
the rotted milk-wharf took the sun
flint-hard on top, dappling below

(remembered children danced up there
spinning their partners, the bright steel cans.
A way of life. But a way of life.)

the snake rose like a Viking ship
signed mud with a scattering flourish and
was into the wale of potato ground

like a whip withdrawn. We punted off.

●

Oar-leather jumping in spaced kicks
against the swivel-screw of rowlocks
we hauled the slow bush headlands near

drinking beer, and talking a bit

such friendliness shone into us, such
dry complex cheer, insouciant calm
out of everything, the brain-shaped trees
the wrinkling middle gleam, the still
indifferently well-wooded hills, it was

like rowing to meet your very best
passionately casual and dead friends
and feast with them on a little island

or an angel leaning down to one
queuing on the Day, to ask
what was the best throw that you did?

that note, raised to the pitch of tears:
tower of joking, star of skill,
gate of sardonyx and worn gold

*Black men and Rosenberg and I
have beliefs in common,* I exclaimed

and you were agreeing that Mao Tse-tung
had somehow come to Dunsinane—

•

any more heightening and it would
have been a test, but the centre we
had stirred stopped down again, one notch

to happiness, and we were let dip
our points in the wide stopped water and
reclaim our motion. Bloodwood trees

round there were in such a froth of bloom
their honey dripped on shale and gummed
blady-grass in wigwams and ant-towns

sweetness, infusing, followed us
Reality is somebody's, you said
with a new and wryly balanced smile

We're country, and Western, I replied.

Spurwing Plover

Foiled hunters sulk homewards at dusk

and the plover, among bitten grass
and the puffed felt of cattle manure
has made his white head and chest
a peg, or a mushroom. His greys
and dark tints are tucked in the gloom.

It is a discipline test
his still white. It faces sharp critics.
Those fellows are burning to shoot:

they'd like the stiff crack in the air
and your struggles, plover, much more
than ever your family-defending
quick dives, or your dinnerplate-scraping
sad cry: *turkey work! turkey work!*

Laconics: The Forty Acres

We have bought the Forty Acres,
prime brush land.

If Bunyah is a fillet
this paddock is the eye.

The creek half-moons it,
log-deep, or parting rocks.

The corn-ground by now
has had forty years' grassed spell.

Up in the swamp
are paperbarks, coin-sized frogs—

The Forty, at last,
our beautiful deep land

it was Jim's, it was Allan's,
it was Reg's, it is Dad's—

Brett wanted it next
but he'd evicted Dad:

for bitter porridge
many cold returns.

That interior machine-gun,
my chainsaw, drops dead timber.

Where we burn the heaps
we'll plant kikuyu grass.

Ecology? Sure.
But also husbandry.

And the orchard will go there,
and we'll re-roof the bare pole barn.

Our croft, our Downs,
our sober, shining land.

Creeper Habit

On Bennelong Point
a two-dimensional tree
drapes the rock cutting.

Bird-flecked, self-espaliered
it issues out of the kerb
feeding on dead sparks
of the old tram depot;

a fig, its muscles
of stiffened chewing gum grip
the flutings and beads
of the crowbar-and-dynamite wall.

The tree has height and extent
but no roundness. Cramponned in cracks
its branches twine and utter
coated leaves.

With half its sky blank rock
it has little choice.
It has climbed high from a tiny sour gall

and spreads where it can,
feeding its leaves on the light
of North Shore windows.

Tanka: The Coffee Shops

Lorenzini's, Vadim's,
Rowe Street, and Repin's upstairs,
all shuttered and gone.
The coffee shops vanished
just as they'd conquered the world.

The Gallery

Stale pasture, midsummer
    going down to the canopy
    that is under the paddocks

tristania trees, laurinas, water gums
are a sinewy corps
    beneath their loot of rosettes

floodwrack hangs jammed
in the lillipilly boughs
    it is campfires fixed above ground
it is wet-season beards

    through root-stumbling cattletrack
doors, below the landscape
to the pavement, cracked floor
    and the bouldery parterres

    bulltussocks ostend
    fierce wheat-heads of their bloom

dead-end water breeds

   still-purposeful water finds ways
   between rock, and the light
   hangs quivering all day.

In the inwardness
it is twilit and tall,
inleaning, with stilled sway.
Flies stay out in the farms.

Parrots sweep in here
from the hacking gunshot corn
for their sip of ancient
and way along the gallery
a great white-cedar tree,
Melia azedarach, burns
in a Christmas of sun.

   The creek is a vein
   like every stream on earth
   going back to the heart

   but the gallery's a bridge
   of the forest across cleared land,
   battalions sheltering
   out of the chainsaw age here.

   The cool of high country
   marches west with the galleries
   shade, verticals, complexity
   hide out from the plains inside
   half-day horizons

whisky of the high
peat maltings, smuggled out
under Antarctic beeches,
runoff from the white man's tent,
washes one's feet here

black thwarts, branched tackle
rotting where they paused
on their way to the lagoons
    deflect and bridge
the fish-scummed spider pools

rust drip, glass gravel,
kingfisher, robin, wren.

All tumbled together, in the vanished flood,
eel bones, the rock of horror,
                            style-test of fellows
and the rock of God who does not rescue flesh.

This skeleton river, soil-shadow feeding the farms:
to be under these terraces
                       understanding your life
that is more than half gone, and your friends dismarrying,

to be here with your country, that will waken when it wakens,
that won't be awakened by contempt
                               or love;
to know you may live and die in colonial times.

    rock-bar of quartz
    why should your life go well?

    rock-bench of basalt
    do we know everything yet?

    despair and attitudes
    might be licensed then

    oar-bench of mahogany
    is all the evidence in?

    courage and largesse
    of hope may, till then, be licensed

    in the middle of the world

Out of the ochre-mined
farm gullies, milky blood
and bottles creep in
but the creek is irreverent
in its riddling way:

> when they stole my hat
> I hid beneath a stone
> and I starved their corn
> and when I got strong
> I ate the bastards' corn

> but the gallery's the interchange
> of some primal worlds
> it points out of every
> evergreen island,
>   it is
> greater than hedgerows
> where doomed pets hang on
> against autumn cultures;
> it leads inland to the heart.

And climbing up, out
through liana cordage, boot-slipping
    on humus, under panicles,
    acmena and syzygium trunks, you

come into the place where fathers and children are sitting
around under paperbark trees. They are eating wrapped tucker
and God-enclosed melons. The daylight moon is rising
over the shoulder of towns, it is putting on flesh
and seeds; it will ripen smoke-red above the white farms.

Employment for the Castes in Abeyance

I was a translator at the Institute:
fair pay, clean work, and a bowerbird's delight
of theory and fact to keep the forebrain supple.

I was Western Europe. *Beiträge, reviste,*
dissertaties, rapports turned English under my
one-fingered touch. Teacup-and-Remington days.

It was a job like Australia: peace and cover,
a recourse for exiles, poets, decent spies,
for plotters who meant to rise from the dead with their circle.

I was getting over a patch of free-form living:
flat food round the midriff, long food up your sleeves—
castes in abeyance, we exchanged these stories.

My Chekhovian colleague who worked as if under surveillance
would tell me tales of real life in Peking and Shanghai
and swear at the genders subsumed in an equation.

The trade was uneasy about computers, back then:
if they could be taught not to render, say, *out of sight*
out of mind as *invisible lunatic*

they might supersede us—not
because they'd be better. More on principle.
Not that our researchers were unkindly folk:

one man on exchange from Akademgorod
told me about Earth's crustal plates, their ponderous
inevitable motion, collisions that raised mountain chains,

the continents rode on these Marxian turtles, it seemed;
another had brought slow death to a billion rabbits,
a third team had bottled the essence of rain on dry ground.

They were translators, too, our scientists:
they were translating the universe into science,
believing that otherwise it had no meaning.

Leaving there, I kept my Larousse and my Leutseligkeit
and I heard that machine translation never happened:
language defeated it. We are a language species.

I gather this provoked a shift in science,
that having become a side, it then changed sides
and having collapsed, continued at full tempo.

Prince Obolensky succeeded me for a time
but he soon returned to Fiji to teach Hebrew.
In the midst of life, we are in employment:

seek, travel and print, seek-left-right-travel-and-bang
as the Chinese typewriter went which I saw working
when I was a translator in the Institute.

The Cardiff Commonwealth Arts Festival
Poetry Conference 1965, Recalled

Three a.m., Tiger Bay. In the only
club still open, the Sheik's Tent,
James McAuley and two Welsh students
are discussing enjambment.

Uptown, the Bomb Culture's just opened
its European run,
discounting many things on its counter:
calm tradition is one;

here, though, cheesecloth, fuzzed menace and Sin
are all mortified to death
to find themselves kindly dismissed
for talk of Wordsworth;

the Pleasure Principle's looking quite haggard,
belching whisky, sweating scent,
the belly dancers rhythmically twitching,
pallid boughs in a current.

Driving to the Adelaide Festival 1976
via the Murray Valley Highway

A long narrow woodland with channels, reentrants, ponds:
the Murray's a mainstream with footnotes, a folklorists' river.

The culture, on both banks, is pure Victoria:
the beer, the footy, the slight earnest flavour, the cray.

Some places there's a man-made conventional width of water
studded with trunks; a cold day in the parrots' high rooms.

Walking on the wharf at Echuca, that skyscraper roof:
sixty feet down timber to a dry-season splash.

In the forest there are sudden cliffs: dusty silken water
moving away: the live flow is particle-green.

Billabongs are pregnant with swirls, and a sunken road
of hyacinth leads to an eerie noonday corner.

Ships rotting in the woods, ships turning to silt in blind
    channels;
one looked like a bush pub impelled by a combine header.

Out in the wide country, channels look higher than the road
even as you glance along them. Salt glittering out there.

Romance is a vine that survives in the ruins of skill:
inside the horizon again, a restored steamboat, puffing.

Thinking, at speed among lakes, of a time beyond denim
and the gardens of that time. Night-gardens. Fire gardens.

Crazed wood, brushed chars, powder-blue leaves. Each year
    the purist
would ignite afresh with a beerbottle lens, a tossed bumper—

Heading for a tent show, thinking stadium thoughts,
a dense bouquet slowing the van through the province of
    sultanas.

The Buladelah-Taree Holiday
Song Cycle

I

The people are eating dinner in that country north of
    Legge's Lake;
behind flywire and venetians, in the dimmed cool, town people
    eat Lunch.
Plying knives and forks with a peek-in sound, with a tuck-in
    sound,
they are thinking about relatives and inventory, they are talking
    about customers and visitors.
In the country of memorial iron, on the creek-facing hills there,
they are thinking about bean plants, and rings of tank water, of
    growing a pumpkin by Christmas;
rolling a cigarette, they say thoughtfully Yes, and their
    companion nods, considering.
Fresh sheets have been spread and tucked tight, childhood rooms
    have been seen to,
for this is the season when children return with their children
to the place of Bingham's Ghost, of the Old Timber Wharf, of
    the Big Flood That Time,
the country of the rationalized farms, of the day-and-night
    farms, and of the Pitt Street farms,
of the Shire Engineer and many other rumours, of the tractor
    crankcase furred with chaff,
the places of sitting down near ferns, the snake-fear places, the
    cattle-crossing-long-ago places.

2

It is the season of the Long Narrow City; it has crossed the
    Myall, it has entered the North Coast,
that big stunning snake; it is looped through the hills, burning
    all night there.
Hitching and flying on the downgrades, processionally balancing
    on the climbs,
it echoes in O'Sullivan's Gap, in the tight coats of the
    flooded-gum trees;
the tops of palms exclaim at it unmoved, there near Wootton.

Glowing all night behind the hills, with a north-shifting glare,
    burning behind the hills;
through Coolongolook, through Wang Wauk, across the
    Wallamba,
the booming tarred pipe of the holiday slows and spurts again;
    Nabiac chokes in glassy wind,
the forests on Kiwarrak dwindle in cheap light; Tuncurry and
    Forster swell like cooking oil.
The waiting is buffed, in timber villages off the highway, the
    waiting is buffeted:
the fumes of fun hanging above ferns; crime flashes in strange
    windscreens, in the time of the Holiday.
Parasites weave quickly through the long gut that paddocks
    shine into;
powerful makes surging and pouncing: the police, collecting
    Revenue.
The heavy gut winds over the Manning, filling northward,
    digesting the towns, feeding the towns;
they all become the narrow city, they join it;
girls walking close to murder discard, with excitement, their
    names.
Crossing Australia of the sports, the narrow city, bringing home
    the children.

3

It is good to come out after driving and walk on bare grass;
walking out, looking all around, relearning that country.
Looking out for snakes, and looking out for rabbits as well;
going into the shade of myrtles to try their cupped climate,
    swinging by one hand around them,
in that country of the Holiday . . .
stepping behind trees to the dam, as if you had a gun,
to that place of the Wood Duck,
to that place of the Wood Duck's Nest,
proving you can still do it; looking at the duck who hasn't
    seen you,
the mother duck who'd run Catch Me (broken wing) I'm Fatter
    (broken wing), having hissed to her children.

4

The birds saw us wandering along.
Rosellas swept up crying out *we think we think*; they settled
    farther along;
knapping seeds off the grass, under dead trees where their eggs
    were, walking around on their fingers,
flying on into the grass.
The heron lifted up his head and elbows; the magpie stepped
    aside a bit,
angling his chopsticks into pasture, turning things over in his
    head.
At the place of the Plough Handles, of the Apple Trees Bending
    Over, and of the Cattlecamp,
there the vealers are feeding; they are loosely at work, facing
    everywhere.
They are always out there, and the forest is always on the hills;
around the sun are turning the wedgetail eagle and her mate,
    that dour brushhook-faced family:
they settled on Deer's Hill away back when the sky was opened,
in the bull-oak trees way up there, the place of fur tufted in the
    grass, the place of bone-turds.

5

The Fathers and the Great-grandfathers, they are out in the
    paddocks all the time, they live out there,
at the place of the Rail Fence, of the Furrows Under Grass, at
    the place of the Slab Chimney.
We tell them that clearing is complete, an outdated attitude,
    all over;
we preach without a sacrifice, and are ignored; flowering bushes
    grow dull to our eyes.
We begin to go up on the ridge, talking together, looking at the
    kino-coloured ants,
at the yard-wide sore of their nest, that kibbled peak, and the
    workers heaving vast stalks up there,
the brisk compact workers; jointed soldiers pour out then, tense
    with acid; several probe the mouth of a lost gin bottle;
Innuendo, we exclaim, *literal minds!* and go on up the ridge,
    announced by finches;

passing the place of the Dingo Trap, and that farm hand it
    caught, and the place of the Cowbails,
we come to the road and watch heifers,
little unjoined Devons, their teats hidden in fur, and the cousin
    with his loose-slung stockwhip driving them.
We talk with him about rivers and the lakes; his polished horse
    is stepping nervously,
printing neat omegas in the gravel, flexing its skin to shake off
    flies;
his big sidestepping horse that has kept its stones; it recedes
    gradually, bearing him;
we murmur *stone-horse* and *devilry* to the grinners under grass.

6

Barbecue smoke is rising at Legge's Camp; it is steaming into the
    midday air,
all around the lake shore, at the Broadwater, it is going up
    among the paperbark trees,
a heat-shimmer of sauces, rising from tripods and flat steel, at
    that place of the cone shells,
at that place of the Seagrass, and the tiny segmented things
    swarming in it, and of the Pelican.
Dogs are running around disjointedly; water escapes from their
    mouths,
confused emotions from their eyes; humans snarl at them
    Gwanout and Hereboy, not varying their tone much;
the impoverished dog people, suddenly sitting down to nuzzle
    themselves; toddlers side with them:
toddlers, running away purposefully at random, among cars,
    into big drownie water (come back, Cheryl-Ann!).
They rise up as charioteers, leaning back on the tow-bar; all
    their attributes bulge at once:
swapping swash shoulder-wings for the white-sheeted shoes that
    bear them,
they are skidding over the flat glitter, stiff with grace, for once
    not travelling to arrive.
From the high dunes over there, the rough blue distance, at
    length they come back behind the boats,
and behind the boats' noise, cartwheeling, or sitting down, into
    the lake's warm chair;

they wade ashore and eat with the families, putting off that
     uprightness, that assertion,
eating with the families who love equipment, and the freedom
     from equipment,
with the fathers who love driving, and lighting a fire between
     stones.

7

Shapes of children were moving in the standing corn, in the
     child-labour districts;
coloured flashes of children, between the green and parching
     stalks, appearing and disappearing.
Some places, they are working, racking off each cob like a lever,
     tossing it on the heaps;
other places, they are children of child-age, there playing jungle:
in the tiger-striped shade, they are firing hoehandle machine-
     guns, taking cover behind fat pumpkins;
in other cases, it is Sunday and they are lovers.
They rise and walk together in the sibilance, finding single rows
     irksome, hating speech now,
or, full of speech, they swap files and follow defiles, disappearing
     and appearing;
near the rain-grey barns, and the children building cattleyards
     beside them;
the standing corn, gnawed by pouched and rodent mice;
     generations are moving among it,
the parrot-hacked, medicine-tasseled corn, ascending all the
     creek flats, the wire-fenced alluvials,
going up in patches through the hills, towards the Steep
     Country.

8

Forests and State Forests, all down off the steeper country;
     mosquitoes are always living in there:
they float about like dust motes and sink down, at the places of
     the Stinging Tree,
and of the Staghorn Fern; the males feed on plant-stem fluid,
     absorbing that watery ichor;

the females meter the air, feeling for the warm-blooded smell,
    needing blood for their eggs.

They find the dingo in his sleeping-place, they find his underbelly
    and his anus;

they find the possum's face, they drift up the ponderous pleats of
    the fig tree, way up into its rigging,

the high camp of the fruit bats; they feed on the membranes and
    ears of bats; tired wings cuff air at them;

their eggs burning inside them, they alight on the muzzles of
    cattle,

the half-wild bush cattle, there at the place of the Sleeper Dump,
    at the place of the Tallowwoods.

The males move about among growth tips; ingesting solutions,
    they crouch intently;

the females sing, needing blood to breed their young; their
    singing is in the scrub country;

their tune comes to the name-bearing humans, who dance to it
    and irritably grin at it.

9

The warriors are cutting timber with brash chainsaws; they are
    trimming hardwood pit-props and loading them;

Is that an order? they hoot at the peremptory lorry driver, who
    laughs; he is also a warrior.

They are driving long-nosed tractors, slashing pasture in the
    dinnertime sun;

they are fitting tappets and valves, the warriors, or giving finish
    to a surfboard.

Addressed on the beach by a pale man, they watch waves break
    and are reserved, refusing pleasantry;

they joke only with fellow warriors, chaffing about try-ons and
    the police, not slighting women.

Making Timber a word of power, Con-rod a word of power,
    Sense a word of power, the Regs. a word of power,

they know belt-fed from spring-fed; they speak of being *stiff*,
    and being *history*;

the warriors who have killed, and the warriors who eschewed
    killing,

the solemn, the drily spoken, the life peerage of endurance;
    drinking water from a tap,

they watch boys who think hard work a test, and boys who
　　　think it is not a test.

10

Now the ibis are flying in, hovering down on the wetlands,
on those swampy paddocks around Darawank, curving down in
　　　ragged dozens,
on the riverside flats along the Wang Wauk, on the Boolambayte
　　　pasture flats,
and away towards the sea, on the sand moors, at the place of
　　　the Jabiru Crane;
leaning out of their wings, they step down; they take out their
　　　implement at once,
out of its straw wrapping, and start work; they dab grasshopper
　　　and ground-cricket
with nonexistence . . . spiking the ground and puncturing it . . .
　　　they swallow down the outcry of a frog;
they discover titbits kept for them under cowmanure lids, small
　　　slow things.
Pronging the earth, they make little socket noises, their
　　　thoughtfulness jolting down and up suddenly;
there at Bunyah, along Firefly Creek, and up through Germany,
the ibis are all at work again, thin-necked ageing men towards
　　　evening; they are solemnly all back
at Minimbah, and on the Manning, in the rye-and-clover
　　　irrigation fields;
city storemen and accounts clerks point them out to their wives,
remembering things about themselves, and about the ibis.

11

Abandoned fruit trees, moss-tufted, spotted with dim lichen
　　　paints; the fruit trees of the Grandmothers,
they stand along the creekbanks, in the old home paddocks,
　　　where the houses were,
they are reached through bramble-grown front gates, they creak
　　　at dawn behind burnt skillions,
at Belbora, at Bucca Wauka, away in at Burrell Creek,
at Telararee of the gold-sluices.

The trees are split and rotten-elbowed; they bear the old-
fashioned summer fruits,
the annual bygones: china pear, quince, persimmon;
the fruit has the taste of former lives, of sawdust and parlour
song, the tang of Manners;
children bite it, recklessly,
at what will become for them the place of the Slab Wall, and of
the Coal Oil Lamp,
the place of moss-grit and swallows' nests, the place of the
Crockery.

12

Now the sun is an applegreen blindness through the swells, a
white blast on the sea face, flaking and shoaling;
now it is burning off the mist; it is emptying the density of trees,
it is spreading upriver,
hovering above the casuarina needles, there at Old Bar and
Manning Point;
flooding the island farms, it abolishes the milkers' munching
breath
as they walk towards the cowyards; it stings a bucket here, a
teatcup there.
Morning steps into the world by ever more southerly gates;
shadows weaken their north skew
on Middle Brother, on Cape Hawke, on the dune scrub toward
Seal Rocks;
steadily the heat is coming on, the butter-water time, the clothes-
sticking time;
grass covers itself with straw; abandoned things are thronged
with spirits;
everywhere wood is still with strain; birds hiding down the creek
galleries, and in the cockspur canes;
the cicada is hanging up her sheets; she takes wing off her
music-sheets.
Cars pass with a rational zoom, panning quickly towards
Wingham,
through the thronged and glittering, the shale-topped ridges, and
the cattlecamps,
towards Wingham for the cricket, the ball knocked hard in front
of smoked-glass ranges, and for the drinking.

In the time of heat, the time of flies around the mouth, the time
of the west verandah;
looking at that umbrage along the ranges, on the New England
side;
clouds begin assembling vaguely, a hot soiled heaviness on the
sky, away there towards Gloucester;
a swelling up of clouds, growing there above Mount George,
and above Tipperary;
far away and hot with light; sometimes a storm takes root there,
and fills the heavens rapidly;
darkening, boiling up and swaying on its stalks, pulling this way
and that, blowing round by Krambach;
coming white on Bulby, it drenches down on the paddocks, and
on the wire fences;
the paddocks are full of ghosts, and people in cornbag hoods
approaching;
lights are lit in the house; the storm veers mightily on its stem,
above the roof; the hills uphold it;
the stony hills guide its dissolution; gullies opening and
crumbling down, wrenching tussocks and rolling them;
the storm carries a greenish-grey bag; perhaps it will find hail
and send it down, starring cars, flattening tomatoes,
in the time of the Washaways, of the dead trunks braiding
water, and of the Hailstone Yarns.

13

The stars of the holiday step out all over the sky.
People look up at them, out of their caravan doors and their
campsites;
people look up from the farms, before going back; they gaze at
their year's worth of stars.
The Cross hangs head-downward, out there over Markwell;
it turns upon the Still Place, the pivot of the Seasons, with one
shoulder rising:
"Now I'm beginning to rise, with my Pointers and my Load . . ."
hanging eastwards, it shines on the sawmills and the lakes, on the
glasses of the Old People.
Looking at the Cross, the galaxy is over our left shoulder, slung up
highest in the east;

there the Dog is following the Hunter; the Dog Star pulsing there
    above Forster; it shines down on the Bikies,
and on the boat-hire sheds, there at the place of the Oyster; the
    place of the Shark's Eggs and her Hide;
the Pleiades are pinned up high on the darkness, away back above
    the Manning;
they are shining on the Two Blackbutt Trees, on the rotted river
    wharves, and on the towns;
standing there, above the water and the lucerne flats, at the place
    of the Families;
their light sprinkles down on Taree of the Lebanese shops, it
    mingles with the streetlights and their glare.
People recover the starlight, hitching north,
travelling north beyond the seasons, into that country of the
    Communes, and of the Banana:
the Flying Horse, the Rescued Girl, and the Bull, burning steadily
    above that country.
Now the New Moon is low down in the west, that remote
    direction of the Cattlemen,
and of the Saleyards, the place of steep clouds, and of the Rodeo;
the New Moon who has poured out her rain, the moon of the
    Planting-times.
People go outside and look at the stars, and at the melon-rind
    moon,
the Scorpion going down into the mountains, over there towards
    Waukivory, sinking into the tree-line,
in the time of the Rockmelons, and of the Holiday . . .
the Cross is rising on his elbow, above the glow of the horizon;
carrying a small star in his pocket, he reclines there brilliantly,
above the Alum Mountain, and the lakes threaded on the Myall
    River, and above the Holiday.

The Swarm

*Of late there has been some loose talk about Australia becoming a
republic . . .*

                              Governor-General Sir John Kerr, 1976

On a stone wall, adrift from their hive
seeking shelter away from the wind
of a bitter blue day, this tight swarm
of brown English bees is adhering.

Poor monarchists, clumped round their queen,
they look like a furry, half-risen
loaf of gingerbread dough, with transparent
mica scales crusted on it: worn wings.

That animal, made up of lives,
drones, queen, dispensable workers—
we feel almost tempted to stroke it
but we know the terror, the venom

in those many clenched loyalists, whose rote
runs simply *Some eat the royal jelly:
most do not. This is Right. Work and die.*
What is, is, the clustered swarm murmurs.

Oh it is, some cool men with a smoke-pot
might smirk, and box them. Not us, though.
We must love and bypass them, like Nature,
since *springtime* or *freedom* would be loose talk indeed.

Four Gaelic Poems

1. Free Kirk Cemetery,
Northern New South Wales

I farmed in the land
of Lazy Fair.

Pipe-music and dancing
when I was young;

lamplight and wireless
as I grew older.

Rabbits shot in a flood
rabbits eaten in drought-time.

Now inside a fence
psalm-flattened silence.

2. A Skirl for Outsets

The sea smooths a page of its folio
and another page:
I lie in the lee of high sand
earning my wage;

pale child of the sunburnt clans
I lie covered there
and try out this pibroch-baseline
on the air:

Purest moment of all venture
is the beginning,
recruits stepping out, tanned and sure,
who, stepping, sing.

It is the first depth of voyage
after stowing all aboard,
a moment, on deck, and on the bridge,
and the lengthening forward.

And then there's the density of
fraught thresholds in
first love, and in first real love.
Some cross them again.

We are mad for fresh starts, for leaps forward,
for this vertigo;
for new Angles, and recycled Breakthroughs,
the 1912 Show,

for the terrorist's clenched joy
when told he, or she,
is to move at the vortex of things
with the Chosen Company.

Connoisseurship of outsets
is required, perhaps,
to say what is shrouds in all this,
what is silk, what straps:

I have loved the absorbed angel
Preparation, and that charge
that gathers in maps, stores, field-glasses
and attracts a charge:

the squadron, the Core Group, the Movement,
Sinn Fein amháinn!—
how briefly we knew not to join
was best for man.

The swimmer into cleanness leaping
spurns the shore,
exultant, out of gravity, acclaimed,
upright in water,

and this is the way the worlds end
after space, after sense:
not by the tin bowl, nor the Bomb,
but by Significance.

3. The Gum Forest

After the last gapped wire on a post,
homecoming for me, to enter the gum forest.

This old slow battlefield: parings of armour,
cracked collars, elbows, scattered on the ground.

New trees step out of old: lemon and ochre
splitting out of grey everywhere, in the gum forest.

In there for miles, shade track and ironbark slope,
depth casually beginning all around, at a little distance.

Sky sifting, and always a hint of smoke in the light;
you can never reach the heart of the gum forest.

In here is like a great yacht harbour, charmed to leaves,
innumerable tackle, poles wrapped in spattered sail,
or an unknown army in reserve for centuries.

Flooded-gums on creek ground, each tall because of each.
Now a blackbutt in bloom is showering with bees
but warm blood sleeps in the middle of the day.
The witching hour is noon in the gum forest.

Foliage builds like a layering splash: ground water
drily upheld in edge-on, wax-rolled, gall-puckered
leaves upon leaves. The shoal life of parrots up there.

Stone footings, trunk-shattered. Non-human lights. Enormous
abandoned machines. The mysteries of the gum forest.

Delight to me, though, at the water-smuggling creeks,
health to me, too, under banksia candles and combs.

A wind is up, rubbing limbs above the bullock roads;
mountains are waves in the ocean of the gum forest.

I go my way, looking back sometimes, looking round me;
singed oils clear my mind, and the pouring sound high up.

Why have I denied the passions of my time? To see
lightning strike upward out of the gum forest.

4. Elegy for Angus Macdonald of Cnoclinn

The oldest tree in Europe's lost
a knotty branch it could ill spare
to make a hump in Sydney ground,
not for the first time. No. But the last.
A genus of honey bees has died out,
a strain that came to us from the lost world.

Anger at that coarse canting fool
who tried to bury you meanings and all
under his turnip-cairn of texts
—you with the knowledge, he with the talk—
kept us from tears, the day you rode
down ropes in your chest of polished wood.

You were as strange in our waters as
the Atlantis-reef Rocabarraidh. Students,
we came for ancestral language, but you,
no teacher of grammar, gave us lore,
a sight down usages to the Bronze Age
and an ideal from then, older than Heaven,
the "harmony of the men of peace".

The highest folk culture in the West
and terms from a lost, non-Greek Agora
mingled in you, our giver of words:
feallsanachd, oine, foidhirlisg.
Late on and far from heirs, you wrote
your oral learning down in a book,
a dense heaped Cadbury Hill of a book,

the history of your island, songs
and steadings of Heisgir under the sea,
black crimes from the Age of Forays, wise
folk government in the Lordship of the Isles,
astronomy and logic of the men
who taught in that curious late druidical
university of the White Mountain;

you were oath-bound to transmit these things
and you did transmit them. The book remains,
cranky, magnificent, pregnant with rethinkings
as the Watts Towers or Fort's museum,
a Celtic history indeed, a line—
for this is the meaning of the drowned lands—
by which to haul from the conqueror's sea
of myth, our alternative antiquity.

Teacher of my heart, you'll not approve
my making this in the conqueror's language
(though Calgacus used their Latin finely:
"You have made a desert and called it peace").
Even the claim I make at times
to writing Gaelic in English words
would make you sniff (but also smile),

but my fathers were Highlanders long ago
then Borderers, before this landfall
—"savages" once, now we are "settlers"
in the mouth of the deathless enemy—
but I am seized of this future now.
I am not European. Nor is my English.

And perhaps you too were better served here
than in Uist of the Sheldrakes and the tides
watching the old life fade, the *toradh*,
the good, go out of the island world.
Exile's a rampart, sometimes, to the past,
a distiller of spirit from bruised grains;
this is a meaning of the New World.

The good does not go out of the past.
Angles of the moving moon and sun
elicit fresh lights from it continually;
now, in the new lands, everyone's Ethnic
and we too, the Scots Australians, who've been
henchmen of much in our self-loss
may recover ourselves, and put off oppression.

This, then, for the good you put on us,
round-tower of Gaelic, grand wrongheaded one,
now you have gone to the dark crofts:
the oldest tree in Europe's shed
a seed to us—and the Otherworld
becomes ancestral, a code of history,
a style of fingering, an echo of vowels,
honey that comes to us from the lost world.

Rainwater Tank

Empty rings when tapped give tongue,
rings that are tense with water talk:
as he sounds them, ring by rung,
Joe Mitchell's reddened knuckles walk.

The cattledog's head sinks down a notch
and another notch, beside the tank,
and Mitchell's boy, with an old jack-plane,
lifts moustaches from a plank.

From the puddle that the tank has dripped
hens peck glimmerings and uptilt
their heads to shape the quickness down;
petunias live on what gets spilt.

The tankstand spider adds a spittle
thread to her portrait of her soul.
Pencil-grey and stacked like shillings
out of a banker's paper roll

stands the tank, roof-water drinker.
The downpipe stares drought into it.
Briefly the kitchen tap turns on
then off. But the tank says Debit, Debit.

The Future

There is nothing about it. Much science fiction is set there
but is not about it. Prophecy is not about it.
It sways no yarrow stalks. And crystal is a mirror.
Even the man we nailed on a tree for a lookout
said little about it; he told us evil would come.
We see, by convention, a small living distance into it
but even that's a projection. And all our projections
fail to curve where it curves.
                              It is the black hole
out of which no radiation escapes to us.
The commonplace and magnificent roads of our lives
go on some way through cityscape and landscape
or steeply sloping, or scree, into that sheer fall
where everything will be that we have ever sent there,
compacted, spinning—except perhaps us, to see it.
It is said we see the start.
                              But, from here, there's a blindness.
The side-heaped chasm that will swallow all our present
blinds us to the normal sun that may be imagined
shining calmly away on the far side of it, for others
in their ordinary day. A day to which all our portraits,
ideals, revolutions, denim and deshabille
are quaintly heartrending. To see those people is impossible,
to greet them, mawkish. Nonetheless, I begin:
"When I was alive—"
                              and I am turned around
to find myself looking at a cheerful picnic party,
the women decently legless, in muslin and gloves,
the men in beards and weskits, with the long
cheroots and duck trousers of the better sort,
relaxing on a stone verandah. Ceylon, or Sydney.
And as I look, I know they are utterly gone,
each one on his day, with pillow, small bottles, mist,
with all the futures they dreamed or dealt in, going
down to that engulfment everything approaches;
with the man on the tree, they have vanished into the Future.

Cowyard Gates

I saw from the road last time, our house
is all down now.
I didn't go to look.

My cousin had prised the last sheet iron off
the rafters of our sleep
and winced the wall-studs down.

He didn't want an untidy widower ageing
on his new farm.
I'll want the timber for cowyard gates, he said.

The floor joists will persist awhile
and the fireplace, that pack-ice of concrete, stained
with the last spilt fat.
I didn't go to look.

I had said goodbye to that house many times
and so helped it fall.
I have even ransacked it,
carried off slants of sunlight and of wind
that used to strike through the bedroom planking, blades
against the upstart.

Many feelings are suspended:
the front verandah feeling, looking away at the west,
the back verandah feeling, wet boards, towel on its nail,
all widowed in the air,

but, half demolished, it was almost an eddy
standing there on the ridge,
memory and loss in a grove of upright boards.

Now Time's free to dissipate all the days trapped there:
books in the sleepout, green walling of branches around
our Christmas table, my mother placing and placing
a tin ring on scone-dough, telling me about French.
The first weeks of her death.

Suppertime lamp,
full moon through the loungeroom door.
I did not go to look.

Immigrant Voyage

My wife came out on the *Goya*
in the mid-year of our century.

In the fogs of that winter
many hundred ships were sounding;
the DP camps were being washed to sea.

The bombsites and the ghettoes
were edging out to Israel,
to Brazil, to Africa, America.

The separating ships were bound away
to the cities of refuge
built for the age of progress.

Hull-down and pouring light
the tithe-barns, the cathedrals
were bearing the old castes away.

•

Pattern-bombed out of babyhood,
Hungarians-become-Swiss,
the children heard their parents:
Argentina? Or Australia?
Less politics, in Australia . . .

Dark Germany, iron frost
and the waiting many weeks
then a small converted warship
under the moon, turning south.

Way beyond the first star
and beyond Cape Finisterre
the fishes and the birds
did eat of their heave-offerings.

      •

The *Goya* was a barracks:
mess-queue, spotlights, tower,
crossing the Middle Sea.

In the haunted blue light
that burned nightlong in the sleeping-decks
the tiered bunks were restless
with coughing, demons, territory.

On the Sea of Sweat, the Red Sea,
the flat heat melted even
dulled deference of the injured.
Nordics and Slavonics
paid salt-tax day and night, being
absolved of Europe

but by the Gate of Tears
the barrack was a village
with accordions and dancing
(Fräulein, kennen Sie meinen Rhythmus?)
approaching the southern stars.

      •

Those who said Europe
has fallen to the Proles
and the many who said
we are going for the children,

the nouveau poor
and the cheerful shirtsleeve Proles,
the children, who thought
No Smoking signs meant men
mustn't dress for dinner,

those who had hopes
and those who knew that they
were giving up their lives

were becoming the people
who would say, and sometimes urge,
in the English-speaking years:
we came out on the *Goya*.

●

At last, a low coastline,
old horror of Dutch sail-captains.

Behind it, still unknown,
sunburnt farms, strange trees, family jokes
and all the classes of equality.

As it fell away northwards
there was one last week for songs,
for dreaming at the rail,
for beloved meaningless words.

Standing in to Port Phillip
in the salt-grey summer light
the village dissolved
into strained shapes holding luggage;

now they, like the dour
Australians below them, were facing
encounter with the Foreign
where all subtlety fails.

●

Those who, with effort,
with concealment, with silence, had resisted
the collapsed star Death,
who had clawed their families from it,
those crippled by that gravity

were suddenly, shockingly
being loaded aboard lorries:
They say, another camp—
One did not come for this—

As all the refitted
ships stood, oiling, in the Bay,
spectres, furious and feeble,
accompanied the trucks through Melbourne,

resignation, understandings
that cheerful speed dispelled at length.

That first day, rolling north
across the bright savanna,
not yet people, but numbers.
Population. Forebears.

·

Bonegilla, Nelson Bay,
the dry-land barbed wire ships
from which some would never land.

In these, as their parents
learned the Fresh Start music:
physicians nailing crates,
attorneys cleaning trams,
the children had one last
ambiguous summer holiday.

Ahead of them lay
the Deep End of the schoolyard,
tribal testing, tribal soft-drinks,
and learning English fast,
the Wang-Wang language.

Ahead of them, refinements:
thumbs hooked down hard under belts
to repress gesticulation;

ahead of them, epithets:
wog, reffo, Commo Nazi,
things which can be forgotten
but must first be told.

And farther ahead
in the years of the Coffee Revolution
and the Smallgoods Renaissance,
the early funerals:

the misemployed, the unadaptable,
those marked by the Abyss,

friends who came on the *Goya*
in the mid-year of our century.

The Craze Field

These lagoons, these watercourses,
streets of the underworld.
Their water has become the trees that stand along them.

Below root-revetments, in the circles of the water's recession
the ravines seem thronged with a legacy of lily pads.
Earth curls and faintly glistens, scumbled painterly and peeling.

Palates of drought-stilled assonance,
they are cupped flakes of grit, crisps of bottom, dried meniscus
lifted at the edges.

Abstracts realized in slime. Shards of bubble, shrivelled viscose
of clay and stopped life:
the scales of the water snake have gone to grey on this channel.

•

Exfoliate bark of the rain tree, all the outer

plaques have a jostling average size.
It is a kind of fire, the invention of networks.

Water's return, however gradual (and it won't be)
however gentle (it won't be) would not re-lay all seamless
this basal membrane;
it has borne excess of clarity.

This is the lush sheet that overlay the first cities,
the mother-goddess towns, but underlay them first;
this they had for mortar.

Laminar, half detached, these cusps are primal tissue,
foreshadowings of leaf, pottery, palimpsest,
the Dead Lagoon Scrolls.

In this hollow season
everything is perhaps to be recapitulated,
hurriedly, approximately. It is a kind of fire.
Saturate calm is all sprung, in the mother country.

●

The lagoon-bed museums meanwhile have a dizzy stillness
that will reduce, with all the steps that are coming,
to meal, grist, morsels.
Dewfall and birds' feet have nipped, blind noons have nibbled
this mineral matzoh.

The warlike peace-talking young, pacing this dominion
in the beautiful flesh that outdoes their own creations,
might read gnomic fragments:
                              corr   lux   Romant   irit
or fragmentary texts:
    *who lose belief in God will not only believe
    in anything. They will bring blood offerings to it*

Bones, snags, seed capsules,
intrinsic in the Martian central pan,
are hidden, in the craze, under small pagoda eaves.

For a Jacobite Lady

Proud heart, since the light of making lace
for an exiled prince died in your eyes
it is above two centuries.

Your Cause grew literary as it died;
it was Gothic in classicizing times
and a wilder gothic extinguished it,

but you are there in the heat of it,
codes, glasses, the waiting on Versailles,
the sin of hope that eats the heart.

Your needle has left what it could trace:
your life's thread, in endless free returns,
making little subjoined worlds of grace.

That was monarchy. At its defeat
earth fell against heaven, and everyone
was exposed to glory in the street.

I write you this from the Land of Peace,
the Plain of Sports of the vision poems;
your wars drove us here; we possess it now.

We are descendants. As was our one Prince.
Not over the water, but in the wine,
he is more assailed now, since more visible,

freed from the robes of any court.
Causes are our courts; they try our lives,
and dispose of them, to prove their own

as if to see both sides of death
truly, at once, in their due weight
were not reserved to the consummate.

The Grassfire Stanzas

August, and black centres expand on the afternoon paddock.
Dilating on a match in widening margins, they lift
a splintering murmur; they fume out of used-up grass
that's been walked, since summer, into infinite swirled licks.

The man imposing spring here swats with his branch, controlling
    it:
only small things may come to a head, in this settlement pattern.

Fretted with small flame, the aspiring islands leave
odd plumes behind. Smuts shower up every thermal
to float down long stairs. Aggregate smoke attracts a kestrel.

Eruption of darkness from far down under roots
is the aspect of these cores, on the undulating farmland;
dense black is withered into web, inside a low singing;
it is dried and loosened, on the surface; it is made weak.

The green feed that shelters beneath its taller death yearly
is unharmed, under new loaf soot. Arriving hawks teeter
and plunge continually, working over the hopping outskirts.

The blackenings are balanced, on a gradient of dryness
in the almost-still air, between dying thinly away
and stripping the whole countryside. Joining, they never gain
more than they lose. They spread away from their high
    moments.

The man carries smoke wrapped in bark, and keeps applying it
starting new circles. He is burning the passive ocean
around his ark of buildings and his lifeboat water;

it wasn't this man, but it was man, sing the agile
exclamatory birds, who taught them this rapt hunting
(strike! in the updrafts, snap! of hardwood pods).
Humans found the fire here. It is inherent. They learn,
wave after wave of them, how to touch the country.

Sterilizing reed distaffs, the fire edges on to a dam;
it circuits across a cow-track; new surf starts riding outward
and a nippy kestrel feeds from its foot, over cooling mergers.

It's the sun that is touched, and dies in expansion, mincing,
making the round dance, foretelling its future, driving
the frantic lives outwards. The sun that answers the bark tip
is discharged in many little songs, to forestall a symphony.

Cattle come, with stilted bounding calves. They look across the
ripple lines of heat, and shake their armed heads at them;
at random, then, they step over. Grazing smudged black country
they become the beasts of Tartarus. Wavering, moving out over
dung-smouldering ground still covered with its uncovering.

Homage to the Launching-place

Pleasure-craft of the sprung rhythms, bed,
                kindest of quadrupeds,
you are also the unrocking boat
                that moves on silence.

Straining hatchway into this world,
                you sustain our collapses
above earth; guarantor of evolution,
                you are our raised base-line.

Resisting gravity, for us and in us,
                you form a planet-wide
unobtrusive discontinuous platform,
                a layer: the mattressphere,
pretty nearly our highest common level
                (tables may dispute it).

                Muscles' sweatprinted solace,
godmother of butt-stubbing dreams,
                you sublimate, Great Vehicle,
all our upright passions;

> midwife of figuring, and design,
you moderate them wisely;
> aiming solitude outwards, at action,
you sigh Think some more. Sleep on it . . .

Solitude. Approaching rest
Time reveals her oscillation
> and narrows into space;
> there is time in that dilation:
> Mansions. Defiles. Continents.
> The living and the greatly living,
> objects that take sides,
> that aren't morally neutral—

you accept my warm absence
> there, as you will accept,
one day, my cooling presence.

> I loved you from the first, bed,
doorway out of this world;
> above your inner springs
I learned to dig my own.

> Primly dressed, linen-collared one,
you look so still, for your speed,
> shield that carries us to the fight
> and bears us from it.

First Essay on Interest

Not usury, but interest. The cup slowed in mid-raise,
the short whistle, hum, the little forwards shift
mark our intake of that non-physical breath

which the lungs mimic sharply, to cancel the gap in pressure
left by our self vanishing into its own alert—
A blink returns us to self, that intimate demeanour

self-repairing as a bow-wave. What we have received
is the ordinary mail of the otherworld, wholly common,
not postmarked divine; no one refuses delivery,

not even the eagle, her face fixed at heavy Menace:
I have juices to sort the relevant from the irrelevant;
even her gaze may tilt left, askance, aloof, right,
fixing a still unknown. Delaying huge flight.

Interest. Mild and inherent with fire as oxygen,
it is a sporadic inhalation. We can live long days
under its surface, breathing material air

then something catches, is itself. Intent and special silence.
This is interest, that blinks our interests out
and alone permits their survival, by relieving

us of their gravity, for a timeless moment;
that centres where it points, and points to centring,
that centres us where it points, and reflects our centre.

It is a form of love. The everyday shines through it
and patches of time. But it does not mingle with these;
it wakens only for each trace in them of the Beloved.

And this breath of interest is non-rhythmical:
it is human to obey, humane to be wary of rhythm
as tainted by the rallies, as marching with the snare drum.
The season of interest is not fixed in the calendar cycle;

it pulls towards acute dimensions. Death is its intimate.
When that Holland of cycles, the body, veers steeply downhill
interest retreats from the face; it ceases to instill
and fade, like breath; it becomes a vivid steady state

that registers every grass-blade seen on the way,
the long combed grain in the steps, free insects flying;
it stands aside from your panic, the wracked disarray;
it behaves as if it were the part of you not dying.

Affinity of interest with extremity
seems to distil to this polar disaffinity
that suggests the beloved is not death, but rather
what our death has hidden. Which may be this world.

The Fishermen at South Head

They have walked out as far as they can go on the prow of the
     continent,
on the undercut white sandstone, the bowsprits of the towering
     headland.
They project their long light canes
or raise them up to check and string, like quiet archers.
Between casts they hold them couched,
a finger on the line, two fingers on a cigarette, the reel cocked.

They watch the junction of smooth blue with far matt-shining
     blue,
the join where clouds enter,
or they watch the wind-shape of their nylon
bend like a sail's outline
south towards, a mile away, the city's floating gruel
of gull-blown effluent.

Sometimes they glance north, at the people on that calf-coloured
     edge
lower than theirs, where the suicides come by taxi
and stretchers are winched up
later, under raining lights
but mostly their eyes stay level with the land-and-ocean glitter.

Where they stand, atop the centuries
of strata, they don't look down much
but feel through their tackle the talus-eddying
and tidal detail of that huge simple pulse
in the rock and in their bones.

Through their horizontal poles they divine the creatures of
        ocean:
a touch, a dip, and a busy winding death gets started;
hands will turn for minutes, rapidly,
before, still opening its pitiful doors, the victim
dawns above the rim, and is hoisted in a flash above the suburbs
—or before the rod flips, to stand
trailing sworn-at gossamer.

On that highest dreadnought scarp, where the terra cotta
waves of bungalows stop, suspended at sky,
the hunters stand apart.
They encourage one another, at a distance, not by talk

but by being there, by unhooking now and then
a twist of silver for the creel, by a vaguely mutual
zodiac of cars TV windcheaters.
Braced, casual normality. Anything unshared,
a harlequin mask, a painted wand flourished at the sun,
would anger them. It is serious to be with humans.

The Doorman

The man applying rules to keep me out
knows if I have to deal with him the rules
apply to me. I am to be kept out.
Naïve to think that he respects the rules;
he knows their purpose. Complicity is out:
if I were his sort I would know the rules.

His genes have seeped down a hundred centuries;
in a slave-ship's hold they pooled to form his eyes,
on a Sunday-school mop they collected to a face
and they formed a skin in the dry air of a palace.
In stripes, in armour, in pinstripes, he stays the same man
and I know his sister, that right-thinking woman.

He is a craftsman, and these are his tools:
unyielding correctness, thin mouth, a nose for clout,
modulations of boredom (let the blusterers threaten).
He guards the status quo as he guards mankind's salvation
and those he protects need never learn the rules:
his contempt is reserved for those who are In, and Out.

Anthropomorphics

Outside the serious media, the violence of animals
is often like a sad cartoon. Tom catches Jerry
and one of them grows less cute, glibbed with saliva,
shivering, darting. But Tom keeps his appealing intent look.
Similarly the snake, having struck and left you with it,
flourishes off quickly, his expression if anything self-righteous.
Hunting, we know, is mostly a form of shopping
where the problem's to make the packages hold still;
Death's best for that, though cheetahs have been seen feeding
on the bulk of a gazelle while the raised head end still bleated:
it was like the companionable sacking of a small Norse ship.
Even with sex, the symbolic beasts can be unreliable:
the great bull, mounting, cramps his lungs on her knobbed spine
and looks winded and precarious. He is more sexual walking.
I praise, nonetheless, our humane and Scythian arts.

The New Moreton Bay
(ON THE CONVERSION TO CATHOLICISM OF THE POET KEVIN HART)

A grog-primed overseer, who later died,
snapped at twenty convicts gasping in a line
That pole ain't heavy! Two men stand aside!
and then two more, *And you, pop-eyes! And you!*
—until the dozen left, with a terrible cry,
broke and were broken
beneath the tons of log they had stemmed aloft desperately.

Because there is no peace in this world's peace
the timber is to carry. Many hands heave customarily,
some step aside, detained by the Happiness Police
or despair's boutiques; it is a continual sway—
but when grace and intent
recruit a fresh shoulder, then we're in the other testament
and the innocent wood lifts line-long, with its leaves and
    libraries.

The Sydney Highrise Variations

1. Fuel Stoppage on Gladesville Road Bridge in the Year 1980

So we're sitting over our sick beloved engine
atop a great building of the double century
on the summit that exhilarates cars, the concrete vault on its
    thousands
of tonnes of height, far above the tidal turnaround.

Gigantic pure form, all exterior, superbly uninhabited
or peopled only by transients at speed, the bridge
is massive outline.
              It was inked in by scaffolding and workers.
Seen from itself, the arch
is an abstract hill, a roadway up-and-over without country,
from below, a ponderous grotto, all entrance and vast shade
framing blues and levels.
From a distance, the flyover on its vaulting drum
is a sketched stupendous ground-burst, a bubble raising surface
or a rising heatless sun with inset horizons.
                        Also it's a space-probe,
a trajectory of strange fixed dusts, that were milled,
boxed with steel rod mesh and fired, in stages,
from sandstone point to point. They docked at apogee.

It feels good. It feels right.
The joy of sitting high is in our judgement.
The marvellous brute-force effects of our century work.
They answer something in us. Anything in us.

2. *View of Sydney, Australia, from Gladesville Road Bridge*

There's that other great arch eastward, with its hanging
    highways;
the headlands and horizons of packed suburb, white among
    bisque-fired; odd smokes rising;
there's Warrang, the flooded valley, that is now the ship-chained
    Harbour,
recurrent everywhere, with its azure and its grains;
ramped parks, bricked containers,
verandahs successive around walls,
and there's the central highrise, multi-storey, the twenty-year
    countdown,
the new city standing on its haze above the city.

      Ingots of sheer
      affluence poles
      bomb-drawing grid
      of columnar profit
      piecrust and scintillant
      tunnels in the sky
      high window printouts
      repeat their lines
      repeat their lines
      credit conductors
      repeat their lines
      bar graphs on blue
      glass tubes of boom
      in concrete wicker
      each trade Polaris
      government Agena
      fine print insurrected
      tall things on a tray

All around them is the old order: brewery brick terrace hospital
horrible workplace; the scale of the tramway era,
the peajacket era, the age of the cliff-repeating woolstores.
South and west lie the treeless suburbs, a mulch of faded flags,
north and partly east, the built-in paradise forest.

3. The Flight from Manhattan

It is possible the heights of this view are a museum:
though the highrise continues desultorily along some ridges,
     canned Housing, Strata Title,
     see-through Office Space,
     upright bedsteads of Harbour View,
     residential soviets,
the cranes have all but vanished from the central upsurge.

     Hot-air money-driers,
     towering double entry,
     Freud's cobwebbed poem
     with revolving restaurant,
they took eighty years to fly here from Manhattan
these variant towers. By then, they were arriving everywhere.

     In the land of veneers,
     of cladding, of Cape Codding
     (I shall have Cape Codded)
     they put on heavy side.

The iron ball was loose in the old five-storey city
clearing bombsites for them. They rose like nouveaux accents
and stilled, for a time, the city's conversation.

     Their arrival paralleled
     the rise of the Consumers
     gazing through themselves
     at iconoclasms, wines,
     Danish Modern ethics.

Little we could love expanded to fill the spaces
of high glazed prosperity. An extensive city
that had long contained the dimensions of heaven and hell
couldn't manage total awe at the buildings of the Joneses.

Their reign coincided
with an updraft of Ideology,
that mood in which the starving
spirit is fed upon the heart.

Employment and neckties and ruling themes ascended
into the towers. But they never filled them.
Squinting at them through the salt
and much-washed glass of her history, the city kept her flavour
fire-ladder high, rarely above three storeys.

In ambiguous battle at length, she began to hedge
the grilles of Aspiration. To limit them to standing
on economic grounds. With their twists of sculpture.

On similar grounds we are stopped here, still surveying
the ridgy plain of houses. Enormous. England's buried Gulag.
The stacked entrepôt, great city of the Australians.

4. The C19–20

The Nineteenth Century. The Twentieth Century.
There were never any others. No centuries before these.
Dante was not hailed in his time as an Authentic
Fourteenth Century Voice. Nor did Cromwell thunder, *After all,
in the bowels of Christ, this* is *the Seventeenth Century!*

The two are one aircraft in the end, the C19-20,
capacious with cargo. Some of it can save your life,
some can prevent it.
The cantilevered behemoth
is fitted up with hospitals and electric Gatling guns
to deal with recalcitrant and archaic spirits.

It rose out of the Nineteenth, steam pouring from venturi
and every man turning hay with a wooden fork
in the Age of Piety (A.D. or B.C.) wants one
in his nation's airline. And his children dream of living
in a palace of packing crates beside the cargo terminal:
No one will see! Everything will be surprises!

Directly under the flightpath, and tuned to listening,
we hear the cockpit traffic, the black box channel
that can't be switched off: Darwinians and Lawrentians
are wrestling for the controls,
We must take her into Space! / We must fly in potent circles!

5. The Recession of the Joneses

The worldwide breath of Catching Up
may serve to keep the mighty, slowing
machine aloft beyond our lifetime:
nearly all of the poor are blowing.

The soaring double century
might end, and mutate, and persist;
as we've been speaking, the shadows of
bridges, cranes, towers have shifted east.

When we create our own high style
skill and the shadow will not then part;
as rhetoric would conceal from art
effort has at best a winning margin.

The sun, that is always catching up
with night and day and month and year,
blazes from its scrolled bare face: *To be
solar, I must be nuclear—*

Six hundred glittering and genteel towns
gathered to be urban in plein air,
more complex in their levels than their heights
and vibrant with modernity's strange anger.

Quintets for Robert Morley

Is it possible that hyper-
ventilating up Parnassus
I have neglected to pay tribute
to the Stone Age aristocracy?
   I refer to the fat.

We were probably the earliest
civilized, and civilizing, humans,
the first to win the leisure,
sweet boredom, life-enhancing sprawl
   that require style.

Tribesfolk spared us and cared for us
for good reasons. Our reasons.
As age's counterfeits, forerunners of the city,
we survived, and multiplied. Out of self-defence
   we invented the Self.

It's likely we also invented some of love,
much of fertility (see the Willensdorf Venus)
parts of theology (divine feasting, Unmoved Movers)
likewise complexity, stateliness, the ox-cart
   and self-deprecation.

Not that the lists of pugnacity are bare
of stout fellows. Ask a Sumo.
Warriors taunt us still, and fear us:
in heroic war, we are apt to be the specialists
   and the generals.

But we do better in peacetime. For ourselves
we would spare the earth. We were the first moderns
after all, being like the Common Man
disqualified from tragedy. Accessible to shame, though,
   subtler than the tall,

we make reasonable rulers.
Never trust a lean meritocracy

nor the leader who has been lean;
only the lifelong big have the knack of wedding
    greatness with balance.

Never wholly trust the fat man
who lurks in the lean achiever
and in the defeated, yearning to get out.
He has not been through our initiations,
    he lacks the light feet.

Our having life abundantly
is equivocal, Robert, in hot climates
where the hungry watch us. I lack the light step then too.
How many of us, I wonder, walk those streets
    in terrible disguise?

So much climbing, on a spherical world;
had Newton not been a mere beginner at gravity
he might have asked how the apple got up there
in the first place. And so might have discerned
    an ampler physics.

Bent Water in the Tasmanian Highlands

Flashy wrists out of buttoned grass cuffs, feral whisky burning
    gravels,
jazzy knuckles ajitter on soakages, peaty cupfuls, soft pots
    overflowing,
setting out along the great curve, migrating mouse-quivering
    water,
mountain-driven winter water, in the high tweed, stripping off
    its mountains
to run faster in its skin, it swallows the above, it feeds where it
    is fed on,
it forms at many points and creases outwards, pleated water

shaking out its bedding soil, increasing its scale, beginning the
        headlong
—Bent Water, you could call this level
between droplet and planetary, not as steered by twisting beds
        laterally
but as upped and swayed on its swelling and outstanding own
        curvatures,
its floating top that sweeps impacts sidelong, its event-horizon,
a harelip round a pebble, mouthless cheeks globed over a
        boulder, a
finger's far-stretched holograph, skinned flow athwart a snag
—these flexures are all reflections, motion-glyphs, pitches of
        impediment,
say a log commemorated in a log-long hump of wave,
a buried rock continually noted, a squeeze-play
through a cracked basalt bar, maintaining a foam-roofed
        two-sided
overhang of breakneck riesling; uplifted hoseless hosings, fully
        circular water,
flattened water off rock sills, sandwiched between an upper
and a lower whizzing surface, trapped in there with airy scatter
and mingled high-speed mirrorings; water groined, produced
        and spiralled
—Crowded scrollwork from events, at steepening white
        velocities
as if the whole outline of the high country were being pulled out
along these joining channels, and proving infinite, anchored
        deeply as it
is in the groundwater scale, in the silence around racy breccia
yet it is spooling out; the great curve, drawing and driving,
of which these are the animal-sized swells and embodiments
won't always describe this upland; and after the jut falls,
        the inverse
towering on gorges, these peaks will be hidden beneath
rivers and tree-bark, in electricity, in cattle, on the ocean
—Meditation is a standing wave, though, on the black-green
        inclines
of pouring and cascading, slate-dark rush and timber-
        worker's tea

bullying the pebble-fans; if we were sketched first at this speed,
sheaths, buttocks, wings, it is mother and history and
　　　swank here
till our wave is drained of water. And as such it includes
　　　the writhing
down in a trench, knees, bellies, the struggling, the slack
　　　bleeding
remote enough perhaps, within its close clean film,
to make the observer a god; do we come here to be gods?
or to watch an alien pouring down the slants of our anomaly
and be hypnotized to rest by it? So much detail's unlikely,
　　　for hypnosis;
it looks like brotherhood sought at a dreamer's remove
and, in either view, laws of falling and persistence:
the continuous ocean round a planetary stone, braiding uptilts
after swoops, echo-forms, arches built from above and standing
on flourish, clear storeys, translucent honey-glazed clerestories—

Equanimity

Nests of golden porridge shattered in the silky-oak trees,
cobs and crusts of it, their glory-box;
the jacarandas' open violet immensities
mirrored flat on the lawns,
weighted by sprinklers; birds, singly and in flocks
hopping over the suburb, eating, as birds do, in detail
and paying their peppercorns;
talk of "the good life" tangles love with will
however; if we mention it, there is more to say:
the droughty light, for example, at telephone-wire
height above the carports, not the middle-ground
distilling news-photograph light of a smoggy Wednesday,
but that light of the north-west wind, hung on the sky
like the haze above cattleyards;
hungry mountain birds, too, drifting in for food, with the sound
of moist gullies about them, and the sound of the pinch-bar;
we must hear the profoundly unwished

garble of a neighbours' quarrel, and see repeatedly
the face we saw near the sportswear shop today
in which mouth-watering and tears couldn't be distinguished.

Fire-prone place-names apart
there is only love; there are no Arcadias.
Whatever its variants of meat-cuisine, worship, divorce,
human order has at heart
an equanimity. Quite different from inertia, it's a place
where the churchman's not defensive, the indignant aren't on the
      qui vive,
the loser has lost interest, the accountant is truant to remorse,
where the farmer has done enough struggling-to-survive
for one day, and the artist rests from theory—
where all are, in short, off the high comparative horse
of their identity.
Almost beneath notice, as attainable as gravity, it is
a continuous recovering moment. Pity the high madness
that misses it continually, ranging without rest between
assertion and unconsciousness,
the sort that makes Hell seem a height of evolution.
Through the peace beneath effort
(even within effort: quiet air between the bars of our attention)
comes unpurchased lifelong plenishment;
Christ spoke to people most often on this level
especially when they chattered about kingship and the Romans;
all holiness speaks from it.

From the otherworld of action and media, this
interleaved continuing plane is hard to focus:
we are looking into the light—
it makes some smile, some grimace.
More natural to look at the birds about the street, their life
that is greedy, pinched, courageous and prudential
as any on these bricked tree-mingled miles of settlement,
to watch the unceasing on-off
grace that attends their nearly every movement,
the same grace moveless in the shapes of trees
and complex in our selves and fellow walkers: we see it's
      indivisible

and scarcely willed. That it lights us from the incommensurable
that we sometimes glimpse, from being trapped in the point
(bird minds and ours are so pointedly visual):
a field all foreground, and equally all background,
like a painting of equality. Of infinite detailed extent
like God's attention. Where nothing is diminished by
    perspective.

The Forest Hit by Modern Use

The forest, hit by modern use,
stands graced with damage.
                        Angled plaques
tilt everywhere, with graphic needle crowns
and trinket saps fixed round their year;
vines spiderweb, flowering, over smashed
intricacies; long rides appear.

Dense growths that were always underbrush
expand in the light, beside bulldozers'
imprinted machine-gun belts of spoor.

Now the sun's in, through breaks and jags,
culled slopes are jammed with replacement; green
and whipstick saplings, every one out
to shade the rest to death.
                      Scabbed chain
feeds leaf-mould its taut rain-cold solution;
bared creeks wash gold; kingfishers hover.

There is still great height: all through the hills
spared hierarchs toughen to the wind
around the punk hearts that got them spared
and scatter seed down the logging roads.

Grease-fungi, scrolls, clenched pipes of bark:
the forest will now be kept like this

for a long time. There are rooms in it
and, paradox for mystery, birds
too tiny, now that we see them, for
their amplitude and carrying flash of song.

On a stump, a sea eagle eats by lengths
their enemy, a coil-whipping dry land fish,
and voids white size to make room for it.

Shower

From the metal poppy
this good blast of trance
arriving as shock, private cloudburst blazing down,
worst in a boarding-house greased tub, or a barrack with
    competitions,
best in a stall, this enveloping passion of Australians:
tropics that sweat for you, torrent that braces with its heat,
inflames you with its chill, action sauna, inverse bidet,
sleek vertical coruscating ghost of your inner river,
reminding all your fluids, streaming off your points, awakening
the tacky soap to blossom and ripe autumn, releasing the
    squeezed gardens,
smoky valet smoothing your impalpable overnight pyjamas off,
pillar you can step through, force-field absolving love's efforts,
nicest yard of the jogging track, speeding aeroplane minutely
steered with two controls, or trimmed with a knurled wheel.
Some people like to still this energy and lie in it,
stirring circles with their pleasure in it—but my delight's
    that toga
worn on either or both shoulders, fluted drapery, silk whispering
    to the tiles
with its spiralling frothy hem continuous round the gurgle-hole;
this ecstatic partner, dreamy to dance in slow embrace with
after factory-floor rock, or even to meet as Lot's abstracted
merciful wife on a rusty ship in dog latitudes,
sweetest dressing of the day in the dusty bush, this persistent

time-capsule of unwinding, this nimble straight well-wisher.
Only in England is its name an unkind word;
only in Europe is it enjoyed by telephone.

The Quality of Sprawl

Sprawl is the quality
of the man who cut down his Rolls-Royce
into a farm utility truck, and sprawl
is what the company lacked when it made repeated efforts
to buy the vehicle back and repair its image.

Sprawl is doing your farming by aeroplane, roughly,
or driving a hitchhiker that extra hundred miles home.
It is the rococo of being your own still centre.
It is never lighting cigars with ten-dollar notes:
that's idiot ostentation and murder of starving people.
Nor can it be bought with the ash of million-dollar deeds.

Sprawl lengthens the legs; it trains greyhounds on liver and beer.
Sprawl almost never says Why not? with palms comically raised
nor can it be dressed for, not even in running shoes worn
with mink and a nose ring. That is Society. That's Style.
Sprawl is more like the thirteenth banana in a dozen
or anyway the fourteenth.

Sprawl is Hank Stamper in *Never Give an Inch*
bisecting an obstructive official's desk with a chainsaw.
Not harming the official. Sprawl is never brutal
though it's often intransigent. Sprawl is never Simon de
    Montfort
at a town-storming: Kill them all! God will know his own.
Knowing the man's name this was said to might be sprawl.

Sprawl occurs in art. The fifteenth to twenty-first
lines in a sonnet, for example. And in certain paintings;

I have sprawl enough to have forgotten which paintings.
Turner's glorious *Burning of the Houses of Parliament*
comes to mind, a doubling bannered triumph of sprawl—
except, he didn't fire them.

Sprawl gets up the nose of many kinds of people
(every kind that comes in kinds) whose futures don't include it.
Some decry it as criminal presumption, silken-robed Pope
    Alexander
dividing the new world between Spain and Portugal.
If he smiled *in petto* afterwards, perhaps the thing did have
    sprawl.

Sprawl is really classless, though. It's John Christopher Frederick
    Murray
asleep in his neighbours' best bed in spurs and oilskins
but not having thrown up:
sprawl is never Calum who, drunk, along the hallways of our
    house,
reinvented the Festoon. Rather
it's Beatrice Miles going twelve hundred ditto in a taxi,
No Lewd Advances, No Hitting Animals, No Speeding,
on the proceeds of her two-bob-a-sonnet Shakespeare readings.
An image of my country. And would that it were more so.

No, sprawl is full-gloss murals on a council-house wall.
Sprawl leans on things. It is loose-limbed in its mind.
Reprimanded and dismissed
it listens with a grin and one boot up on the rail
of possibility. It may have to leave the Earth.
Being roughly Christian, it scratches the other cheek
and thinks it unlikely. Though people have been shot for sprawl.

Three Poems in Memory of My Mother, Miriam Murray née Arnall
BORN 23.5.1915, DIED 19.4.1951

Weights

Not owning a cart, my father
in the drought years was a bowing
green hut of cattle feed, moving,
or gasping under cream cans. No weight
would he let my mother carry.

Instead, she wielded handles
in the kitchen and dairy, singing often,
gave saucepan-boiled injections
with her ward-sister skill, nursed neighbours,
scorned gossips, ran committees.

She gave me her factual tone,
her facial bones, her will,
not her beautiful voice
but her straightness and her clarity.

I did not know back then
nor for many years what it was,
after me, she could not carry.

Midsummer Ice

Remember how I used
to carry ice in from the road
for the ice chest, half running,
the white rectangle clamped in bare hands
the only utter cold
in all those summer paddocks?

How, swaying, I'd hurry it inside
en bloc and watering, with the butter
and the wrapped bread precarious on top of it?
"Poor Leslie," you would say,

"your hands are cold as charity—"
You made me take the barrow
but uphill it was heavy.

We'd no tongs, and a bag
would have soaked and bumped, off balance.
I loved to eat the ice,
chip it out with the butcher knife's grey steel.
It stopped good things rotting
and it had a strange comb at its heart,
a splintered horizon rife with zero pearls.

But you don't remember.
A doorstep of numbed creek water the colour of tears
but you don't remember.
I will have to die before you remember.

The Steel

I am older than my mother.
Cold steel hurried me from her womb.
I haven't got a star.

What hour I followed
the waters into this world
no one living can now say.
My zodiac got washed away.

The steel of my induction
killed my brothers and sisters;
once or twice I was readied for them

and then they were not mentioned
again, at the hospital
to me or to the visitors.
The reticence left me only.

I think, apart from this,
my parents' life was happy,
provisional, as lives are.

Farming spared them from the war,
that, and an ill-knit blue shin
my father had been harried back

to tree-felling with, by his father
who supervised from horseback.
The times were late pioneer.

So was our bare plank house
with its rain stains down each crack
like tall tan flames,
magic swords, far matched perspectives:

it reaped Dad's shamed invectives—
Paying him rent for this shack!
The landlord was his father.

But we also had fireside ease,
health, plentiful dinners, the radio;
we'd a car to drive to tennis.

Country people have cars
for more than shopping and show,
our Dodge reached voting age, though,
in my first high school year.

I was in the town at school
the afternoon my mother
collapsed, and was carried from the dairy.
The car was out of order.

The ambulance was available
but it took a doctor's say-so
to come. This was refused.
My father pleaded. Was refused.

The local teacher's car was got finally.
The time all this took didn't pass,
it spread through sheets, unstoppable.

Thirty-seven miles to town
and the terrible delay.
Little blood brother, blood sister,
I don't blame you.
How can you blame a baby?
or the longing for a baby?

Little of that week
comes back. The vertigo,
the apparent recovery—
She will get better now.
The relapse on the Thursday.

In school and called away
I was haunted, all that week,
by the spectre of dark women,
Murrays dressed in midday black

who lived on the river islands
and are seen only at funerals;
their terrible weak authority.

Everybody in the town
was asking me about my mother;
I could only answer childishly
to them. And to my mother,

and on Friday afternoon
our family world
went inside itself forever.

Sister Arnall, city girl
with your curt good sense,
were you being the nurse
when you let them hurry me?
being responsible

when I was brought on to make way
for a difficult birth in that cottage hospital
and the Cheers child stole my birthday?

Or was it our strange diffidence,
unworldly at a pinch, unresentful,
being a case among cases,

a relative, wartime sense,
modern, alien to fuss,
that is not in the Murrays?

I don't blame the Cheers boy's mother:
she didn't put her case.
It was the steel proposed
reasonably, professionally,
that became your sentence

but I don't decry unselfishness:
I'm proud of it. Of you.
Any virtue can be fatal.

In the event, his coming gave no trouble
but it might have, I agree;
nothing you agreed to harmed me.
I didn't mean to harm you
I was a baby.

For a long time, my father
himself became a baby
being perhaps wiser than me,
less modern, less military;

he was not ashamed of grief,
of its looking like a birth
out through the face

bloated, whiskery, bringing no relief.
It was mainly through fear
that I was at times his father.
I have long been sorry.

Caked pans, rancid blankets,
despair and childish cool
were our road to Bohemia
that bitter wartime country.

What were you thinking of,
Doctor MB, BS?
Were you very tired?
Did you have more pressing cases?

Know panic when you heard it:
Oh you can bring her in!
Did you often do
diagnosis by telephone?

Perhaps we wrong you,
make a scapegoat of you;
perhaps there was no stain
of class in your decision,

no view that two framed degrees
outweighed a dairy.
It's nothing, dear:
just some excited hillbilly—

As your practice disappeared
and you were cold-shouldered in town
till you broke and fled,
did you think of the word *Clan*?

It is an antique
concept. But not wholly romantic.
We came to the river early;
it gives us some protection.

You'll agree the need is real.
I can forgive you now
and not to seem magnanimous.

It's enough that you blundered
on our family steel.

Thirty-five years on earth:
that's short. That's short, Mother,
as the lives cut off by war

and the lives of spilt children are short.
Justice wholly in this world
would bring them no rebirth
nor restore your latter birthdays.
How could that be justice?

My father never quite
remarried. He went back
by stages of kindness to me
to the age of lonely men,
of only men, and men's company

that is called the Pioneer age.
Snig chain and mountain track;
he went back to felling trees

and seeking justice from his
dead father. His only weakness.
One's life is not a case

except of course it is.
Being just, seeking justice:
they were both of them right,
my mother and my father.

There is justice, there is death,
humanist: you can't have both.
Activist, you can't serve both.
You do not move in measured space.

The poor man's anger is a prayer
for equities Time cannot hold
and steel grows from our mother's grace.
Justice is the people's otherworld.

Machine Portraits with
Pendant Spaceman

FOR VALERIE

The bulldozer stands short as a boot on its heel-high ripple soles;
it has toecapped stumps aside all day, scuffed earth and
      trampled rocks
making a hobnailed dyke downstream of raw clay shoals.
Its work will hold water. The man who bounced high on the box
seat, exercising levers, would swear a full frontal orthodox
oath to that. First he shaved off the grizzled scrub
with that front-end safety razor supplied by the school of hard
      knocks
then he knuckled down and ground his irons properly; they
      copped many a harsh rub.
At knock-off time, spilling thunder, he surfaced like a sub.

•

Speaking of razors, the workshop amazes with its strop,
its elapsing leather drive-belt angled to the slapstick flow
of fast work in the Chaplin age; tightened, it runs like syrup,
streams like a mill-sluice, fiddles like a glazed virtuoso.
With the straitlaced summary cut of Sam Brownes long ago
it is the last of the drawn lash and bullocking muscle
left in engineering. It's where the panther leaping, his swift
      shadow
and all such free images turned plastic. Here they dwindle, dense
      with oil,
like a skein between tough factory hands, pulley and diesel.

•

Shaking in slow low flight, with its span of many jets,
the combine seeder at nightfall swimming over flat land
is a style of machinery we'd imagined for the fictional planets:
in the high glassed cabin, above vapour-pencilling floodlights,
      a hand,
gloved against the cold, hunts along the medium-wave band
for company of Earth voices; it crosses speech garble music—
the Brandenburg Conch the Who the Illyrian High Command—

as seed wheat in the hoppers shakes down, being laced into the thick
night-dampening plains soil, and the stars waver out and stick.

•

Flags and a taut fence discipline the mountain pasture
where giant upturned mushrooms gape mildly at the sky
catching otherworld pollen. Poppy-smooth or waffle-ironed, each armature
distils wild and white sound. These, Earth's first antennae
tranquilly angled outwards, to a black, not a gold infinity,
swallow the millionfold numbers that print out as a risen
glorious Apollo. They speak control to satellites in high
bursts of algorithm. And some of them are tuned to win
answers to fair questions, viz. What is the Universe in?

•

How many metal-bra and trumpet-flaring film extravaganzas
underlie the progress of the space shuttle's Ground Transporter Vehicle
across macadam-surfaced Florida? Atop oncreeping house-high panzers,
towering drydock and ocean-liner decks, there perches a gridiron football
field in gradual motion; it is the god-platform; it sustains the bridal
skyscraper of liquid Cool, and the rockets borrowed from the Superman
and the bricked aeroplane of Bustout-and-return, all vertical,
conjoined and myth-huge, approaching the starred gantry where human
lightning will crack, extend, and vanish upwards from this caravan.

•

Gold-masked, the foetal warrior
unslipping on a flawless floor,

I backpack air; my life machine
breathes me head-Earthwards, speaks the Choctaw
of tech-talk that earths our discipline—

but the home world now seems outside-in;
I marvel that here background's so fore
and sheathe my arms in the unseen

a dream in images unrecalled
from any past takes me   I soar
at the heart of fall on a drifting line

this is the nearest I have been
to oneness with the everted world
the unsinking leap   the stone unfurled

                        •

In a derelict village picture show I will find a projector,
dust-matted, but with film in its drum magazines, and the lens
mysteriously clean. The film will be called *Insensate Violence*,
no plot, no characters, just shoot burn scream beg claw
bayonet trample brains—I will hit the reverse switch then, in
        conscience,
and the thing will run backwards, unlike its coeval the
        machine-gun;
blood will unspill, fighters lift and surge apart; horror will be
        undone
and I will come out to a large town, bright parrots round the
        saleyard pens
and my people's faces healed of a bitter sophistication.

                        •

The more I act, the stiller I become;
the less I'm lit, the more spellbound my crowd;
I accept all colours, and with a warming hum
I turn them white and hide them in a cloud.
To give long life is a power I'm allowed

by my servant, Death. I am what you can't sell
at the world's end—and if you're still beetle-browed
try some of my treasures: an adult bird in its shell
or a pink porker in his own gut, Fritz the Abstract Animal.

•

No riddles about a crane. This one drops a black clanger on cars
and the palm of its four-thumbed steel hand is a raptor of
     wrecked tubing;
the ones up the highway hoist porridgy concrete, long spars
and the local skyline; whether raising aloft on a string
bizarre workaday angels, or letting down a rotating
man on a sphere, these machines are inclined to maintain
a peace like world war, in which we turn over everything
to provide unceasing victories. Now the fluent lines stop, and
     strain
engrosses this tower on the frontier of junk, this crane.

•

Before a landscape sprouts those giant stepladders that pump oil
or before far out iron mosquitoes attach to the sea
there is this sortilege with phones that plug into mapped soil,
the odd gelignite bump to shake trucks, paper scribbling out
     serially
as men dial Barrier Reefs long enfolded beneath the geology
or listen for black Freudian beaches; they seek a miles-wide
     pustular
rock dome of pure Crude, a St Paul's-in-profundis. There are
     many
wrong numbers on the geophone, but it's brought us some
     distance, and by car.
Every machine has been love and a true answer.

•

Not a high studded ship boiling cauliflower under her keel
nor a ghost in bootlaced canvas—just a length of country road
afloat between two shores, winding wet wire rope reel-to-reel,

dismissing romance sternwards. Six cars and a hay truck are her
    load
plus a thoughtful human cast which could, in some dramatic
    episode,
become a world. All machines in the end join God's creation
growing bygone, given, changeless—but a river ferry has its
    timeless mode
from the grinding reedy outset; it enforces contemplation.
We arrive. We traverse depth in thudding silence. We go on.

The International
Poetry Festivals Thing

Those conventions of the trade
in affluent stone cities:
we travel to them up the long shaft
polished by Europe's victims;

since few books can ascend that,
we walk out past the airport submachine-guns
carrying the mirrors we hold up
to the life of our people.

Those scenes at the first
usually luxurious breakfast:
Ciao Allen! Zhenia moi!
polished brevity of attention,
hooded senior repartee,
witty switching of small table flags

but always the unspoken
question, too: how many
divisions, with that fellow?

You notice, on lone walks,
how the city was rebuilt.
Yet you do the unspeakable

among competitive nonchalances
and the polite who've seen Hell:
you are unguarded.
No one is that distinguished!

At last the readings,
super-cool or impassioned recitals
very largely of subtitles
even in fair translation.

Hour on stylish hour of it:
Who is to read now—the Pole?
No, the opposite Pole—
Nothing worthwhile is lost:
the poetry is in print somewhere.

And afterwards, always,
an Englishman quoting cliché
with a heavy archness,
often doing it out of friendliness.

Some things do get through,
your relief at quiet praise
tells you how unguarded
you really were not, previously.

To your terror, you find
you have earned the admiration
of that bright girl who
for always coming down on one side
you had nicknamed Winter Sunlight:

now you may have to say it—
il me serait trop
distingué, ton prolétariat—

Meanwhile, the spirit follows
its curious own nose
collecting, for its lasting life,

south sun. A Gothic square.
Café lamps. Two conversations.
Icecreamed tongues in the horse chestnut trees.

Declining, conjugating,
the week ends in embraces
of love, of career,
Will you be now in Cambridge?
in real regard and book exchanges.

And we carry home our sleek
mirrors cram-full of chic
to show our people.

Little Boy Impelling a Scooter

Little boy on a wet pavement
near nightfall, balancing his scooter,
his free foot spurring it along,
his every speeding touchdown
striking a match of spent light,
the long concrete patched with squeezed-dry impacts
coming and going, his tyres' rubber edge
splitting the fine water. He jinks the handlebars
and trots around them, turning them
back, and stamps fresh small impulsions
maddeningly on and near, off and behind
his earlier impulses.
                        Void blurring pavement stars,
void blurring wheel-noise, uneven with hemmed outsets
as the dark deepens over town. To bear his rapture,
to smile, to share in it, require attitudes
all remote from murder,
watching his bowed intent face and slackly trailing
sudden pump leg passing and hemm! repassing
under powerlines and windy leaves
and the bared night sky's interminable splendours.

Self-portrait from a Photograph

If this picture has survived
its subject's absorption in the absolute
which is either God or death

it will first have been obsolete
for many years, till its style
was wholly defused, its life

glazed over by pathos, by summary
and it could grow timeless,
a midcentury face, taken late in that century.

A high hill of photographed sun-shadow
coming up from reverie, the big head
has its eyes on a mid-line, the mouth
slightly open, to breathe or interrupt.

The face's gentle skew to the left
is abetted, or caused, beneath the nose
by a Heidelberg scar, got in an accident.
The hair no longer meets across the head

and the back and sides are clipped ancestrally
Puritan-short. The chins are firm and deep
respectively. In point of freckling
the bare and shaven skin is just over

halfway between childhood ginger
and the nutmeg and plastic death-mottle
of great age. The large ears suggest more
of the soul than the other features:

dull to speech, alert to language,
tuned to background rustle, easily agonised,
all too fond of monotony, they help
keep the eyes, at their sharpest, remote,

half-turned to another world
that is poorer than this one, but contains it.
The short bulb nose is propped firmly
by flesh ridges. In decline, slow or steep,

this face might have wrinkled copiously
by the shoalwater webbing near the eyes.
With temples this military-naked
you see muscles chewing in the head.

That look of dawning interest, or objection
in which we glimpse dread of dentists,
could be shifting to enjoy a corny joke
out of friendship, or in reflex defiance

of claimant Good Taste and display;
such moods were one edge of his loyalty.
Another is the biceps tourniquet
of rolled sleeves, just out of frame,

a fashion of darkening carriers,
farmers, labourers and their sons
for more than a century.

Wardrobe, this precise relation
between a pinstriped business shirt
and its absent tie can never be recaptured,

and slighter factors, in this drapery and skin:
like impulses deflected by the saints
they end here, short of history.

The Hypogeum

Below the moveable gardens of this shopping centre
down concrete ways

                    to a level of rainwater,
a black lake glimmering among piers, electric lighted,
windless, of no depth.
                    Rare shafts of daylight
waver at their base. As the water is shaken, the few
cars parked down here seem to rock. In everything
there strains that silent crash, that reverberation
which persists in concrete.
                    The cardboard carton
Lorenzo's Natural Flavour Italian Meat Balls has foundered
into a wet ruin. Dutch Cleanser is propped at a high
featureless wall. Self-raising Flour is still floating
and supermarket trolleys hang their inverse harps,
silver leaking from them.
                    What will help the informally religious
to endure peace? Surface water dripping into
this underworld makes now a musical blip,
now rings from nowhere.
                    Young people descending the ramp
pause at the water's brink, banging their voices.

An Immortal

Beckoner of hotheads, brag-tester, lord of the demi-suicides,
in only one way since far before Homer have you altered:
when now, on wry wheels still revolving, the tall dust showers
    back
and tongue-numbing Death stills a screaming among the jagged
    images,
you disdain to strip your victims' costly armour, bright with fire
    and duco,
or even to step forth, visible briefly in your delusive harness,
glass cubes whirling at your tread, the kinked spear of frenzy in
    your hand.

Do you appear, though, bodily to your vanquished challengers
with the bare face of the boy who was large and quickest at it,

the hard face of the boss and the bookie, strangely run together,
the face of the expert craftsman, smiling privately, shaking his
  head?
Are you sometimes the Beloved, approaching and receding
  through the glaze?
Or is this all merely cinema? Are your final interviews wholly
  personal
and the bolt eyes disjunct teeth blood-vomit all a kind mask lent
  by physics?

We will never find out, living. The volunteers, wavering and firm,
and the many conscripted to storm the house of meaning
have stayed inside, with the music. Or else they are ourselves,
sheepish, reminiscent, unsure how we made it past the Warrior
into our lives—which the glory of his wheeled blade has infected
so that, on vacant evenings, we may burn with the mystery of
  his face,
his speed, his streetlights pointing every way, his unbelief in
  joking.

Second Essay on Interest: the Emu

Weathered blond as a grass tree, a huge Beatles haircut
raises an alert periscope and stares out
over scrub. Her large olivine eggs click
oilily together; her lips of noble plastic
clamped in their expression, her head-fluff a stripe
worn mohawk style, she bubbles her pale-blue windpipe:
the emu, *Dromaius novaehollandiae*,
whose stand-in on most continents is an antelope,
looks us in both eyes with her one eye
and her other eye, dignified courageous hump,
feather-swaying condensed camel, Swift Courser of New
  Holland.

Knees backward in toothed three-way boots, you stand,
Dinewan, proud emu, common as the dust

in your sleeveless cloak, returning our interest.
Your shield of fashion's wobbly: you're Quaint, you're Native,
even somewhat Bygone. You may be let live
but beware: the blank zones of Serious disdain
are often carte blanche to the darkly human.
Europe's boats on their first strange shore looked humble
but, Mass over, men started renaming the creatures.
Worship turned to interest and had new features.
Now only life survives, if it's made remarkable.

Heraldic bird, our protection is a fable
made of space and neglect. We're remarkable and not;
we're the ordinary discovered on a strange planet.
Are you Early or Late, in the history of birds
which doesn't exist, and is deeply ancient?
My kinships, too, are immemorial and recent,
like my country, which abstracts yours in words.
This distillate of mountains is finely branched, this plain
expanse of dour delicate lives, where the rain,
shrouded slab on the west horizon, is a corrugated revenant
settling its long clay-tipped plumage in a hatching descent.

Rubberneck, stepped sister, I see your eye on our jeep's load.
I think your story is, when you were offered
the hand of evolution, you gulped it. Forefinger and thumb
project from your face, but the weighing palm is inside you
collecting the bottletops, nails, wet cement that you famously
    swallow,
your passing muffled show, your serially private museum.
Some truths are now called *trivial*, though. Only God approves
    them.
Some humans who disdain them make a kind of weather
which, when it grows overt and widespread, we call *war*.
There we make death trivial and awesome, by rapid turns about,
we conscript it to bless us, force-feed it to squeeze the drama
    out;

indeed we imprison and torture death—this part is called *peace*—
we offer it murder like mendicants, begging for significance.

You rustle dreams of pardon, not fleeing in your hovercraft
     style,
not gliding fast with zinc-flaked legs dangling, feet making high-
     tensile
seesawing impacts. Wasteland parent, barely edible dignitary,
the disinterested spotlight of the lords of interest
and gowned nobles of ennui is a torch of vivid arrest
and blinding after-darkness. But you hint it's a brigand
     sovereignty
after the steady extents of God's common immortality
whose image is daylight detail, aggregate, in process yet plumb
to the everywhere focus of one devoid of boredom.

A Retrospect of Humidity

All the air conditioners now slacken
their hummed carrier wave. Once again
we've served our three months with remissions
in the steam and dry iron of this seaboard.
In jellied glare, through the nettle-rash season,
we've watched the sky's fermenting laundry
portend downpours. Some came, and steamed away,
and we were clutched back into the rancid
saline midnights of orifice weather,
to damp grittiness and wiping off the air.

Metaphors slump irritably together in
the muggy weeks. Shark and jellyfish shallows
become suburbs where you breathe a fat towel;
babies burst like tomatoes with discomfort
in the cotton-wrapped pointing street markets;
the lycra-bulging surf drips from non-swimmers
miles from shore, and somehow includes soil.
Skins, touching, soak each other. Skin touching
any surface wets that and itself
in a kind of mutual digestion.
Throbbing heads grow lianas of nonsense.

It's our annual visit to the latitudes
of rice, kerosene and resignation,
an averted, temporary visit
unrelated, for most, to the attitudes
of festive northbound jets gaining height—
closer, for some few, to the memory
of ulcers scraped with a tin spoon
or sweated faces bowing before dry
where the flesh is worn inside out,
all the hunger-organs clutched in rank nylon,
by those for whom exhaustion is spirit:

an intrusive, heart-narrowing season
at this far southern foot of the monsoon.
As the kleenex flower, the hibiscus
drops its browning wads, we forget
annually, as one forgets a sickness.
The stifling days will never come again,
not now that we've seen the first sweater
tugged down on the beauties of division
and inside the rain's millions, a risen
loaf of cat on a cool night verandah.

Flowering Eucalypt in Autumn

That slim creek out of the sky
the dried-blood western gum tree
is all stir in its high reaches:

its strung haze-blue foliage is dancing
points down in breezy mobs, swapping
pace and place in an all-over sway

retarded en masse by crimson blossom.
Bees still at work up there tack
around their exploded furry likeness

and the lawn underneath's a napped rug
of eyelash drift, of blooms flared
like a sneeze in a redhaired nostril,

minute urns, pinch-sized rockets
knocked down by winds, by night-creaking
fig-squirting bats, or the daily

parrot gang with green pocketknife wings.
Bristling food for tough delicate
raucous life, each flower comes

as a spray in its own turned vase,
a taut starburst, honeyed model
of the tree's fragrance crisping in your head.

When the Japanese plum tree
was shedding in spring, we speculated
there among the drizzling petals

what kind of exquisitely precious
artistic bloom might be gendered
in a pure ethereal compost

of petals potted as they fell.
From unpetalled gum-debris
we know what is grown continually,

a tower of fabulous swish tatters,
a map hoisted upright, a crusted
riverbed with up-country show towns.

The Chimes of Neverwhere

How many times did the Church prevent war?
Who knows? Those wars did not occur.
How many numbers don't count before ten?
Treasures of the Devil in Neverwhere.

The neither state of Neverwhere
is hard to place as near or far
since all things that didn't take place are there
and things that have lost the place they took:

Herr Hitler's buildings, King James' cigar,
the happiness of Armenia,
the Abelard children, the Manchus' return
are there with the Pictish Grammar Book.

The girl who returned your dazzled look
and the mornings you might have woke to her
are your waterbed in Neverwhere.
There shine the dukes of Australia

and all the great poems that never were
quite written, and every balked invention.
There too are the Third AIF and its war
in which I and boys my age were killed

more pointlessly with each passing year.
There too half the works of sainthood are
the enslavements, tortures, rapes, despair
deflected by them from the actual

to beat on the human-sacrifice drum
that billions need not die to hear
since Christ's love of them struck it dumb
and his agony keeps it in Neverwhere.

How many times did the Church bring peace?
More times than it happened. Leave it back there:
the children we didn't let out of there need it,
for the Devil's at home in Neverwhere.

The Smell of Coal Smoke

John Brown, glowing far and down,
wartime Newcastle was a brown town,
handrolled cough and cardigan, rain on paving bricks,
big smoke to a four-year-old from the green sticks.
Train city, mother's city, coming on dark,
Japanese shell holes awesome in a park,
electric light and upstairs, encountered first that day,
sailors and funny ladies in Jerry's Fish Café.

It is always evening on those earliest trips,
raining through the tram wires where blue glare rips
across the gaze of wonderment and leaves thrilling tips.
The steelworks' vast roofed débris unrolling falls
of smoky stunning orange, its eye-hurting slump walls
mellow to lounge interiors, cut pile and curry-brown
with the Pears-Soap-smelling fire and a sense of ships
mourning to each other below in the town.

This was my mother's childhood and her difference,
her city-brisk relations who valued Sense
talking strike and colliery, engineering, fowls and war,
Brown's grit and miners breathing it, years before
as I sat near the fire, raptly touching coal,
its blockage, slick yet dusty, prisms massed and dense
in the iron scuttle, its hammered bulky roll
into the glaring grate to fracture and shoal,

its chips you couldn't draw with on the cement
made it a stone, tar crockery, different—
and I had three grandparents, while others had four:
where was my mother's father, never called Poor?
In his tie and his Vauxhall that had a boat bow
driving up the Coalfields, but where was he now?
Coal smoke as much as gum trees now had a tight scent
to summon deep brown evenings of the Japanese war,

to conjure gaslit pub yards, their razory frisson
and sense my dead grandfather, the Grafton Cornishman,

rising through the night schools by the pressure in his chest
as his lungs creaked like mahogany with the grains of John
    Brown.
His city, mother's city, at its starriest
as swearing men with doctors' bags streamed by toward the
    docks
past the smoke-frothing wooden train that would take us home
    soon
with our day-old Henholme chickens peeping in their box.

The Mouthless Image of God
in the Hunter-Colo Mountains

Starting a dog, in the past-midnight suburbs, for a laugh,
barking for a lark, or to nark and miff, being tough
or dumbly meditative, starting gruff, sparking one dog off
almost companionably, you work him up, playing the rough riff
of punkish mischief, get funky as a poultry-farm diff
and vary with the Prussian note: *Achtung! Schar, Gewehr' auf!*
starting all the dogs off, for the tinny chain reaction and stiff
far-spreading music, the backyard territorial guff
echoing off brick streets, garbage cans, off every sandstone cliff
in miles-wide canine circles, a vast haze of auditory stuff
with every dog augmenting it, tail up, mouth serrated, shoulder
    ruff
pulsing with its outputs, a continuous clipped yap from a
    handmuff
Pomeranian, a Labrador's ascending fours, a Dane grown great
    enough
to bark in the singular, many raffish bitzers blowing their gaff
as humans raise windows and cries and here and there the roof
and you barking at the epicentre, you, putting a warp to
    the woof,
shift the design with a throat-rubbing lull and ill howl,
dingo-vibrant, not shrill, which starts a howling school
among hill-and-hollow barkers, till horizons-wide again a tall
pavilion of mixed timbres is lifted up eerily in full call
and the wailing takes a toll: you, from playing the fool,
move, behind your arch will, into the sorrow of a people.

•

And not just one people. You've entered a sound-proletariat
where pigs exclaim *boff-boff!* making off in fright
and fowls say *chirk* in tiny voices when a snake's about,
quite unlike the rooster's *Chook Chook*, meaning look,
   a good bit:
hens, get stoock into it! Where the urgent boar mutters *root-root*
to his small harassed sow, trotting back and forth beside her,
   rut-rut
and the she-cat's curdling *Mao?* where are kittens? mutating
   to *prr-mao,*
come along, kittens, are quite different words from *prr-au,*
general-welcome-and-acceptance, or extremity's portmanteau
   mee-EU!
Active and passive at once, the boar and feeding sow
share a common prone *unh*, expressing repletion and
   bestowing it,
and you're where the staid dog, excited, emits a mouth-skirl
he was trying to control, and looks ashamed of it
and the hawk above the land calls himself Peter P. P. Pew,
where, far from class hatred, the rooster scratches up some
   for you
and edgy plovers sharpen their nerves on a blurring wheel.
Waterbirds address you in their neck-flexure language, hiss and
   bow
and you speak to each species in the seven or eight
planetary words of its language, which ignore and include the
   detail
God set you to elaborate by the dictionary-full
when, because they would reveal their every secret,
He took definition from the beasts and gave it to you.

•

If at baying time you have bayed with dogs and not humans
you know enough not to scorn the moister dimensions
of language, nor to build on the sandbanks of Dry.
You long to show someone non-human the diaphragm-shuffle
which may be your species' only distinctive cry,
the spasm which, in various rhythms, turns our face awry,

contorts speech, shakes the body, and makes our eyelids liquefy.
Approaching adulthood, one half of this makes us shy
and the other's a touchy spear-haft we wield for balance.
Laughter-and-weeping. It's the great term the small terms qualify
as a whale is qualified by all the near glitters of the sea.
Weightless leviathan our showering words overlie and modify,
it rises irresistibly. All our dry-eyed investigations
supply that one term, in the end; its occasions multiply,
the logics issue in horror, we are shattered by joy
till the old prime divider bends and its two ends unify
and the learned words bubble off us. We laugh because we cry:
the crying depth of life is too great not to laugh
but laugh or cry singly aren't it: only mingled are they spirit
to wobble and sing us as a summer dawn sings a magpie.
For spirit is the round earth bringing our flat earths to bay
and we're feasted and mortified, exposed to those momentary
    Heavens
which, speaking in speech on the level, we work for and deny.

Time Travel

To revisit the spitfire world
of the duel, you put on a suit
of white body armour, a helmet
like an insect's composite eye
and step out like a space walker
under haloed lights, trailing a cord.

Descending, with nodding foil in hand
towards the pomander-and-cravat sphere
you meet the Opponent, for this journey
can only be accomplished by a pair
who semaphore and swap quick respect
before they set about their joint effect

which is making zeroes and serifs so
swiftly and with such sprung variety
that the long steels skid, clatter, zing,

switch, batter, bite, kiss and ring
in the complex rhythms of that society
with its warrior snare of comme il faut

that has you facing a starched beau
near stable walls on a misty morning,
striking, seeking the surrender in him,
the pedigree-flaw through which to pin him,
he probing for your own braggadocio,
confusion, ennui or inner fawning—

Seconds, holding stakes and cloths, look grim
and surge a step. Exchanges halt
for one of you stands, ageing horribly,
collapses, drowning from an entry
of narrow hurt. The other gulps hot chocolate
a trifle fast, but talking nonchalant—

a buzzer sounds. Heads are tucked
under arms, and you and he swap
curt nods in a more Christian century.

Three Interiors

The mansard roof of the Barrier Industrial Council's
pale-blue Second Empire building in Broken Hill
announces the form of a sprightly, intricately painted
pressed metal ceiling, spaciously stepped and tie-beamed
high over the main meeting hall. The factual light
of the vast room is altered, in its dusty rising
toward that coloured mime of myriadness, that figured
carpet of the mind, whose marvel comes down the clean walls
almost to the shoulder-stain level, the rubbings of mass defiance
which circle the hall miner-high above worn-out timber flooring.
Beauty all suspended in air—I write from memory
but it was so when we were there. A consistent splendour,
quite abstract, bloc-voted, crystalline with colour junctions
and regulated tendrils, high in its applied symphonic theory

above the projection hatch, over sports gear and the odd steel
      chair
marooned on the splintery extents of the former dance floor.

                    •

The softly vaulted ceiling of St Gallen's monastic library
is beautifully iced in Rococo butter cream with scrolled
      pipework
surf-dense around islands holding russet-clad, vaguely heavenly
personages who've swum up from the serried volumes below.
The books themselves, that vertical live leather brickwork,
in the violin-curved, gleaming bays, have all turned their backs
on the casual tourist and, clasped in meditation, they pray
in coined Greek, canonical Latin, pointed Hebrew.
It is an utterly quiet pre-industrial machine room
on a submarine to Heaven, and the deck, the famous floor
over which you pad in blanket slippers, has flowed in
honey-lucent around the footings, settled suavely level and
      hardened:
only the winding darker woods and underwater star-points
of the parquetry belie that impression. What is below
resembles what's above, but just enough, as cloud-shadow,
runways and old lake shores half noticed in mellow wheat land.

                    •

The last interior is darkness. Befuddled past-midnight
fear, testing each step like deep water, that when you open
the eventual refrigerator, cold but no light will envelop you.
Bony hurts that persuade you the names of your guides now
are balance, and gravity. You can fall up things, but not far.
A stopping, teeming caution. As of prey. The dark is arbitrary
delivering wheeled smashes, murmurings, something that
      scuttled,
doorjambs without a switch. The dark has no subject matter
but is alive with theory. Its best respites are: no surprises.
Nothing touching you. Or panic-stilling chance embraces.
Darkness is the cloth for pained eyes, and lovely in colour,
splendid in the lungs of great singers. Also the needed matrix

of constellations, flaring Ginzas, desert moons, apparent snow,
verandah-edged night rain. Dark is like that: all productions.
Almost nothing there is caused, or has results. Dark is all one
    interior
permitting only inner life. Concealing what will seize it.

Morse

Tuckett. Bill Tuckett. Telegraph operator, Hall's Creek,
which is way out back of the Outback, but he stuck it,
quite likely liked it, despite heat, glare, dust and the lack
of diversion or doctors. Come disaster you trusted to luck,
ingenuity and pluck. This was back when nice people said pluck,
the sleevelink and green eyeshade epoch.
                        Faced, though, like Bill Tuckett
with a man needing surgery right on the spot, a lot
would have done their dashes. It looked hopeless (dot dot dot)
Lift him up on the table, said Tuckett, running the key hot
till Head Office turned up a doctor who coolly instructed
up a thousand miles of wire, as Tuckett advanced slit by slit
with a safety razor blade, pioneering on into the wet,
copper-wiring the rivers off, in the first operation conducted
along dotted lines, with rum drinkers gripping the patient:
d-d-dash it, take care, Tuck!
                        And the vital spark stayed unshorted.
Yallah! breathed the camelmen. Tuckett, you did it, you did it!
cried the spattered la-de-dah jodhpur-wearing Inspector of Stock.
We imagine, some weeks later, a properly laconic
convalescent averring Without you, I'd have kicked the bucket . . .

From Chungking to Burrenjuck, morse keys have mostly gone
    silent
and only old men meet now to chit-chat in their electric
bygone dialect. The last letter many will forget
is dit-dit-dit-dah, V for Victory. The coders' hero had speed,
resource and a touch. So ditditdit daah for Bill Tuckett.

Late Snow in Edinburgh

Snow on the day before Anzac!
A lamb-killing wind out of Ayr
heaped a cloud up on towering Edinburgh
in the night, and left it adhering
to parks and leafing trees in the morning,
a cloud decaying on the upper city,
on the stepped medieval skyscrapers there,
cassata broadcast on the lower city
to be a hiss on buzzing cobblestones
under soaped cars, and cars still shaving.

All day the multiplying whiteness
persisted, now dazzling, now resumed
into the spectral Northern weather,
moist curd out along the Castle clifftops,
linen collar on the Mound, pristine pickings
in the Cowgate's blackened teeth, deposits
in Sir Walter Scott's worked tusk, and under
the soaked blue banners walling Princes Street.
The lunchtime gun fired across dun distances
ragged with keen tents. By afternoon, though,
derelicts sleeping immaculate in wynds
and black areas had shrivelled to wet sheep.
Froth, fading, stretched thinner on allotments.

As the melting air browned into evening
the photographed city, in last umber
and misty first lights, was turning into
the stones in a vast furrow. For that moment
half a million moved in an earth cloud
harrowed up, damp and fuming, seeded
with starry points, with luminous still patches
that wouldn't last the night. No Anzac Day
prodigies for the visitor-descendant.
The snow was dimming into Spring's old
Flanders jacket and frieze trousers. Hughie Spring,
the droll ploughman, up from the Borders.

Art History: the Suburb
of Surrealls

We dreamed very wide awake
those days, for obedience's sake:

In the suburb of Surrealls
horse families board the airline bus
to sell packages of phlegm.
My notebook is hugely swollen.
For some reason I am American.

Such dreaming is enforceable.
Everyone became guarded;
a tinkling of symbols was heard.
It's the West occupying the dreamworld
because the East has captured reason,
some said. Many ceased to listen.

In fact we'd gone to the dream
for supplies of that instant
paint of the twilight kingdom
which colours every object
supernal, deeply important.
Spirit-surrogate. We even synthesised it.

Exposed to the common air, it
weathered quickly to the tone
of affectless weird despair,
elegant barely contained anger
our new patrons demanded
when we had trained them to it.

False dreamings are imperial
but we couldn't disappoint them
(Few others now read us by choice.
Woolf! Woolf! our master's voice).

To be fair, many of us
had now joined the creative class

and become our masters
—but the paint, when stolen
and breathed straight from the tin,
gave a noble deathly rush
that replaced imagination.

The Dialectic of Dreams

Dream harbours Sin, and Innocence, and Magic,
re-stews mundane cabbage, stacks a shifting Tarot,
equivocates naïvely about Death, the secular Absolute—

things Rationality, the replacement aristocrat
approves only for enhancement. By midday
it has clarified its twinship with that relic—

but it comes round again, by deep night at the latest,
in a skin boat sailing on the blood
for dream lives its life engorged. It owns tumescence,

makes eerie conquests, can engender children—
though few who see the sun. The real takes some joint
    permission
and all of ourself not in the dream lies flaccid.

Every night, stepped mast or unfurled sail,
we reach a land where nothing is held trivial.

  •

Real dreams are from home • back there. The light as it was,
will be, might have been • all the receding dream-tenses.

The dreamer is even yourself • or you're aware it is.
There in the action, unsafe • greater than the action, passive,

rarely uttering, in the endless • preparations, for horror, for
                                     happiness,

220

those appalling formulae   •   other-directed at us

which may persist as salt foam   •   on the margin of lapsed
                                                    scenes
or, like the filmed cities, be resumed   •   into their own
                                                    presence.

And that otherworld incongruence   •   spindling faintly through
                                                    the day,
heightening thought, blanking it   •   silvering, beckoning away:

preternatural, those interiors   •   half-recalled by consciousness,
they were never in this world   •   nor in your life, those wet
                                                    bossed lanes.

Yet this is the heart of work   •   *the human sage, the butterfly*
to be conscious at the source of worlds   •   rapt, raising the
                                                    ante.

      •

The daylight oil, the heavier grade of Reason,
reverie's clear water, that of the dreamworld ocean
agitate us and are shaken, forming the emulsion

without which we make nothing much. Not art,
not love, not war, nor its reasoned nightmare methods,
not the Taj, not our homes, not the Masses or the gods

—but the fusion persists in the product, not in us.
A wheel shatters, drains our pooled rainbow. It was a moment:
the world is debris and museum of that moment,

its prospectus and farm. The wheel is turned by this engine.
I think of the people and buildings in a business street,
how they lack a perfect valve to take on and release

unceasing fusions. And will be pulled down for it,
their walls dreamed on in the milk of obsolete children.

      •

Dream surrounds, is infused with this world. It is not
　　subordinate.
We come from it; we live at tangents and accords with it; we go
back into it, at last, through the drowsing torture chambers to it.

We have gills for dream-life, in our head; we must keep them
　　wet
from the nine-nights' immense, or dreams will emerge bodily,
　　and enforce it.
Hide among or deny the shallow dreadful ones, and they may
　　stay out:

moor things in Heaven and earth then, Ratio, anyhow you can
because dream's the looseleaf book, not of fiction, but of raw
　　Pretend,
incalculable as this world when the God of Mercy intervened
　　often.

It is the free splitting from God that parts Nature from dream.
They refresh each other with bafflement, each as the other's
　　underground
freeing lives to be finite, because more; to be timeless, yet pure
　　preparation—

while those spaces, sacred as the poor, of the haloed russet
　　kingdom
are tigers impelling us, full of futures and pasts, toward a
　　present.

Satis Passio

Elites, levels, proletariat:
the uniting cloth crowns
of Upper and Lower Egypt
suggest theories of poetry

which kindness would accept
to bestow, like Heaven, dignity
on the inept and the ept,
one Papuan warrior's phallocrypt
the soaring equal of its fellowcrypt.

By these measures, most knowledge
in our heads is poetry,
varied crystals of detail, chosen
by dream-interest, and poured spirally
from version to myth, with spillage,
from theory to history
and, with toppings-up, to story,
not metered, lined or free
but condensed by memory
to roughly vivid essences:
most people's poetry is now this.
Some of it is made by poets.

God bless the feral poetries,
littératures and sensibilities,
theory, wonder, the human gamut
leaping cheerfully or in heavy earnest
—but there is this quality to art
which starts, rather than ends, at the gist.
Not the angle, but the angel.

Art is what can't be summarised:
it has joined creation from our side,
entered Nature, become a fact
and acquired presence,
more like ourselves or any subject
swirled around, about, in and out,
than like the swirling poetries.

Art's best is a standing miracle
at an uncrossable slight distance,
an anomaly, finite but inexhaustible,
unaltered after analysis
as an ancient face.

Not the portrait of one gone
merely, no pathos of the bygone
but a section, of all that exist,
a passage, a whole pattern
that has shifted the immeasurable
first step into Heaven.
A first approximation.
Where is Heaven? Down these roads.

The fine movement of art's face
before us is a motionless traffic
between here and remote Heaven.
It is out through this surface,
we may call it the Unfalling Arrow,
this third mode, and perhaps by art first
that there came to us the dream-plan
of equality and justice,
long delayed by the poetries—

but who was the more numinous,
Pharaoh or the hunted Nile heron?
more splendid, the iris or Solomon?
Beauty lives easily with equities
more terrible than theory dares mean.
Of the workers set free to break stone
and the new-cracked stone, which is more luminous?

God bless the general poetries?
This is how it's done.

Flood Plains on the Coast
Facing Asia

Hitching blur to a caged propeller
with its motor racket swelling
barroom to barrage, our aluminium

airboat has crossed the black coffee
lagoon and swum out onto
one enormous crinkling green.
Now like a rocket loudening
to liftoff, it erects the earsplitting
wigwam we must travel in
everywhere here, and starts skimming
at speed on the never-never
meadows of the monsoon wetland.

Birds lift, scattering before us
over the primeval irrigation,
leaf-running jacanas, twin-boomed
with supplicant bare feet for tails;
knob-headed magpie geese
row into the air ahead of us;
waterlilies lean away, to go
under as we overrun them
and resurrect behind us.
We leave at most a darker green
trace on the universal glittering
and, waterproof in cream and blue,
waterlilies on their stems, circling.

Our shattering car
crossing exposed and seeping spaces
brings us to finely stinking places,
yet whatever riceless paddies
we reach, of whatever grass,
there is always sheeting spray
underhull for our passage;
and the Intermediate Egret leaps
aloft out of stagnant colours
and many a double-barrelled crossbow
shoots vegetable breath emphatically
from the haunts of flaking buffalo;
water glinting everywhere, like ice,
we traverse speeds humans once reached
in such surroundings mainly
as soldiers, in the tropic wars.

At times, we fold our windtunnel
away, in its blackened steel sail
and sit, for talk and contemplation.
For instance, off the deadly islet,
a swamp-surrounded sandstone knoll
split, cabled, commissured
with fig trees' python roots.
Watched by distant plateau cliffs
stitched millennially in every crevice
with the bark-entubed dead
we do not go ashore.
Those hills are ancient stone gods
just beginning to be literature.

We release again the warring sound
of our peaceful tour, and go sledding
headlong through mounded paperbark
copses, on reaches of maroon
grit, our wake unravelling
over green curd where logs lie digesting
and over the breast-lifting deeps
of the file snake, whom the women here
tread on, scoop up, clamp head-first in their teeth
and jerk to death, then carry home as meat.

Loudest without speech, we shear
for miles on the paddock of nymphaeas
still hoisting up the paired pied geese,
their black goslings toddling below them.
We, a family with baby and two friends,
one swift metal skin above the food-chains,
the extensible wet life-chains of which
our civility and wake are one stretch,
the pelicans circling over us another
and the cat-napping peace of the secure,
of eagles, lions and two-year-old George
asleep beneath his pink linen hat as
we enter domains of flowering lotus.

In our propeller's stiffened silence
we stand up among scalloped leaves

that are flickering for hundreds of acres
on their deeper water. The lotus
prove a breezy nonhuman gathering
of this planet, with their olive-studded
rubbery cocktail glasses, loose carmine roses,
salmon buds like the five-fingertips-joined
gesture of summation, of *ecco!*
waist-high around us in all their greenery
on yeasty frog water. We receive this
sidelong, speaking our wiry language
in which so many others ghost and flicker.

We discuss Leichhardt's party and their qualities
when, hauling the year 1845
through here, with spearheads embedded in it,
their bullock drays reached and began skirting
this bar of literal water
after the desert months which had been
themselves a kind of swimming,
a salt undersea plodding, monster-haunted
with odd very pure surfacings.
We also receive, in drifts of calm
hushing, which fret the baby boy,
how the fuzzed gold innumerable cables
by which this garden hangs skyward
branch beneath the surface, like dreams.

The powerful dream of being harmless,
the many chains snapped and stretched hard for that:
both shimmer behind our run back
toward the escarpments where stallion-eyed
Lightning lives, who'd shiver all heights
down and make of the earth
one oozing, feeding peneplain.
Unprotected Lightning: there are his wild horses
and brolgas, and far heron not rising.
Suddenly we run over a crocodile.
On an unlilied deep, bare even
of minute water fern, it leaped out,
surged man-swift straight under us. We ran over it.
We circle back. Unhurt, it floats, peering

from each small eye turret, then annuls
buoyance and merges subtly under,
swollen leathers becoming gargoyle stone,
chains of contour, with pineapple abdomen.

Cumulus

Repeatedly out of grazed plateaux, the Dividing
Range assumes, soaring after gliding,
into high countries, not peaked but cumulus
in evergreen black and mossy bleached khaki
out under antarctic grey and razory blues,
horizons above the nation, now visited rarely
except in polemic hiking, or on the ski niveaux.
We turned away to ochre and surf sands long ago
and secret cattleyards never formed a traceable city.

White cloud still assembles daily along each island
far above our South Sea levels. Mist forest, tussock sops
under redoubled height drink fog along the Tops
and newly earthed rivers edge out of sphagnum overloads
to shin down human clay and unhuman cobbled roads
to the short east, to the brown west ocean of land;
the cello necks of tree ferns spread as they come uncurled
and screech-red parrots fly, with many stops,
toward the beech trees of the southern world.

On the varying heights where stupendous heights are brewed
out of clear air by pitch and altitude
few have yet lived, in all the centuries. Some have stayed.
Many themes attended the hibernation of Ned Kelly:
the fat moth-feast of the tribes, whip bird and rifle bird,
moleskin prospectors each working his vein of solitude;
Thunderbolt emerging from the wet cave of his treasure
sights a coach down through timber, spurs into ballad measure—
but these disappear down the crumples of the possum-skin rug,

the great ravines of catchment. Jindabygone, Adamemory.
Of Governors fleeing heat on the hill stations, we recall Jimmy,
but the sleepout in the dark ranges has weakened its tug
and retreat is continually modelled. Our plateau capital
avoids its own heights and nearby mountains. They are all
cloud-shadowed with new dry forest. The vixen feeds her cubs,
and kangaroos fold down to graze, above the human suburbs.
Neither fantasy nor fear has built an eagle's nest fortress
to top our nonfiction poetry. We've put the wild above us.

Federation Style on the Northern Rivers

And entering on the only smooth road
this steamer glides past the rattling shipyard
where they're having the usual Aboriginal
whale-feast in reverse, with scaffolding and planking;
engine smoke marching through blue sheoak trees
along the edge of Jack Robertson farms,
the river opens and continually opens

and lashed on deck, a Vauxhall car,
intricate in brass, with bonnet grooves,
a bulb to squawk, great guillotine levers,
high diamond-buttoned leather club chairs
and dressing-table windscreen to flash afar:
in British cherry metal, detailed in mustard
it cruises up country with a moveless wheel.

In the town it approaches, a Habsburg-yellow store
Provisions—Novelties—J. Cornwell Prop.
contains a knot of debt that has reached
straining point, tugging between many poor
selector farmers and several not necessarily
rich city suppliers. Mobilised, it can tear
the store apart, uproot many families

and tomorrow the auditor will be in town
and the car will be parked just where he comes
after a prolonged hilarious midday dinner
I see your town's acquired a motor—
You fancy those beasts, do you, Stickney?
One face grows inspired, in step with the other.
What is that sly joker Cornwell at?

asks the Bank of Australasia's swank bow window:
How can he have afforded a motor?
but a schooner bee deflects the questioner.
Would you like to take a spin in her,
Stickney?—I daresay your books will wait
for half an hour . . . One mounts from the left,
one hoists the crankhandle. Directly, indirectly

they wind down the street over horsemanures
of varying fatness, past the Coffee Palace
unconcerned with ales—*Stickney, you're a marvel!*
Just aim her straight and don't shout Whoa!
Tread on that to slow her: don't tug the wheel—
Children running, neighbours cheering, *Go it, Jim!*
Mr Cornwell lifts his hat to the faces greeting him.

Smashing water-windows along the parallel
wheeltracks of the cart-cut river road
they pass the deeply laden Cornwell shop-boat
Turn inland here: we will have drier going.
I agree she'd be a buy, Stickney: I'd have to think—
Think how to waste more afternoon
with the tall affection of local tales:

. . . And old Tom Beattie managing himself
along, like a bad horse; you hear him curse it:
Hold up, you bugger! Walk!—Mr Cornwell,
we should get back, to your ledgers.—Yes.
Take the left fork two miles on. A shortcut—
The shortcut ends in blackpudding bog
and no country curricles bowling by it.

Dear God, Cornwell, I must catch tomorrow's boat!
but heaving, corduroying, pole-levering all fail
and Cornwell must vanish through the rung timber.
For Stickney there will now accrue a wait
heavy as blacksoil around buried wheels.
Shanks' pony? Not I. Not through snaky bush.
He watches a swamp pheasant's sailing flight

and on the creekbank, in a place where cattle,
and white man's firesticks, can't come
he finds a child's small bowerbird farm:
scraped roads, wharf, little twig cattleyards,
clay beasts. A new world, already immemorial.
He will tighten his coat against evening chill
long before Cornwell reappears with helpers.

That night the yellow store will burn
in a jammed eye-parching abolishment of proof
and the car, strangely spotless, will not be harmed.
Tomorrow the innocent owner will collect it.
The steamer hoots. *Cornwell, now that you're*
safely ruined: where did you go yesterday?
—*I had to dodge certain bandicoot farms*

where the little ones bolt up under the house
at the sight of a stranger. I've never cared
to be a stranger who threatens children.
They part, across water, with the ghost of a salute.
Certain surnames will now survive in the district.
As the town declines through the mulberry years
Cornwell will receive odd grateful sovereigns.
The rebuilt store will be kept by a Hogan.

Easter 1984

When we saw human dignity
healing humans in the middle of the day

we moved in on him slowly
under the incalculable gravity

of old freedom, of our own freedom,
under atmospheres of consequence, of justice

under which no one needs to thank anyone.
If this was God, we would get even.

And in the end we nailed him,
lashed, spittled, stretched him limb from limb.

We would settle with dignity
for the anguish it had caused us,

we'd send it to be abstract again,
we would set it free.

•

But we had raised up evolution.
It would not stop being human.

Ever afterwards, the accumulation
of freedom would end in this man

whipped, bloodied, getting the treatment.
It would look like man himself getting it.

He was freeing us, painfully, from freedom,
justice, dignity—he was discharging them

of their deadly ambiguous deposit,
remaking out of them the primal day

in which he was free not to have borne it
and we were free not to have done it,

free never to torture man again,
free to believe him risen.

•

Remember the day when life increased,
explainably or outright, was haloed in poignancy,

straight life, given not attained, unlurching ecstasy,
arrest of the guards for once, and ourself released,

splendour taking detail, beyond the laughter-and-tears
as if these were gateway to it, a still or moving utterness

in and all around us? Some have been this human
night and day, steadily. Flashes of it have drawn others on.

A laser of this would stand the litter-bound or Lazarus
upright, stammering, or unshroud absent Jesus

whose anguish was to be for a whole day lost to this,
making of himself the companionway of our species

up from where such love is an unreal, half-forgotten
peak, and not yet the baseline of the human.

Physiognomy on the Savage Manning River

Walking on that early shore, in our bodies,
the autumn ocean has become wasp-waisted:
a scraped timber mansion hung in showering
ropework is crabbing on the tide's flood,

swarming, sway, and shouting,
entering the rivermouth over the speedy bar.

As it calms into the river, the Tahitian
helmsman, a pipe-smoking archer,
draws and tightens the wheel. The spruce captain
meanwhile celebrates the bohême of revolutions
with a paper cigarette, and the carpenter,
deepwater man, combs his sulky boy's hair.

Seo abhainn mar loch—the polished river is indeed
like a loch, without flow, clear to the rainforest islands
and the Highland immigrants on deck, remarking it,
keep a hand, or a foot, on their bundles and nail-kegs.
No equipment is replaceable: there's only one of anything,
experience they will hand down.

Beyond the river brush extends the deserted
Aboriginal hunting park. There is far less blue
out in the grassland khaki than in our lifetime
though the hills are darkening, sprinkling outward,
closing on crusted lagoons. Nowhere a direct line;
no willows yet, nor any houses.
Those are in the low hills upriver.
Beyond are the ranges, edge over edge, like jumbled sabres.

Crocodile chutes slant out of the riverbank forest
where great logs have been launched.
It is the feared long-unburnable
dense forest of the dooligarl. The cannibal solitary
humanoid of no tribe. Here, as worldwide, he and she
are hairy, nightmare-agile, with atavisms of the feet.
Horror can be ascribed and strange commissions given
to the fireless dooligarl. Killer, here, of gingery bat-hunters.

Tiptoeing after its slung leadline, the ship moves forward
for hours into the day. Raising the first dogleg paddocks,
the first houses, the primal blowflies.
Soup and clothing
boil in a fire-hut, in cauldrons slung on steel saws
there where next century's pelicans will haunt the Fish
    Cooperative.

The gossip on the river is all Miss Isabella Kelly:
triumphing home with her libel case now won
and, for her months in jail, a thousand pounds compensation;
she has found her stations devastated:
yards smashed, homestead burnt, cattle lifted
(irrecoverable nods are winked here).
Now she has sailed to England in her habitual
infuriated self esteem.
She will have Charles Dickens write her story.
Voices, calling God to forgive them, wish her drownded.

Isabella Mary Kelly. The shadowy first landholder.
Now she has given the district a larger name
to drop than her own. She, who rode beside
her walking convicts three days through the wilderness
to have them flogged half-insane in proper form
at Port Macquarie and Raymond Terrace
then walked them immediately back,
her crosshatched harem,
she who told the man who dragged her from swift floodwater
"You waste your gallantry. You are still due a lashing.
Walk on, croppy."

Isabella Kelly, of the sidesaddle acerbities,
grazier and pistol shot
throned and footless in her hooped midcentury skirts,
for some years it has been she,
and perhaps it really was she, who had the deadly crystals
mixed into scones for the natives at Belbora,
Miss Kelly all alone. The colonies' earlier Kelly.
Jilted in Dublin—or is that an acanthus leaf
of motivation, modelled over something barer?
Suddenly her time has passed.
Death in a single room in chilly Sydney
still lies ahead—and being confused with Kate Kelly—
but she has moved already into her useful legend.

Now up every side creek a youth in a cabbagetree hat
is rocking like a steersman, feinting like a boxer:
every stone of gravel must go a round or two
in a circling dish, and the pouring of waters be adjusted.

The same on every track round the heads of rivers:
men escaping the black mills
and families tired of a thousand years' dim tenancy
are entering the valley beside their jolting stacks;
there is even the odd spanker,
reins in hand behind trotters, on a seat like a chocolate éclair,
though he is as yet rare;
more are riding through horse-high grass, and into timber
that thickens, like work, to meet their mighty need of it.

The ship is tied up meanwhile in a sort
of farmyard dockland:
pigs under the wharf, saddles, pumpkin patches, corn boats.
The men unloading her, who never doff their shirts,
are making whips of tin;
this one who has worn the white clay girdle of the Bora,
of sung rebirth, now plies a lading hook
to keep his Kentish wife.
At spell-oh time, they will share a pipe of tobacco
which she has shaved from the succulent twist with her
        case-knife.

Farther upriver, men are rolling out onto their wharf
big solid barrels of a mealy wetness
and others with axes are dismembering downed cattle
in jarring sight of yarded herds. They heave the pieces
into huge smoking trypots. It is the boiling-down,
a kind of inland sealing.
The boiled-out meat is pitched down a cloacal gully.

All that can be exported of the squatter's cattle,
of the spinster Kelly's cattle and the others',
is their tallow, for candles.
Lights for the sickroom, lustre for pianoforte sconces.
Cattle distilled to a fluted wax, and sea creatures
sublimated to a liquor light the readers
of Charles Darwin and Charles Dickens.
On sleeping skins, snorting boys drip melted cattle.

Now the gently wrecking cornfields relax, and issue
parents and children. What do families offer us?

Some protection from history,
a tough school of forgiveness.
After the ship has twitched minutely out of
focus and back, as many times as there were barrels
and night has assumed the slab huts and sawn houses,
the faces drinking tea by their various lights
include some we had thought modern. The mask of
     unappeasable
rage is there, and those of scorn's foundling aristocracy,
among the timeless sad and contented faces,
the vacant and remote faces. Only the relative
licensing of expressions is wholly different.
Blame is not yet privileged.

And, walking on that early shore in our bodies
(perhaps the only uncowardly way to do history)
if we asked leading questions, we might hear,
short of a ringing ear,
something like: We do what's to be done
and some things because we can.
Don't be taking talk out of me.

Such not only from the haughtily dreaming,
intelligent, remorseless, secretly amused still face
of Isabella Kelly.
As the Highlandman said
eating his first meal of fresh beef and cornmeal porridge
after landing today:
Thig lá choin duibh fhathast. The black dog will have his day yet.
Not every dog, as in English, but the black dog.

The Dream of Wearing Shorts Forever

To go home and wear shorts forever
in the enormous paddocks, in that warm climate,
adding a sweater when winter soaks the grass,

to camp out along the river bends
for good, wearing shorts, with a pocketknife,
a fishing line and matches,

or there where the hills are all down, below the plain,
to sit around in shorts at evening
on the plank verandah—

If the cardinal points of costume
are Robes, Tat, Rig and Scunge,
where are shorts in this compass?

They are never Robes
as other bareleg outfits have been:
the toga, the kilt, the lava-lava
the Mahatma's cotton dhoti;

archbishops and field marshals
at their ceremonies never wear shorts.
The very word
means underpants in North America.

Shorts can be Tat,
Land-Rovering bush-environmental tat,
socio-political ripped-and-metal-stapled tat,
solidarity-with-the-Third-World tat tvam asi,

likewise track-and-field shorts worn to parties
and the further humid, modelling negligée
of the Kingdom of Flaunt,
that unchallenged aristocracy.

More plainly climatic, shorts
are farmers' rig leathery with salt and bonemeal,
are sailors' and branch bankers' rig,
the crisp golfing style
of our youngest male National Costume.

Most loosely, they are Scunge,
ancient Bengal bloomers or moth-eaten hot pants

worn with a former shirt,
feet, beach sand, hair
and a paucity of signals.

Scunge, which is real negligée
housework in a swimsuit, pyjamas worn all day,
is holiday, is freedom from ambition.
Scunge makes you invisible
to the world and yourself.

The entropy of costume,
scunge can get you conquered by more vigorous cultures
and help you to notice it less.

Satisfied ambition, defeat, true unconcern,
the wish and the knack for self-forgetfulness
all fall within the scunge ambit
wearing board shorts or similar;
it is a kind of weightlessness.

Unlike public nakedness, which in Westerners
is deeply circumstantial, relaxed as exam time,
artless and equal as the corsetry of a hussar regiment,

shorts and their plain like
are an angelic nudity,
spirituality with pockets!
A double updraft as you drop from branch to pool!

Ideal for getting served last
in shops of the temperate zone
they are also ideal for going home, into space,
into time, to farm the mind's Sabine acres
for product or subsistence.

Now that everyone who yearned to wear long pants
has essentially achieved them,
long pants, which have themselves been underwear
repeatedly, and underground more than once,
it is time perhaps to cherish the culture of shorts,

to moderate grim vigour
with the knobble of bare knees,
to cool bareknuckle feet in inland water,
slapping flies with a book on solar wind
or a patient bare hand, beneath the cadjiput trees,

to be walking meditatively
among green timber, through the grassy forest
towards a calm sea
and looking across to more of that great island
and the further topics.

At the Aquatic Carnival

Two racing boats seen from the harmonic railing
of this road bridge quit their wakes,
plane above their mirroring shield-forms
and bash the river, flat out, their hits batts of appliqué
violently spreading, their turnings eiderdown
abolishing translucency before the frieze of people,
and rolled-over water comes out to the footings of the carnival.

Even up drinking coffee-and-froth in the town
prodigious sound rams through arcades and alleyways
and burrs in our teeth, beneath the slow nacelle
of a midsummer ceiling fan.
No wonder pelicans vanish from their river at these times.
How, we wonder, does that sodden undersized one
who hangs around the Fish Co-op get by?
The pert wrymouth with the twisted upper beak.

It cannot pincer prey, or lid its lower scoop,
and so lives on guts, mucking in with the others
who come and go. For it to leave would be death.
Its trouble looks like a birth defect, not an injury,
and raises questions.

There are poetics would require it to be pecked
to death by fellow pelicans, or kids to smash it with a stick,
preserving a hard cosmos.

In fact it came with fellow pelicans, parents maybe,
and has been around for years. Humans who feed it
are sentimental, perhaps—but what to say
of humans who refused to feed a lame bird?
Nature is not human-hearted. But it is one flesh
or we could not imagine it. And we could not eat.

Nature is not human-hearted. So the animals
come to man, at first in their extremity:
the wild scrub turkeys entering farms in drought-time,
the done fox suddenly underfoot among dog-urgers
(that frantic compliment, that prayer never granted by dogs)
or the shy birds perching on human shoulders and trucks
when the mountains are blotted out in fiery dismemberment.

Such meetings enlarge the white middle term of claim
which quivers between the dramatic red and blue poles
of fight-or-flight.
The claim exercised by pelicans
on the riverbank lawn who tap you for a sandwich
or the water-dragon in flared and fretted display
who opened its head at me, likewise for a sandwich,

by the tiny birds who materialised and sang
when my wife sang in the sleeper-cutting forest
down Stoney Creek Road. And the famous dolphins.
Today, though, men are fighting
the merciful wars of surplus, on the battered river,
making their own wide wings, and water skiers
are hoisting the inherent white banner, making it stretch
and stream both ways at once, like children's drawings
of ships or battle, out in front of the carnival.

The Sleepout

Childhood sleeps in a verandah room
in an iron bed close to the wall
where the winter over the railing
swelled the blind on its timber boom

and splinters picked lint off warm linen
and the stars were out over the hill;
then one wall of the room was forest
and all things in there were to come.

Breathings climbed up on the verandah
when dark cattle rubbed at a corner
and sometimes dim towering rain stood
for forest, and the dry cave hunched woollen.

Inside the forest was lamplit
along tracks to a starry creek bed
and beyond lay the never-fenced country,
its full billabongs all surrounded

by animals and birds, in loud crustings,
and something kept leaping up amongst them.
And out there, to kindle whenever
dark found it, hung the daylight moon.

Tropical Window

Out through a long bright window
are three headlands ruched together
on an ivory drawstring of beach. Salad and jade
over freckled pancake rock, each
is washed at foot by noonday suds intermittently
and some yachts are pinned with tall spears to the bay.

This horizontal window
is lamp and sole brilliant picture
to a shadowy cane room
where people stir instant drinks. There is the man
with sunglasses at his throat like sleek electrodes
or a very high tech bow tie
and the woman with the luminous
ruby signet of the smoker. And another
figure saying We need more passive verbs:

I am sneezed, for example (and just try to resist!) or:
You are coughed. More coughed about than coughing—
But the windowed littoral
distracts them again and again. The motionless
shellburst palms, on the skyline, over the golf course,
the sea's lucent linoleum,
the near trees with green-ants' nests
square-folded out of living leaves, like Japanese packages.

If the three stepped out
into that scene, humidity and glare would sandbag them,
make them fretful tourists.
Not coated glass but simple indoor contrast
has tuned the hyaline
to a sourceless cerebral light
and framing has made the window photo-realist,
a style of art everybody now feels they have been
in. And will be in again
at any immortal democratic moment.

Louvres

In the banana zone, in the poinciana tropics
reality is stacked on handsbreadth shelving,
open and shut, it is ruled across with lines
as in a gleaming gritty exercise book.

The world is seen through a cranked or levered
weatherboarding of explosive glass
angled floor-to-ceiling. Horizons which metre
the dazzling outdoors into green-edged couplets.

In the louvred latitudes
children fly to sleep in triplanes, and
cool nights are eerie with retracting flaps.

Their houses stand aloft among bougainvillea,
covered bridges that lead down a shining hall
from love to mystery to breakfast,
from babyhood to moving-out day

and visitors shimmer up in columnar gauges
to touch lives lived behind gauze
in a lantern of inventory,
slick vector geometries glossing the months of rain.

There, nudity is dizzily cubist, and directions
have to include: stage left, add an inch of breeze
or: enter a glistening tendril.

Every building of jinked and slatted ledges
is at times a squadron of inside-out
helicopters, humming with rotor fans.

For drinkers under cyclonic pressure, such
a house can be a bridge of scythes—
groundlings scuffing by stop only for dénouements.

But everyone comes out on platforms of command
to survey cloudy flame-trees, the plain of streets, the future:
only then descending to the level of affairs

and if these things are done in the green season
what to do in the crystalline dry? Well
below in the struts of laundry is the four-wheel drive

vehicle in which to make an expedition
to the bush, or as we now say the Land,
the three quarters of our continent
set aside for mystic poetry.

The Edgeless

Floodwater from remote rains has spread out
of the riverine scrub, resuming its mirages.
Mostly shallow, mild water
it ties its hidden drowning strains
taut around odd trees, in that low forest
whose skinny shade turns the water taupe. Nests float
and the vaster flat shine is cobbled at wave-shadow points
with little brown melons, just starting to smell rank.

The local station manager, his eyes
still squinting from the greenest green on the place,
the computer screen, strolls out of his office
onto the verandah. Tiny native bees
who fly standing up, like angels, shimmer the garden.
His wife points out their dog Boxer,
pads slipping, tongue slipping out, nails
catching in unseen lurch mineshafts, gamely
teetering along the round top rail of the killing yard.

Where does talk come from? the two ask each other
over teacups.—From the same place as the world.
We have got the word and we don't understand it.
It is like too much.—So we made up a word of our own
as much like nothing else as possible
and gave it to the machines. It made them grow—
And now we can't see the limits of that word either.

Come down off there, Boxer! Who put you up there?

The Drugs of War

On vinegar and sour fish sauce Rome's legions stemmed
  avalanches
of whirling golden warriors whose lands furnished veterans'
  ranches;
when the warriors broke through at last, they'd invented sour
  mash
but they took to sugared wines and failed to hold the lands
  of hash.

By beat of drum in the wars of rum flogged peasant boys faced
  front
and their warrior chiefs conversed coolly, attired for the hunt,
and tobacco came in, in a pipe of peace, but joined the pipes
  of war
as an after-smoke of battle, or over the maps before.

All alcohols, all spirits lost strength in the trenches, that belt-fed
  country
then morphine summoned warrior dreams in ruined and would-
  be gentry;
stewed tea and vodka and benzedrine helped quell that
  mechanized fury—
the side that won by half a head then provided judge and jury.

In the acid war the word was Score; rising helicopters cried
  Smack! Smack!
Boys laid a napalm trip on earth and tried to take it back
but the pot boiled over in the rear; fighters tripped on their lines
  of force
and victory went to the supple hard side, eaters of fish sauce.

The perennial war drugs are made in ourselves: sex and
  adrenalin,
blood, and the endomorphias that transmute defeat and pain
and others hardly less chemical: eagles, justice, loyalty, edge,
the Judas face of every idea, and the fish that ferments in the
  brain.

Letters to the Winner

After the war, and just after marriage and fatherhood
ended in divorce, our neighbour won the special lottery,
an amount then equal to fifteen years of a manager's
salary at the bank, or fifty years' earnings by
a marginal farmer fermenting his clothes in the black
marinade of sweat, up in his mill-logging paddocks.

The district, used to one mailbag, now received two
every mailday. The fat one was for our neighbour.
After a dip or two, he let these bags accumulate
around the plank walls of the kitchen, over the chairs,
till on a rainy day, he fed the tail-switching calves,
let the bullocks out of the yard, and, pausing at the door
to wash his hands, came inside to read the letters.

Shaken out in a vast mound on the kitchen table
they slid down, slithered to his fingers. *I have 7 children*
I am under the doctor if you could see your way clear
equal Pardners in the Venture God would bless you lovey
assured of our best service for a mere fifteen pounds down
remember you're only lucky I knew you from the paper
straightaway

Baksheesh, hissed the pages as he flattened them, baksheesh!
mate if your interested in a fellow diggers problems
old mate a friend in need—the Great Golden Letter
having come, now he was being punished for it.
You sound like a lovely big boy we could have such times
her's my photoe Doll Im wearing my birthday swimsuit
with the right man I would share this infallible system.

When he lifted the stove's iron disc and started feeding in
the pages he'd read, they clutched and streamed up the
    corrugated
black chimney shaft. And yet he went on reading,
holding each page by its points, feeling an obligation
to read each crude rehearsed lie, each come-on, flat truth,
    extremity:
We might visit you the wise investor a loan a bush man like you

remember we met on Roma Street for your delight and mine
a lick of the sultana—the white moraine kept slipping
its messages to him *you will be accursed* he husked them like
    cobs
Mr Nouveau Jack old man my legs are all paralysed up.
Black smuts swirled weightless in the room *some good kind*
    person
like the nausea of a novice free-falling in a deep mine's cage
now I have lost his pension and formed a sticky nimbus round
    him

but he read on, fascinated by a further human range
not even war had taught him, nor literature glossed for him
since he never read literature. Merely the great reject pile
which high style is there to snub and filter, for readers.
That his one day's reading had a strong taste of what he and
    war
had made of his marriage is likely; he was not without
    sympathy,

but his leap had hit a wire through which the human is policed.
His head throbbed as if busting with a soundless shout
of immemorial sobbed invective *God-forsaken, God-forsakin*
as he stopped reading, and sat blackened in his riches.

The China Pear Trees

The power of three China pear trees
standing in their splintery timber bark
on an open paddock:

the selector's house that staked and watered them
in Bible times, beside a shaded patch,
proved deciduous; it went away in loads,

but after sixty years of standing out,
vanishing in autumn, blizzarding in spring,
among the farmlands' sparse and giant furniture,

after sixty crops gorged on from all directions,
so that no windfalls, fermenting, shrank to lizard-skinned
puree in the short grazed grass,

the trees drew another house, electrified and steaming
but tin-roofed as before for blazing clouds to creak over
and with tiny nude frogs upright again on lamplit glass;

they drew another kitchen garden, and a dam
half scintillating waterlily pleasance, half irrigation,
an ad hoc orchard, Christmas pines, a cud-dropping mower;

they drew a wire fence around acres of enclosure
shaped like a fuel tin, its spout a tunnel of trees
tangled in passionflower and beige-belled wonga vine,

down inside which a floodtime waterfall churns
millet-sized gravel. And they called lush water-leaved trees
like themselves to the stumpholes of gone rainforest

to shade with four seasons the tattered evergreen
oil-haloed face of a subtle fire landscape
(water forest versus fire forest, ancient war of the southern
     world).

It was this shade in the end, not their coarse bottling fruit
that mirrored the moist creek trees outward, as a culture
containing the old gardener now untying and heaping up

one more summer's stems and chutneys,
his granddaughter walking a horse the colour of her boots
and his tree-shaping son ripping out the odd failed seedling,
"Sorry, tree. I kill and I learn."

The Vol Sprung from Heraldry

Left wing, right wing:
two wings torment our lives,
two wings without a body,
joined, turkey wing and vulture wing

like the badge of an airborne army.
Each has its clients to enfold
and shed lice on. It gets quite underarm
and the other wing lashes at them.

Two wings without a bird—
is called a *vol* in heraldry—
spinning, fighting, low to the ground,
whomping up evil dusts for our breath.

Sometimes they borrow a head
like the bride-head on a Scots grave,
stone, pitiless in pursed absorption,
drinking blood to digest into thought,

biting out sinews to weave
into an agenda of trap questions.
Only on abstract figures,
statues of the past or future,

does it have mercy.
Discarded, it drops from the wings
to burst in the street like a car bomb
—and the lightened, whipping

wings stiffen to a double kinked sword,
left tip up, right point down,
in wingovers shedding diseased feathers
and the slashed air bleeds oppression.

Two wings, longing for a body:
left wing, right wing, flexing

still from the noble secret spring
that launched, propels and will exhaust them:

that everything in the end grows boring.

The Megaethon: 1850, 1906–29

I.M. LEO PORT

Farmer Cleve, gent., of the Hunter
Valley has ordained that his large
Sydney-built steam engine shall be walked
home under its own power, on iron
shoes serially laid beneath its wheels.
Making four miles a day, it's no fizzer.
He has christened it the Megaethon,
Greek for the Ruddy Big Fiery Thing.

On black iron plates that lean down
and flatten successively, imprinting
rectangular billets of progression
it advances on the Hawkesbury district
hissing, clanking, stoked by freed men.
People run from oat-field and wash-house,
from pot-house and cockpit to gape
at its shackled gait, its belt-drive pulsation:

"Look, Mother, it walks on its knees!" "Aye,
it's praying its way to Wiseman's Ferry,
coughing black smoke out of its steeple!"
Sparks canter by it, cracking whips. Small
native children scream "Buggy-buggy!"
and the iron gangs straighten from their sad
triangular thoughts to watch another
mighty value approach along their spadework.

In that last, dissolving convict year
what passes their wedged grins is a harbinger
not merely of words like *humdinger*, but
of stumpjump ploughs, metal ores made float,
ice plants, keel wings, a widening vote,
the world's harvesters, the utility truck, rotary
engines pipemoulds lawnmowers—this motor the
slaves watch strikes a ringing New World note.

As, tilting, stayed with ropes and pulleys,
the Megaethon descends a plateau edge,
casting shoes, crushing sandstone, only
the poorest, though, watching from dry bush
in that chain-tugging year, last before the gold rush,
know that here is a centre of the world
and that one who can rattle the inverted
cosmos is stamping to her stamping ground.

Not guided by such truth, the Megaethon
veers towards rum-and-opium stops,
waits, cooling, beside a slab bordello
and leans at last in upland swamp,
flat-footed, becoming salvage,
freight for ribald bullockies. Its polygonal
rhythms will engender no balladry;
it won't break the trench-lines at Vicksburg.

The engine goes home to make chaff
and the idea of the Megaethon
must travel underground. Stockmen gallop
above it. It travels underground.
Secret ballots and boxkites are invented,
unions form, national purposes gather
above it. It travels underground;
for fifty years it travels underground

losing its first name. It surfaces
in Melbourne at last, in the mind
of one Frank Bettrill, who calls
his wheel of three sliding plates

the Pedrail or Dreadnaught wheel
"for travelling across country in all
conditions, where roads may be absent."
In all but name, the Megaethon

is abroad again, now clearing country,
now ploughing the new farms. Its jointed
wheel-plates go to war on artillery
lashing back the Ottoman Empire
from Suez to Damascus. The monster
guns of Flanders advance and recoil
on many-slatted wheels. Tanks grind by them,
collateral descendants of the Megaethon

which itself remains in innocent
rebirth in its own hemisphere.
Its largest example, Big Lizzie
spends the mid-war years crossing Victoria
and following the Murray through Gunbower,
Mystic Park and Day Trap to Mildura.
From its cab eighteen feet above ground
crews wave to the river paddlesteamers:

"Gutter sailors! Our ship don't *need* water!"
Submarine in the mallee forests
Big Lizzie leaves a shattered wake;
she wades marsh, crosses grass fires' negative
landscape: black ground, bleached rattling trees;
her slamming gait shuts the earth down
but her following ploughs reopen it
in long rising loaves. Soldiers follow her

and turn into farmers sewing full
wheat bags with a large darning needle.
Giant workhorse born between the ages
of plodding feet and highway speeds
it takes lorries a decade to catch
and relegate Lizzie's oil-engined shuffle.
The Megaethon thus re-enters quaintness
at two miles an hour, having,

though ponderous, only lightly existed
(twice so far) and never directly
shed blood. And there, repaired with wire
from strict fences, it still walks the trackless,
slow as workaday, available for metaphor,
laying down and picking up the squeezed-
fragrant iron suit-cards of its patience,
crews making mugs of tea from its boiler.

Fastness

I am listening for words the eldest
of three brothers must have uttered
magically, out of their whole being,

to make a sergeant major look down
at the stamped grass, and not have them stopped
as they walked, not trooped, off his shouting
showground parade, in the brown
fatal clothes and pink boots they'd been given,

to retrieve their own horses and vanish
bearing even the unloaded strap rifles
the Government would still be pursuing
a decade later, along with the brothers.

I have come as far as officials
and sergeants ever came, telling their
hillbilly yarns: the boy-headed calf,
the barbed wire across the teenage bedroom,
the dead wife backpacked forty miles
in a chaff bag, but gutted to save weight.
I have passed where their cars' spoke wheels
slid and stopped, and the silent vines hung.

Since beyond the exact words, I need
the gesture with which they were said,
the horizons and hill air that shaped them,
the adze-faceted timbers of the kitchen
where they were repeated to the old people

who, having heard nothing about war,
had sent the boys three days round trip
in to town for saltpetre and tobacco.
I need the angle of cloud forest
visible through that door, the fire chains
and the leaf tastes of tank water there.

I will only have history, lacking these,
not the words as they have to be
spoken out, in such moments:

centrally, so as to pass the mind
of cheerful blustering authority
and paralyse it in its dream—
right in the unmeant nick of time
even as the rails were shutting
on the wide whooping yard of adventure
and making it a cattle chute
that led through jokes and accoutrements
to the long blood trail a-winding.

I need not think the brothers were
unattracted by a world venture
in aid of the woman Belgium
or not drawn by herd-warmth towards
the glorious manhunting promised them
by fellows round pipe-drawing fires
outside the beast-pavilions they slept in.

I need remember only the angel
poverty wrestles with in vast places
to know the power of abandon
people want, with control, to touch
when they tell hillbilly stories

and knowing it well, to uncover
how the brothers missed their legendary
Anzac chance, I need only
sit on this rusty bedstead, on a known
vanished sleepout verandah and reflect

how the lifelong lordly of space
might speak, in discernment of spirits
at the loud surcingled overseer's
very first bawled genial insult
to any of theirs. Not the camel's-back-
breaking, trapped slight, but the first.

1980 in a Street of Federation Houses

In 1980, in a street of Federation houses
a man is brushing his hair inside a car
while waiting for his children. It is his access day.

Men down the street—one perched high
as an oldtime sailor, others hauling long lines—
are dismantling a tree, from the top down. A heavy
branch drops, out of keen gristing noise, and runs
dragging all the stumpy hauliers
inwards on their ropes, then hangs swinging.

In 1964, the same man, slightly plumper,
is proclaiming in the Union bar *Now let
us watch the angels dance on the head of a pill!*
He does not mean, but swallows, a methedrine tablet.

In the same year he consents for the first time
to find the woodchoppers at the Easter Show
faintly comical, in their cricketing whites and singlets,

starting in handicap order to knock on wood:
one chopper, two choppier, then a clobbering
increment of cobbers, down in the grunting arena—

he assigns them to 1955, an obsolete year,
and the whole Labor Movement
shifts and re-levels in his mind
like mercury, needing new calibrations.

In 1824 in another country
present to his albums, small children run all day
breathing lint in a cavernous tropic factory
lit by weak globes on which older lint has caramelled.

They work from dawn to palm-frond-clattering dark
loading bales of packaged shirts onto trucks
driven by tribesmen who smoke, as they do themselves,
like the Industrial Revolution, paper chimneys in their cursing
    mouths.

Upcountry, men of the Thirties in 1950s uniform
instruct youths and girls of the starving fourteen hundreds
how to conjure with rifles the year 1792.
Their ammunition is the first packaged goods they have handled.

To reproduce yourself is to admit defeat!
His dashing friend had said it, in the year
he was told about cadmium fish, and blamed for the future.
To reproduce oneself? Who ever did that?

Most perhaps, before the Industrial Revolution
but then permanent death came in; all the years,
all the centuries now had to fit into one lifetime.

As did Heaven. Which drew Hell.
The Bomb and the Club Méditerranée had to lie
down together—. He begins to see his educators
as missionaries of the new unending death.

He shifts to another year, along the band
of his car's stereo, and his children are playing
in a tent on sandy grass;
can there be a time in which this scene is not a bibelot?

Now that up the suburban street that leads to the past
a figure is leading not greyhounds but Afghan hounds
and on the beach beyond, women who enter the surf
shielding a web of dusty lint emerge
and each is wearing a feather!

The Milk Lorry

Now the milk lorry is a polished submarine
that rolls up at midday, attaches a trunk and inhales
the dairy's tank to a frosty snore in minutes

but its forerunner was the high-tyred barn of crisp mornings,
reeking Diesel and mammary, hazy in its roped interior
as a carpet under beaters, as it crashed along potholed lanes

cooeeing at schoolgirls. Long planks like unshipped oars
butted, levelling in there, because between each farm's
stranded wharf of milk cans, the work was feverish slotting

of floors above floors, for load. It was sling out the bashed
paint-collared empties and waltz in the full,
stumbling on their rims under ribaldry, tilting their big gallons

then the schoolboy's calisthenic, hoisting steel men man-high
till the glancing hold was a magazine of casque armour,
a tinplate 'tween-decks, a seminar engrossed

in one swaying tradition, behind the speeding doorways
that tempted a truant to brace and drop, short of town,
and spend the day, with book or not, down under

the bridge of a river that by dinnertime would be
tongueing like cattledogs, or down a moth-dusty reach
where the fish-feeding milk boat and cedar barge once floated.

The Butter Factory

It was built of things that must not mix:
paint, cream and water, fire and dusty oil.
You heard the water dreaming in its large
kneed pipes, up from the weir. And the cordwood
our fathers cut for the furnace stood in walls
like the sleeper-stacks of a continental railway.

The cream arrived in lorried tides; its procession
crossed a platform of workers' stagecraft: *Come here
Friday-Legs! Or I'll feel your hernia—*
Overalled in milk's colour, men moved the heart of milk,
separated into thousands, along a roller track—*Trucks?
That one of mine, son, it pulls like a sixteen-year-old—*
to the tester who broached the can lids, causing fat tears,
who tasted, dipped and did his thin stoppered chemistry
on our labour, as the empties chattered downstage and fumed.

Under the high roof, black-crusted and stainless steels
were walled apart: black romped with leather belts
but paddlewheels sailed the silvery vats where muscles
of the one deep cream were exercised to a bullion
to be blocked in paper. And between waves of delivery
the men trod on water, hosing the rainbows of a shift.

It was damp April even at Christmas round every
margin of the factory. Also it opened the mouth
to see tackles on glibbed gravel, and the mossed char louvres
of the ice-plant's timber tower streaming with
heavy rain all day, above the droughty paddocks
of the totem cows round whom our lives were dancing.

Bats' Ultrasound

Sleeping-bagged in a duplex wing
with fleas, in rock-cleft or building
radar bats are darkness in miniature,
their whole face one tufty crinkled ear
with weak eyes, fine teeth bared to sing.

Few are vampires. None flit through the mirror.
Where they flutter at evening's a queer
tonal hunting zone above highest C.
Insect prey at the peak of our hearing
drone re to their detailing tee:

ah, eyrie-ire, aero hour, eh?
O'er our ur-area (our era aye
ere your raw row) we air our array,
err, yaw, row wry—aura our orrery,
our eerie ü our ray, our arrow.

A rare ear, our aery Yahweh.

Roman Cage-cups

Excavate, at a constant curving interval,
a layer of air between the inner and outer
skins of a glass beaker, leaving only odd struts integral;

at the same time, at the same ablative atom-
by-atom rate, sculpt the outer shell to an openwork
of rings, or foliage, or a muscular Elysium—

It made for calm paste and a steady file
that one false stroke, one twitch could cost a year's time,
a good billet, your concubine. Only the cups were held noble.

Plebs and immigrants fashioned them, punters
who ate tavern-fried pike and talked Vulgate.
The very first might have been made as a stunt, as

the life-gambit of a slave. Or a joke on the feasting scene:
a wine-bowl no one coarsely drunk could handle
nor, since baseless, easily put down,

a marvel of undercutting, a glass vessel
so costly it would exact that Roman gravity,
draw blood, and feud, if grasped without suavity.

The one depicting Thracian Lycurgus
strangled by amorous vines for slighting Bacchus
could hardly have survived an old-time bacchanal.

Where polish is cutting and festivity an ice
and most meaning paradox, it is an age of cool.
Culture has lifted off and impends above us

on brittle legs, always more or less transparent.
Splendour of social vertigo. Even to describe it serves its luxury.
But this is the fourth, that is, the eleventh century:

war-chiefs are coming whose descendants in turn
will learn to exalt, and suspend the new fraternal
faith that triumphed lately. So the engravers groove on

under the fixed heavens, into that driest liquid,
miming a low but vast space, never roofed entirely—
as between the idea and its word, a global interstice.

The glass flowers of Harvard, monks' micro pen-lace, a
       chromosome
needled to grow wings on a horse (which they'd also have done),
the freely moving ivory dragons-inside-a-dragon

ball of Cathay—the impossible is a groove:
why else do we do it? Even some given a choice
would rather work the metaphors than live them, in society.

But nothing, since sparkle became permanent in the thumbs
and rib-cages of these craftsmen, has matched their handiwork
for gentleness, or edge. They put the gape into agapé,

these factory products, of all Rome's underground Gothic:
cups transfigured by hand, too delicate to break.
Some, exported beyond the Rhine as a *miss-*

ion civilisatrice, have survived complete and unchipped
a sesquimillennium longer than the trumpets (allude,
allude) of the arena. Rome's very hardest rock.

The Lake Surnames

There are rental houseboats down the lakes now.
Two people facing, with drinks, in a restaurant party
talk about them: *That idiot, he ran us aground
in the dark! These fishermen rescued us,
towed us off the mudbank. They were frightening actually,
real inbred faces, Deliverance people
when we saw them by torchlight in their boat—*

For an instant, rain rattles at the glass
and brown cardboards of a kitchen window
and drips lamplight-coloured out of soot
in the fireplace, hitching steam off stove-iron.

Tins of beeswax, nails and poultice mixture
stick to shelves behind the door. Triangular
too, the caramel dark up under rafters
is shared, above one plank wall, by the room

where the English housekeeper screamed
at a crisp bat on the lino. Guest room,
parents' room, always called *the room*
with tennis racquet and rifle in the lowboy.

Quick steps jingle the glassed cabinet
as a figure fishes spoons from scalding water
("what's not clean's sterilised") in the board-railed
double triangle of a kerosene-tin sink,

a real Bogan sink, on the table.
The upright wireless, having died when valves vanished,
has its back to the wall. It is a *plant* for money
guarded by a nesting snake, who'll be killed when
     discovered.

The new car outside, streaming cricket scores,
is a sit-in radio, glowing, tightly furnished
but in the Auburn wood stove, the fire laps
and is luxury too, in one of them flood years.

—With only the briefest pause, the other
answers: *There aren't that many full-time*
surnames down the lakes. If you'd addressed them
as Mr Blanche, Mr Woodward, Mr Legge,
Mr Bramble, or Palmer, your own surname,
you'd probably have been right. And more at ease.

Nocturne

Brisbane, night-gathered, far away
estuarine imaginary city
of houses towering down one side
of slatted lights seen under leaves

confluence of ranginess with lush,
Brisbane, of rotogravure memory
approached by web lines of coke and grit
by sleepers racked in corridor trains

weatherboard incantatory city
of the timber duchess, the strapped port
in Auchenflower and Fortitude Valley
and bottletops spat in Vulture Street

greatest of the floodtime towns
that choked the dictionary with silt
and hung a navy in the tropic gardens.
Brisbane, on the steep green slope to war

brothel-humid headquarters city
where commandos and their allies fought
down café stairs, belt buckle and boot
and once with a rattletrap green gun.

In midnight nets, in mango bombings
Brisbane, storied and cable-fixed,
above your rum river, farewell and adieu
in marble on the hill of Toowong

by golfing pockets, by deep squared pockets
night heals the bubbled tar of day
and the crab moon, rising, reddens above
Brisbane, rotating far away.

Lotus Dam

Lotus leaves, standing feet above the water,
collect at their centre a perfect lens of rain
and heel, and tip it back into the water.

Their baby leaves are feet again, or slant lips
scrolled in declaration; pointed at toe and heel
they echo an unwalked sole in their pale green crinkles

and under blown and picket blooms, the floor
of floating leaves rolls light rainwater marbles
back and forth on sharkskins of anchored rippling.

Each speculum, pearl and pebble of the first water
rides, sprung with weight, on its live mirroring skin
tipped green and loganberry, till one or other sky

redeems it, beneath bent foils and ferruled canes
where cupped pink bursts all day, above riddled water.

At Min-Min Camp

In the afternoon, a blue storm walloped and split
like a loose mainsail behind us. Then another
far out on the plain fumed its corrugated walls.

A heavy dough of cloud kept rising, and reached us.
The speeding turbid sky went out of focus, fracturing
continually, and poured. We made camp on a verandah

that had lost its house. I remembered it: pitsawn pine
lined with newspaper. People lived on treacle and rabbit
by firelight, and slept under grain-bag quilts there.

It was a lingering house. Millions had lived there
on their way to the modern world. Now they longed for and
    feared it.
It had been the last house, and the first.

Dark lightnings tore the ground as we ripped up firewood
and when the rain died away to conversation, and parted
on refreshed increasing star-charts, there arose

an unlikely bushfire in the ranges. The moon leaped from it,
slim, trim in perfect roundness. Spiderwebs palely yellow
by firelight changed sides, and were steel thread, diamante.

Orange gold itself, everything the moon gave, everywhere
was nickel silver, or that lake-submerged no-colour
native to dreams. Sparse human lights on earth

were solar-coloured, though: ingots of a homestead,
amoebae that moved and twinned on distant roads
and an unfixed anomaly, like a star with land behind it.

We were drinking tea round a sheet-iron fire on the boards
bearing chill on our shoulders, like the boys who'd slept
on that verandah, and gone to be wandering lights

lifelong on the plains. You can't catch up to them now
though it isn't long ago: when we came from the
    Rift Valley
we all lived in a small star on the ground.

From the Rift we also carried the two kinds of fear
humans inherit: the rational kind, facing say weapons,
and the soul's kind, the creeps. Awe, which warns of law.

The two were long bound together, in the sacred
cultures of fright, that called shifting faces to the light's edge:
none worse than our own, when we came dreaming of houses.

Then the sacred turned fairytale, as always. And the new thing,
holiness, a true face, constant in all lights,
was still very scattered. It saved some. It is still scattered.

Many long for the sacred lights, and would renew their lore
in honoured bantustans—no faery for the laager of the
    lagerphone—
but they are unfixed now, and recede, and suddenly turn pale as

an escaped wife dying of a dread poem. Or her child
who sniffs his petrol, and reels like a shot kangaroo:
something else, and not the worst, that happens in a shifting
    light.

Holiness is harder to inhale, for adventure or desperation.
It cleanses awe of fear, though not of detailed love,
the nomads' other linkage, and maps the law afresh with it.

We left that verandah next day, and its ruined garden
of wire and daylilies, its grassy fringe of ancient pee scalds,
and travelled further west on a truck that had lost its body.

Hearing Impairment

Hearing loss? Yes, loss is what we hear
who are starting to go deaf. Loss
trails a lot of weird puns in its wake, viz.
Dad's a real prism of the Left—
you'd like me to repeat that?
THE SAD SURREALISM OF THE DEAF.

It's mind over mutter at work
guessing half what the munglers are saying
and society's worse. Punchlines elude to you
as Henry Lawson and other touchy drinkers
have claimed. Asides, too, go pasture.
It's particularly nasty with a wether.

First you crane at people, face them
while you can still face them. But grudgually
you give up dinnier parties; you begin
to think about Beethoven; you Hanover
next visit here on silly Narda Fearing—I SAY
YOU CAN HAVE AN EXQUISITE EAR
AND STILL BE HARD OF HEARING.

It seems to be mainly speech, at first,
that escapes you—and that can be a rest,
the poor man's escape itch from Babel.
You can still hear a duck way upriver,
a lorry miles off on the highway. You
can still say boo to a goose and
read its curt yellow-lipped reply.
You can shout SING UP to a magpie,

but one day soon you must feel
the silent stopwatch chill your ear
in the doctor's rooms, and be wired
back into a slightly thinned world
with a faint plastic undertone to it
and, if the rumours are true, snatches
of static, music, police transmissions:
it's a BARF minor Car Fourteen prospect.

But maybe hearing aids are now perfect
and maybe it's not all that soon.
Sweet nothings in your ear are still sweet;
you've heard the human range by your age
and can follow most talk from memory;
the peace of the graveyard's well up
on that of the grave. And the world would
enjoy peace and birdsong for more moments

if you were head of government, enquiring
of an aide Why, Simpkins, do you tell me
a warrior is a ready flirt?
I might argue—and flowers keep blooming
as he swallows his larynx to shriek
our common mind-overloading sentence:
I'M SORRY, SIR, IT'S A RED ALERT!

At Thunderbolt's Grave in Uralla

The New England Highway was formed
by Christian men who reckoned
Adam and Eve should have been
sodomized for the curse of work
they brought on humankind,
not drudgery, but work.
No luxury of distinctions.

None ever went to Bali. Some set out.
But roads were game reserves to Thunderbolt
when a bridge was a leap, and wheels
were laborious, trundling through the splashways.
There were two heights of people: equestrians
and those foreshortened on foot.
All were more dressed, because more naked.

That German brass band that Thunderbolt,
attended by a pregnant boy,
bailed up on Goonoo Goonoo Gap:
"Gentlemen, if you are that poor
I'll refund your twenty pound, provided
a horse I mean to shake wins at Tenterfield."
And it did, arching its neck, and he did
by postal note at Warwick.
Hoch! Public relations by trombone!

No convict ever got off Cockatoo
Island by swimming except Thunderbolt.
His lady, Yellow Long or Long Yella,
whichever way the name points, swam
the channel from Balmain before him
bringing tucker and clothes, and she got
him past the sharks when he swam for it.

But who wouldn't swim, and wear trousers
for a man pinched and bearded as the nine
lions on the courthouse coat of arms
with their tongues saying languish and lavish,
who took her from men who gasped romance
into her lungs and offered sixpence
from her own heart-gelded tribesfolk
and white women's dreadful eyes?

Though Uralla creek is floored with planks now
the amethystine light of New England
still seems augmented from beneath
both horizons; tin outside chimneys
still squeeze woodsmoke into the air

but the police cars come wailing their
unerotic In-Out In-Out,
red-shifting over Goonoo Goonoo.

Of all the known bushrangers,
those cropped in the floggers' gulag,
those jostled by its Crown guards,
the bolters and the hoods were merely shot
or ironed or hanged. Only three required
frenzied extermination, with rituals:
Jackey Westaway, made monstrous by torture,
Fred Ward shot and head-pulped, Ben Hall
shot dead, and for several minutes afterwards.

All three were thieves. They likely never met.
All three stole the Crown's magic pallium
and trailed it through the bush, a drag
for raging pursuit. On every snag
they left some white or blue—the red part
they threw away at once, disdaining murder.
Robbery with mock menaces? Why that is subsidy!
The part they died hard for was the part
they wouldn't play, not believing the game worth murder.

Criminal noncomplicity! It was something nameless
above all stations, that critical magic
haloed in laughter. *Tell Fred I need to be robbed Friday
or I'm jiggered!* A deadly style suddenly felt lumbering,
battered with a slapstick. Our only indigenous revolution.
It took Ned Kelly to reassure policemen.

Why don't we kill like Americans?
We started to. The police were pushing it
but we weren't a republic for bringing things to a head
and these, even dying—*Are you a married man?*
cried Ward, and fired wide—helped wrong-foot mortal drama
and leave it decrepit, a police atmosphere.
In a few years, the game was boss and union.
Now society doesn't value individuals
enough for human sacrifice.

You were a cross swell, Fred. You alone never
used a gang. Those always kill, as Hall learned.
I hope your children found your cache
and did good with it. They left some on deposit.

Infra Red

FOR PROF. FRED HOYLE AND THE *IRAS* TELESCOPE

Dark stars that never fire,
brown dwarfs, whose deepening collapse
inward on themselves never tightens to fuse glory,
scorched dust the size of worlds, and tenuous
sandbars strung between the galaxies,
a universe dull with life:

with the eye and eye-adjuncts
mind sees only what is burning, the peak nodes of fury
that make all spiralling in on them
or coronally near, blowing outward from them,
look eager, intense, even brave. Most of the real
however is obscurely reflective, just sauntering along,
yarning across a ditch, or watching television,
vaguely dreaming, perhaps about pubic stuff,

getting tea ready. This absorbs most of the light
but is also family. It impoverishes to unreality
not to consider the dim, cannon fodder of stardom,
the gravities they are steepening to,
the unfathomable from which the trite is spoken.
And starry science is an evening-paper astrology
without the unknown bodies registered
only by total pain, only by dazzled joy,
the transits marked by a tight grip of the heart.

That the visible stars are suburbs and slow towns
hyped to light speed is the testimony of debris
and the serious swarms at rest in migrant trajectories.

271

Brilliance stands accused of all their losses.
Presence perhaps, and the inference of presence,
not light, should found a more complete astronomy.

It will draw in absence, too:
the pain-years between a love and its fulfilment,
the intricate spiral space of suppressed tradition
and all the warmth, whose peaks aren't those of heat,
that the white dwarfs froze out of their galaxies.

Poetry and Religion

Religions are poems. They concert
our daylight and dreaming mind, our
emotions, instinct, breath and native gesture

into the only whole thinking: poetry.
Nothing's said till it's dreamed out in words
and nothing's true that figures in words only.

A poem, compared with an arrayed religion,
may be like a soldier's one short marriage night
to die and live by. But that is a small religion.

Full religion is the large poem in loving repetition;
like any poem, it must be inexhaustible and complete
with turns where we ask Now why did the poet do that

You can't pray a lie, said Huckleberry Finn;
you can't poe one either. It is the same mirror:
mobile, glancing, we call it poetry,

fixed centrally, we call it a religion,
and God is the poetry caught in any religion,
caught, not imprisoned. Caught as in a mirror

that he attracted, being in the world as poetry
is in the poem, a law against its closure.
There'll always be religion around while there is poetry

or a lack of it. Both are given, and intermittent,
as the action of those birds—crested pigeon, rosella parrot—
who fly with wings shut, then beating, and again shut.

Inverse Ballad

Grandfather's grandfather rode down from New England
that terrible steep road. One time there, his horse
shat over his shoulder. It's not so steep now.
Anyway he was riding, and two fellows came
out of the brush with revolvers pointed at him:

Bail up! What joy have you got for the poor, eh?
Bail up? Ye're never bushrangers? Wad ye shoot me?
My oath we'd shoot yer—. He looked them up and down,
poor weedy toerags both. Ye'd really shoot, then?
Masel, I never find it necessary.

Eh? You're on our lay, are you?—Aye, I am.
Ward's the name.—Not Thunderbolt? By Hell. Hmm.
They muttered some asides. Well, Mister Ward, you
are money on the hoof. A thousand's a fair screw
for turning you in. Dead *or* alive, so ride!

We're going to town to sell your pretty hide.
It must have felt lonely, riding ahead of them
knowing they could just as easily turn you in,
head lolling and blood dripping, strapped over your saddle.
When they reached the police post, the old sergeant listened

a moment, then snapped: Ye'll gie me thae barkers;
hand them over! Constable, handcuff yon men!

Ye ignorant puir loons, did ye no ken
Thunderbolt's no Scots. He disnae talk like me.
Ye'll hae time tae regret bailing up Mister Murray!

Ward's wintertime employer, had the police or he known.

Relics of Sandy

Beside the odd gene
just three pictures remain
of Uncle Sandy Beattie,
big fair man:

He used to swim his horse
through the flooded rivers
with bags tied on the saddle
when he was the mailman;
he'd hang on to its tail:
he couldn't swim at all.

Once for a bet he
humped a ton of iron
sheets up from the jetty
to the pub at Tinonee
and found a man had ridden
up, clinging on the load:
Ye've bowed my legs, laddie.

A loudmouth in the pub
was needling Sandy
one night, talking fight,
all the men he'd stiffened,
how the big raw ones were easy.
Yes, McMahon, I hear ye.
He finished his beer.
It's hard to take, McMahon,

and I'll not take any more.
Barman, give me a room key.
And he took the bareknuckle man
upstairs to the room,
pushed him in, locked the door:
Now, man, it's what you wanted,
no audience, we're private.
Just you and me for it!

There was thunder up there.
All the bottles jinked about
in the bar, and the fighter
squealed like a poor rabbit.
The barman got a pound
when Sandy came downstairs:
Yon man shouldn't have to
pay twice, for accommodation.
Sandy Beattie. Big fair man.

Joker as Told

Not a latch or lock could hold
a little horse we had
not a gate or paddock.

He liked to get in the house.
Walk in, and you were liable
to find him in the kitchen
dribbling over the table
with a heap behind him

or you'd catch a hoof
right where it hurt bad
when you went in your bedroom.

He grew up with us kids,
played with us till he got rough.
Round then, they cut him,

but you couldn't ride him:
he'd bite your bum getting on,
kick your foot from the stirrup

and he could kick the spurs off
your boots. Almost hopped on with you,
and if he couldn't buck you
he'd lie down plop! and roll
in his temper, and he'd squeal.

He was from the Joker breed,
we called him Joker;
no joke much when he bit you
or ate the Monday washing.

They reckon he wanted to be
human, coming in the house.
I don't think so. I think he
wanted something people had.
He didn't do it from love of us.

He couldn't grow up to be a
full horse, and he wouldn't be a slave one.
I think he was looking for his childhood,
his foalhood and ours, when we played.

He was looking for the Kingdom of God.

Writer in Residence
(OR: DROP ONE OF YOUR OWN)

I was good at the Common Room game
but when Dr X dropped a name
it hung in the air
like a parachute flare
far over my head, to my shame.

A Public Figure

To break the Judaeo-Christian mould was his caper
but the ethic he served torched him with its newspaper.

The Young Woman Visitor

I never heard such boasting.
For two whole days while I was there
he never let up. He was the best axeman,
driver, horsebreaker, farmer, bullocky and judge
of standing timber "that ever God put guts in".
He'd also had the best dog, the best car,
the best crop of corn and the very best eight-day clock
and he'd been the best psalm-singer in his church, too.
Someone had let a little boy grow old;
I saw that all these things were a posy of flowers
snatched out of a funeral wreath and offered
to me, or to anyone,
not a wreath that would lie heaped on his grave
but the little special one that would go down
diminishing past clay, and trembling, on his coffin.

The Grandmother's Story

Just a few times in your life, you speak
those strange words. Or they speak themselves
out of you, before you can bite your tongue.
They are there, like a dream. You're not sure you've spoken
but you see them hit the other person
like a stone into floodwater. No splash much
but they go right to the bottom. To the soul.
No use saying you're sorry, or didn't mean them.

I never liked Ted Quarrie. Partly the way
he treated women. More, and it's the same,
the way he made poor Annie behave like him,
drinking and dribbling with Harold's whisky friends,
falling on the floor. The way they drank it:
Heere's luck! and pitch it down like castor oil;
they almost held their noses. They were like that at the show
when Ted sneaked up and pinched me. Hard, to hurt

and I hit him. Not slapped him. Shut my fist
and flattened him, in front of the whole showground.
I'd lumped more iron camp ovens, butter churns, and logs too
than ever he had. He stayed out for minutes.
When he came around, he cursed me. Called me every kind
of low-bred bitch. That's when I said—that other.
What did I say? That doesn't matter. I silenced him.
It would be a sin to do on purpose. To practise.

He hated me, ever after. And he hung round home
so I'd see him and know. But I've got a strong back;
I could bear it. You could still buy revolvers then
and he had one. But it took him years to creep away
round the verandahs, one Sunday, from where they were
        drinking
and lean in at our window, where I lay sick in bed.
He opened his coat, took out that thieves' gun, said
See this, Emily? It's for you. Poor thing. I nearly laughed.

Of course, I might have been shot for that. So I had to
look frightened, when really I was sick and tired
of the whole silliness. He went away, but my third boy
heard him, and followed. He was only seventeen
and Ted was a grown man. But he made him hand over
that gun in front of everyone. Harold never spoke, as usual.
The boys climbed up and dropped the thing down inside
the walling of this kitchen. It's still rusting there, I fancy.

The Line

Opium and vitriol and a plug of twist
added to the rum have left the Tiger prostrate,
snoring on his stripes in the sun.
        Mickeen and Hoojah
step gingerly around him. Their own headache-bones
wince at the long saw's bare-fanged undulant clangour.

At the palace of a felled tree's crown, they strike up a fire,
share a pannikin of tea, then mix burnt bark with the dregs
and immerse a string in it.
        Hold your end, Mickeen!
They walk either side of the sawdust-mealy pit
and pass the string above a chocked log. Precisely as Mercator

the wet black twine hovers half an inch above
the timber's knocked continents, tautens, is minutely
aligned. Then Hoojah plucks it.
        The whipped note lays the first
straight line of a city, the first rectilinear thought
realised on that landscape. And marks it for division.

*Down in the hole, now. Sheeus late, a Vickeen!**
And keep yer feet on the ground, ye Fenyan bolter!
The black blade angles down,
        is gripped: a rhythmic chaff
starts modelling sweat, choking ripe Donegal curses.
As each plank slats off, the saw sings its future as cattlebells.

The line has been printed six times, when the Tiger stumbles
across from their tent with bread and three pounds of salt beef
stuck on a bayonet.
        At least it's not the poisonous snake
he slung into the pit last time the rum clawed at him.
Belching after a feed, he rips the handles downward

as if to pull the merciful saw through himself
or drag work itself down on his anguish, like Samson.

*Down with you, Micky! (Anglicised Irish)

279

Don't jerk a woman
           right through the cut, there, Tiger!
Shouts Hoojah, laughing, *or I'll be narrer and flat.*
Taste, reverence and polemic close over the gang after that.

Extract from a Verse Letter to Dennis Haskell

Dear Dennis,
               Warm thanks for your letter
in verse. It's very much better,
nicer and more thoughtful than those
postcards packed with minuscule prose
I write even to friends, like the harassed
editor I once was. I'm impressed.
Moved, too, that you should miss my company
—I never quite expect that, perhaps funnily,
of people. Yes, too much ochre
separates us now, joker from joker.
It's a bore that the width of the continent
can't be secretly folded or bent
so's to let us yarn here on the crest
of Deer's Hill, watching sunsets on Rottnest,
or strolling, well fed, by the Swan
as it flows beside our vegie garden.
I think you'd like it here, in our glade
of fruit saplings that now nearly manage shade
and soft grass, beside the lotus dam
and our other trees. Some year you must see them.
Trees, space, waterbirds—things of that ilk,
plus people of my own kind, are the milk
and honey I came home for. Not dairying,
that drudgery, poor, imprisoning, unvarying.
At eighteen, I made a great vow
I'd never milk another bloody cow.
It was only after I won my battle
to be free of them, that I came to love cattle.
Few dairy here now, anyway. It's gone largely bung.

I'm forty-eight next week. I won't die a dairyman. Or young.
The bush permits allusion, not illusion:
I didn't come for any past that's gone.
More for Dad, who had stopped getting on
and was getting old and sick. Our eldest children
too had already missed a country childhood
and we didn't think the younger three should
have to. Also there was this choice I had:
get out of Yuppie City or go mad.
No perhaps in that either. But enough.
Life here is scarcely tough:
Valerie's wryly and happily learning bush ways
and would have mastered the harder ones, too, of the old days.
She's on leave from teaching. Alec goes to special school by bus,
Clare to a local school. I'm running my export business
out of this room from which, well, four bean rows
and two of turnips are visible. Peter, our smallest boy,
is enjoying his babyhood, but sometimes gets wistful for Sydney.
Dad's had a cataract op. and sees well for his age
but now he's got shingles, nailed not to rafters but his rib-cage.
Ouch! Still, spring here delivers days you could dance to,
given a chance to. And that is our news.

Max Fabre's Yachts*

Towers of swell fabric
leaning on the ocean
go about in salt haze
to race for the rocked gun.

Straining theory makes the world
equivocal as miracles
ever were. Between spear and sphere
here tussle in purified war

*Max Fabre, of Sydney, made pioneering designs in the early 1960s of trifoil "winged" keel forms for ocean racing yachts.

the souls of rich men,
of syndicates and winch-winders
but no longer do they skate
on a sunk ice of ambition.

Nothing turns on a blade: all
now glide on a lucky trefoil,
a trinitarian trifoil,
vision of a drowning man

and first unveiled off Newport:
Hermes, messenger of Heaven,
speeding with one winged foot
dipped in the ocean.

The Man with the Hoe

I

Thinking about air conditioning's Willis Carrier
who also won the West, I am turning
earth in on a long potato drill,
which is like folding history down on trench lines

of unnumbered mild faces. The day
is overcast, with rain pricking the air
and us to hurry, plying our hoes along this promontory
above Horses Creek. The channel-billed cuckoo

shouts, flying, and the drug squad helicopter
comes singing *I'll spot it, your pot plot*.
O Lord of love, look from above,
sang the churches, but what looks down

from beyond the sky now's the television
of a spy satellite, feeding the coordinates
of today's cloud nations into spinning
tapes for the updating screens of judgement.

The Lord of love is in decay. Relievedly.
He's in worn flanks of stonework, in weathering
garden posts, in the survival of horses,
in humans' long survival after mating, in ticky-tacky

buildings that mean the builders were paid properly
and not always by magnates. He is more apparent
in the idea, verandahs and visitings of a hospital
than the stunning theatre. More in surrounds than the centre

where he is ground against, love versus love, he lives
in the bantering pauses. The pattern of love's also
behind our continuing to cover these potatoes
which, by her mercy, also look like potatoes.

2

Warmth makes cool. The mystery of refrigeration—
but now three fighter aircraft distil out
of the north hills, fast, ahead of their enormous
collapse of sound. Cloud resorbs them. As in the bra ad

the heart lifts and separates, shrivelled with exultation
that is the angel of history: a boy bored rigid
with farmwork sights along a noble light-draining
sword blade held at the level of his mouth.

Cold. Burning cold. The old tremendous imagery
of the Judgement recycles cold, in a bitter age
where love is passion, and passion is the action.
Who could trust a God of love, now we have seen

the love that ignites stars, and ourselves possess such ignition?
Who would trust a god on heat nearer than the stars?
Who can trust heat, that may now freeze the planet?
Who can trust coldness, matrix of utter heat?

We cry for cool, because we long for warmth.
When the fighters grow obsolete, and their pipes cool,
warmth reinvests them. It seems a reversing cycle.
Let the Lord be warm and cool, and judgement be

a flower I'm not good enough to unfold yet,
as I stitch down this earth, and my uncle comes driving
his skittish young tractor over our holey paddock,
my uncle the ex-smoker—not pot: we're older than the
    pot lot—

who starts conversations with a ruminative ahaanh,
not *aha! I've caught you!* A shyer reconnecting ahaanh
warm from past meetings. This is among my people
whom I do understand, but not before they speak.

Aspects of Language and War
on the Gloucester Road

I travel a road cut through time
by bare feet and boots without socks,
by eight-year-old men droving cattle,
by wheels parallel as printed rhyme
over rhythms of hill shale and tussocks.
    In the hardest real trouble of my life
    I called this Gloucester road to mind,
    which cuttings were bare gravel, which rife
    with grass, which ones rainforest-vined.
The road starts at Coolongolook
which means roughly Leftward Inland
from *gulunggal*, the left hand,
runs west between Holdens' and James'
where new people have to paint names
on their mailboxes, and stumps have board-slots
from when tall trees were jibbed like yachts
and felled above their hollow tones.
Later logs lie about like gnawed bones.
The road comes on through Sawyers Creek
where the high whaleback ridge becomes a peak
and where my father, aged nine years,
faced down the Bashing Teacher, a Squeers
who cut six-foot canes in the scrub
and, chewing his tongue in a sub-

jective ecstasy, lashed back-arching children.
Mind your mhisness!—Time someone chipped you!—
Short blazed at tall—and the knobbed cane withdrew.
My father was cheered shoulder-high in the playground then
and the flogging rods vanished. But previously slack
parents loomed, shouting. And behind them, the sack.

    Here too a farmer heard *Give up*
    cigarettes or your life! He coughed a sup
    of Flanders gas, cried *Jesus Christ and that,*
    Doctor, I'll give up my life! And what
    was burning inside him smouldered on
    for decades, disclosed only once
    in '39, teaching dodges to his sons.
    (1939, smiles an aunt, *the year*
    when no woman had to stay a spinster.)

The road runs through Bunyah, meaning bark
for shelters, or firelighters' candlebark
blown on in a *gugri* house, a word
for fire-hut that is still heard
though few farms still use a googery.
Few? None now. I was gone a generation.
Even parrot-eating's stopped:—*The buggers,*
they'd been eating that wild-tobacco berry:
Imagine a soup of boiled cigars!—

    I'm driving to Gloucester station
    to collect my urban eldest from the train,
    and there are the concrete tips
    of bridge piles, set like a tank trap
    up a farm entryway. The huge rap
    of a piledriver shivered few chips
    off the bedrock when they were banged stubbornly
    by an engineer who would not be told
    Black rock at eight feet'll stop you cold!
    What did locals know, lacking a degree?
    I loved the old bridge, its handrails,
    ballast logs and deck, an inland ship.
    Kids watched how floods' pewter rip
    wracked limbs over it. Floods were our folktales.
    Now we drive above missed schooldays, high
    on the Shire's concrete second try.

There at the hall, drums and accordions

still pump, and well-lit dancers glide.
In the dark outside move, single and duo,
the angrily shy and the bawdy ones:
blood and babies from the dancing outside.

   We held Free Church services too, though,
   in that hall. For months I'd cry aloud
   at the rise in the east of any cloud
   no bigger than a man's hand.
   A cloud by day led me out of Babyland
   about when Hiroshima had three years to go.

The Free Church, knuckle-white on its ridge,
now looks north at the Lavinia Murray Bridge,
at my great-grandmother's Chinese elm tree
and the Dutchman tractoring peaceably.
That faint scar across the creek is butts
of a range for aligned wartime rifle shots.

   What fearsome breach of military law
   sent you, Lieutenant Squance, to command
   that platoon of worried men-on-the-land
   the Bunyah Volunteer Defence Corps
   in those collapsing months after Singapore,
   brassbuttoned fathers, deadly afraid
   for life and family? Your British parade
   manner gave them some diversion:
   milky boots, casual mutiny, aspersion,
   your corporal raving death-threats in your face
   for calling his clean rifle a disgrace,
   brownpaper sandwiches sent to you with tea
   after parade one Saturday—
   I think, though, you'd have stayed and defended
   us, and died as our world ended,
   Mr Squance. Belated thanks are extended.

There's a house where I had hospitality
without fuss for years when I needed it.
Now it's dying, of sun-bleach, of shadowed
scarlet lichen, the poisons of abandonment.
I'm thinking, over the next rises,
of children who did not have their lives,
who died young, and how one realises
only at home that, unknown to younger wives,
faces lie in wait in finger-felted albums'

gapless groupings of family. The sums
of those short lifetimes add to one's own age,
to its weight, having no light yarns to lift them.
Peace or war, all die for our freedom.
The innocent, the guilty, the beasts, all die for our freedom.
I was taught the irreparable knowledge
by a baby of thirty next door in his wheelchair
who'd thrash and grimace with happiness when I went there.
I see the road, and many roads before,
through a fawn snap of him as a solemn little boy
before meningitis. And it is first for him
that I insist on a state where lives resume.

> The squatter style grinds eastward here, or "down"
> (both *ba:rung* in the old language) and spreads out from
> town.
>
> One property here was Something Downs for a bit:
> over there through the hills I can glimpse part of it
> just short of the pines round my gone one-teacher school
> with its zigzag air raid trench and morning flagpole;
> from there I remember birthdays, and how to shin
> fast over fence rails: *You're last!—I'll be first in Heaven!*
> I pass by Lavinia's gate,
> the first woman Shire President in the State
> and not dowager at eighty, but reigning, in her fox fur,
> descending on Parliament, ascending with the cropduster
> whose rent for an airfield was shopping flights to Gloucester.

A flagman stops me with a circled word.
I halt beside him, wait till he can be heard
over a big steel roller's matt declensions
as it tightens gravel down into two dimensions.
He points at a possum curled like an ampersand
around a high dead branch, spending the day
miserably where its light caught her away
from her cache of darkness.—*There's her baby's hand
out of her pouch.—She's dreaming.—Wonder if we
are in her dream?—Wonder if she's ever seen a hill?—
What lights would we have, on what cars, if we were nocturnal?
Look lower, native bees.*—Round a knothole spout
a thought-balloon of grist breathes in and out.
*Look, one on your arm.—Their mixture must need salt.
Hell will have icecream before this road gets asphalt.*

I drive off, on what sounds like a shore.
In Upper Bunyah there are more
settlers without nicknames, or
none they know. The widower on that hill
used to have one (and he was the raving corporal).
He once had some evangelists staying
in his house, demonstratively praying,
so one day his two dozen cats annoyed him
and he took the small rifle and destroyed them,
shot them off rafters, sniped eyes under his bed—
cups exploded in the kitchen as poor Tibby fled—
the men of prayer too ran headlong from his charity.
Sweet, for one, are the uses of barbarity.
His later wife had a chequebook and painted in France.
Why does so much of our culture work through yarns
equivalent to the national talent for cartoons?
It is an old war brought from Europe
by those who also brought poverty and landscape.
They had scores to settle, even with themselves. Tradition
is also repeating oneself, expecting inattention,
singing dumb, expecting scorn. Or sly mispronunciation
out of loyalty to the dead: *You boiling them bikinis
in that Vichy sauce?* We were the wrong people risen
—forerunners in that of nearly everyone—
but we rose early, on small farms, and were family.
A hard yarn twangs the tension
and fires its broad arrow out of a grim space
of Old Australian smells: toejam, tomato sauce,
semen and dead singlets the solitary have called peace
but which is really an unsurrendered trench. Really prison.
It is a reminder all stories are of war.
Peace, and the proof of peace, is the verandah
absent from some of the newer houses here.
It is also a slight distance—as indeed
grows between me and the farm of my cousin
who recently was sold treated seed grain
in mistake for cattle-feed grain:
it killed cows, but he dared not complain
or sue the feed merchant, for fear
he'd be barred as a milk supplier
to the Milk Board, and ruined, and in consequence

see his house become somebody's rural residence.
Such things can make a farmer look down, at his land
between his boots, and dignity shrink in his hand.
Now the road enters the gesture of the hills
where they express geologic weather
and contend with landscape in spills
of triangular forest down fence lines
and horse-and-scoop dams like filled mines.
What else to say of peace? It is a presence
with the feeling of home, and timeless in any tense.
I am driving *waga*, up and west.
Parting cattle, I climb over the crest
out of Bunyah, and skirt Bucca Wauka,
A Man Sitting Up With Knees Against His Chest:
baga waga, knees up, the burial-shape of a warrior.
Eagles flying below me, I will ascend Wallanbah,
that whipcrack country of white cedar
and ruined tennis courts, and speed up on the tar.
In sight of the high ranges I'll pass the turnoff to Bundook,
Hindi for musket—which it also took
to add to the daylight species here, in the prim-
al 1830s of our numbered Dreamtime
and under the purple coast of the Mograni
and its trachyte west wall scaling in the sky
I will swoop to the valley and Gloucester Rail
where boys hand-shunted trains to load their cattle
and walk on the platform, glancing west at that country
of running creeks, the stormcloud-coloured Barrington,
the land, in lost Gaelic and Kattangal, of Barandan.

The Idyll Wheel:
Cycle of a Year at Bunyah,
New South Wales,
April 1986–April 1987

An east-running valley where two hooded creeks make junction
and two snoring roads make a rainguttered cross of function:

there, each hamlet of house-and-sheds stands connected and
    alone
and the chimneys of old houses are square bottles cut from iron.

Gum forest is a solid blue cloud on the hills to the south
and bladygrass and chain rust round its every wheeltracked
    mouth.

Being back home there, where I am all my ages,
I wanted to trace a year through all its stages.

I would start after summer, to catch a subtly vernal effect
(April is also when I conceived the project).

At one poem per month, it would take a baker's dozen
to accommodate the stretch and overlap of season

into season, in any single year—
and to be real, the year had to be particular

since this wasn't to be a cyclic calendar
of miniature peasantry painted as for a proprietor.

No one can own all Bunyah. Names shouted over coal-oil lamps
cling to their paddocks. Bees and dingoes tax the cattlecamps.

As forefather Hesiod may have learned too, by this time,
things don't recur precisely, on the sacred earth: they rhyme.

To illuminate one year on that known ground
would also draw light from the many gone underground

with steel wedges and glass and the forty thousand days lost or
worked, daylight to dark, there between Forster and Gloucester.

So: as grass tips turn maroon in a further winter
I present how time revolved through the spiral of a year

average, says experience, in erosions and deposit of seeds.
I thank Rosalind Atkins, whose burin opens up further leads

into the heart of it, making the more exquisite lines—
and I thank Alec Bolton for a book that dresses ours to the
    nines.

APRIL

Leaf Spring

The long-limbed hills recline high
in Disposals khaki boiled in tankwater
or barbed-wire-tattered navy wool.
A dust of oil blues the farther air.

Crotches of black shade timber
thicken, and walled sky insets;
friezes of the one tree are repeated
along ridgelines, and the gesture of the heights

continues beneath the valley floor,
outcrops stepping toward the roofed creeks'
greener underground forest, spacing
corrugated corn flats. Contour-line by contour

cattle walk the hills, in a casual-seeming
prison strung from buried violins.
Sparse houses sit unpacked for good, each
among sheds, in its wheeltracked star.

Hobnail and elastic-side, bare and cloven feet:
you can't know this landscape in shoes, or with ideas
like relevance. It is a haughty pastoral
bent fitfully to farming's fourteen-hour days.

Disked-up ground in unseasonable heat
burns purple, and the tracks of a foam-white
longed-for watersnake are brown down every incline.
Season of smoke and parrots pecking the road,

half-naturalized autumn. Fruit is almost done
though few deciduous imports have yet decided;
no rain, and the slow tanks fill with dew;
nothing flowering, yet colour is abundant:

it is leaf spring, that comes on after heat.
The paperbark trees that suck on swampy clay
are magnified in skims of leek and sherry.
Though growth's gone out of grass, and cattle nose

green from underneath its tawny pelt,
the creek trees cluster, showered with pale expansion
from inside themselves, as if from dreams of rain;
heightening gum trees are tipped bronze and citrine

and grey-barked apple trees are misted round
with rosy blue—the aged angophora trees
that sprout from every live part of themselves
and drop their heavy death along the ground

on just such a still day here
as shade broadens south of everything
and fugitive whisky-bottle blink
and windscreen glance point the paddock air.

MAY

When Bounty is Down
To Persimmons and Lemons

In May, Mary's month,
when snakes go to sleep,
sunlight and shade lengthen,
forest grows deep,

wood coughs at the axe
and splinters hurt worse,
barbed wire pulls through
every post in reverse,

old horses grow shaggy
and flies hunker down
on curtains, like sequins
on a dead girl's ball gown.

Grey soldier-birds arrive
in flickers of speed
to hang upside down
from a quivering weed

or tremble trees' foliage
that they trickle down through.
Women's Weekly summer fashions
in the compost turn blue.

The sun slants in under things
and stares right through houses;
soon pyjamas will peep, though,
from the bottoms of trousers.

Night-barking dogs quieten
as overcast forms
and it rains, with far thunder,
in queer predawn storms;

then the school bus tops ridges
with clay marks for effort,
picking up drowsy schoolkids,
none of them now barefoot,

and farmers take spanners
to the balers, gang ploughs
and towering diesel tractors
they prefer to their cows.

The Kitchens

This deep in the year, in the frosts of then
that steeled sheets left ghostly on the stayed line,
smoked over verandah beds, cruelled water taps rigid,
family and visitors would sit beside the lake
of blinding coals, that end of the detached kitchen,
the older fellows quoting qoph *and* resh
from the Book of Psalms, as they sizzled phlegm
(some still did it after iron stoves came
and the young moved off to cards and the radio)
and all told stories. That's a kind of spoken video:

> We rode through from the Myall
> on that road of the cedarcutter's ghost.
> All this was called Wild Horses Creek then;
> you could plait the grass over the pommel
> of your saddle. That grass don't grow now.
> I remember we camped on Waterloo that night
> there where the black men gave the troopers a hiding.

The garden was all she had: the parrots were at it
and she came out and said to them, quite serious
like as if to reasonable people They are *my* peas.
And do you know? They flew off and never come back.

> If you missed anything: plough,
> saddle, cornplanter, shovel,
> you just went across to Uncle Bob's
> and brought it home. If he
> was there, he never looked ashamed:
> he'd just tell you a joke,
> some lies, sing you a poem,
> keep you there drinking all night—

Bloody cruel mongrels, telling me the native bear
would grow a new hide if you skun it alive.
Everybody knows that, they told me. I told them
if I caught any man skinning bears alive
on my place, he'd bloody need a new hide himself.

Tommy Turpin the blackfellow said to me More better
you walk behind me today, eh boss.
Might be devil-devil tell me hit you with the axe
longa back of the head. I thought he was joking
then I saw he wasn't. My word I stayed behind
that day, with the axe, trimming tongues on the rails
while he cut mortises out of the posts. I listened.

I wis eight year old, an Faither gied me the lang gun
tae gang doon an shuit the native hens at wis aitin
aa oor oats. I reasoned gin ye pit ae chairge
i the gun, pouder waddin an shot, ye got ae shot
sae pit in twa, ye'd get twa. Aweel, I pit in seven,
liggd doon ahint a stump, pu'd the trigger—an the warld
gaed milky white. I think I visited Scotland
whaur I had never been. It was a ferlie I wis seean.
It wis a sonsy place. But Grannie gard me gang back.
Mither wis skailan watter on ma heid, greetin. Aa they found
o the gun wis stump-flinders, but there wis a black scour thro
    the oats,
an unco ringan in ma ears, an fifteen deid native hens.

Of course long tongue she laughed about that other
and they pumped her about you can guess and hanging
    round there
and she said He's got one on him like a horse, Mama,
and I like it. Well! And all because of you know—

Father couldn't stand meanness.
When Uncle you-know-who
charged money for milking our cows
that time Isabel took bad
Father called him gutless,
not just tin-arsed, but gutless.
Meanness is for cowards, Father reckoned.

The little devil, he says to the minister's wife
Daddy reckons we can't have any more children,
we need the milk for the pigs. Dear I was mortified—

Poor Auntie Mary was dying Old and frail
all scroopered down in the bedclothes pale as cotton
even her hardworking old hands Oh it was sad
people in the room her big daughters performing
rattling the bedknobs There is a white angel
in the room says Mary in this weird voice And then
NO! she heaves herself up Bloody no! Be quiet!
she coughed and spat Phoo! I'll be damned if I'll die!
She's back making bread next week Lived ten more years.

Well, it was black Navy rum; it buggered Darcy.
Fell off his horse, crawled under the cemetery fence.
Then some yahoos cantered past Yez all asleep in there?
All but me, croaks Darcy. They off at a hand gallop,
squealing out, and his horse behind them, stirrups belting it.

The worst ghost I ever saw
was a policeman and (one of the squatters)
moving cattle at night.
I caught them in my headlights.
It haunted me. Every time
I went in to town after that
somehow I'd get arrested—

I'll swear snakes have got no brains!
The carpet snake we had in the rafters
to eat rats, one day it et a chook.
I killed it with the pitchfork, ran a tine
through the top of its head, and chucked it
down the gully. It was back in a week
with a scab on its head and another under its chin.
They bring a house good luck but they got no brain.

Then someone might cup his hand short of the tongue
of a taut violin, try each string to be wrung
by the bow, that spanned razor of holy white hair
and launch all but his earthly weight into an air
that breathed up hearth fires strung worldwide between
the rung hills of being and the pearled hills of been.

In the language beyond speaking they'd sum the grim law,
speed it to a daedaly and foot it to a draw,
the tones of their scale five gnarled fingers wide
and what sang were all angles between love and pride.

JULY

Midwinter Haircut

Now the world has stopped. Dead middle of the year.
Cloud all the colours of a worn-out dairy bucket
freeze-frames the whole sky. The only sun is down
intensely deep in the dam's bewhiskered mirror
and the white-faced heron hides in the drain with her spear.

Now the world has stopped, doors could be left open.
Only one fly came awake to the kitchen heater
this breakfast time, and supped on a rice bubble sluggishly.
No more will come inside out of the frost-crimped grass now.
Crime, too, sits in faraway cars. Phone lines drop at the horizon.

Now the world has stopped, what do we feel like doing?
The district's former haircutter, from the time before barbers,
    has shaved
and wants a haircut. So do I. No longer the munching hand
    clippers
with locks in their gears, nor the scissors more pointed than a
    beak
but the buzzing electric clipper, straight from its cardboard
    giftbox.

We'll sit under that on the broad-bottomed stool that was
the seat for fifty years of the district's only sit-down job,
the postmistress-telephonist's seat, where our poor great-aunt
who trundled and spoke in sour verdicts sat to hand-crank
the tingling exchange, plugged us into each other's lives

and tapped consolation from gossip's cells as they unlidded.
From her shrewd kind successor who never tapped in, and
    planes

along below the eaves of our heads, we'll hear a tapestry
of weddings funerals surgeries, and after our sittings
be given a jar of pickle. Hers won't be like the house

a mile down the creek, where cards are cut and shuffled
in the middle of the day, and mortarbombs of beer
detonate the digestion, and they tell world-stopping yarns
like: I went to Sydney races. There along the rails,
    all snap brims and cold eyes, flanked by senior police

and other, stony men with their eyes in a single crease
stood the entire Government of New South Wales
watching Darby ply the whip, all for show, over this fast colt
It was young and naïve. It was heading for the post in a bolt
while the filly carrying his and all the inside money

strained to come level. Too quick for the stewards to note him
Darby slipped the colt a low lash to the scrotum.
It checked, shocked, stumbled—and the filly flashed by.
As he came from weighing in, I caught Darby's eye
and he said *Get out of it, mug,* quite conversationally.—

AUGUST

Forty Acre Ethno

The Easter rains are late this year
at this other end of a dry hard winter.
Low clouds grow great rustling crops of fall
and all the gully-courses braid and bubble,
their root-braced jugs and coarse lips pour
and it's black slog for cows when, grass lake to puddle,
a galloping dog sparks on all four.
It'll be plashy England here for a while
or boggy Scotland, by the bent straw colour
and the breaks of sun mirror-backed with chill.

Coming home? It was right. And it was time.
I had been twenty-nine years away
after books and work and society
but society vanished into ideology

and by then I could bring the other two home.
We haven't been out at night since we came
back, except last month, in the United Kingdom.
The towns ranged like footlights up the highway
and coastline here rehearse a subtle play
that's only staged in private by each family.

Sight and life restored by an eye operation
my father sits nightly before the glass screen
of a wood-burning slow combustion stove. We see
the same show, with words, on television.
Dad speaks of memories, and calls his fire homely:
when did you last hear that word without scorn
for something unglossy, or some poor woman?
Here, where thin is *poor*, and fat is *condition*,
"homely" is praise and warmth, spoken gratefully.
Its opposite lurks outside in dark blowing rain.

Horses are exposed to it, wanly stamping out
unglazed birth ware for mosquitoes in the coming season
and already peach trees are a bare wet frame
for notional little girls in pink dots of gingham.
Cars coming home fishtail and harrow the last mile,
their undersea headlights kicking gum trees around eerily;
woodducks wake high in those trees, and peer from the door
they'll shove their ducklings out of, to spin down in their down,
sprawl, and swim to water. Our children dog the foot-
steps of their grandfather, learning their ancient culture.

SEPTEMBER

Mercurial

Preindustrial haze. The white sky rim
forecasts a hot summer. Burning days
indeed are rehearsed, with flies and dinnertime fan,
but die out, over west mountains
erased with azure, into spring-cool nights
and the first flying insects
which are the small weeds of a bedroom window.

Early in the month, the valley was a Friesian cow:
knobbed black, whitened straw.
Alarming smokes bellied up behind the heights of forest.
Now green has invested fires'
fixed cloud-shadows; lower gum boughs are seared chestnut.
Emerald kingparrots, crimson-breasted, whirr
and plane out of open feed sheds.

Winds are changeable. We're tacking.
West on rubbed blue days,
easterlies on hot, southerly and dead calm for rain.
Mercury is near the moon, Venus at perigee
and frogs wind their watches all night on swampy stretches
where waterhens blink with their tails at dusk, like rabbits
and the mother duck does her cripple act.

Dams glitter like house roofs again.
The first wasp comes looking for a spider to paralyse:
a flimsy ultralight flier
who looks like a pushover, but after one pass lifts
you, numb, out of your trampoline. Leaves together
as for prayer or diving, bean plants erupt
into the grazing glory. Those unnibbled spread their arms.

Poddy calves wobbling in their newborn mushroom colours
ingest and make the pungent custard of infancy.
Sign of a good year, many snakes lie flattened
on the roads again. Bees and pollens drift
through greening orchards. And next day it pours rain:
smokes of cloud on every bushland slope,
that opposite, wintry haze. The month goes out facing
     backwards.

OCTOBER

Freshwater and Salt

It's the opening of the surf season
thirty miles away east;

most things speak a different dialect
over there on the coast.

Here, the rising wave comes as
grass. The animals drink it
thirstily. It's a sweetwater ocean.
If your house is fenced in, it'll sink it.

Fire and snakes swim in it;
you have to slash and mow.
Time for rotary blades, and weeping salt water
with your whole skin as you make them go.

It isn't in fact such a whelming
tide. But it's an ever-swelling one
you have to keep in balance, like the Dutch.
Much worse when it doesn't run

and even the cities are stranded
by the fresh sea they're really built on,
the shark-free, drown-you-quick, money-devious
child not of moons but the sun.

Between us and the saltwater breakers
there's that rind, too, of chip-frying city
twelve thousand miles long, that locals
will come home from soon with gritty

trunksful and running shoes full
of ground bottle, ground coral, ground shell.
I guess we're all flesh of that shell
and will broach it by New Year, and wade gingerly

up to our nacres in salt swirl,
even we freshwater pearlers
and privately pale herbage hurlers
happiest on the grassed forms of groundswell.

The Misery Cord
IN MEMORY OF F. S. MURRAY

Misericord. The Misery Cord.
It was lettered on a wall.
I knew that cord, how it's tough to break
however hard you haul.

My cousin sharefarmed, and so got half:
half dignity, half hope, half income,
for his full work. To get a place
of his own took his whole lifetime.

Some pluck the misery chord from habit
or for luck, however they feel,
some to deceive, and some for the tune—
but sometimes it's real.

Milking bails, flannel shirts, fried breakfasts,
these were our element,
and doubling on horses, and shouting Score!
at a dog yelping on a hot scent—

but an ambulance racing on our back road
is bad news for us all:
the house of community is about
to lose a plank from its wall.

Grief is nothing you can do, but do,
worst work for least reward,
pulling your heart out through your eyes
with tugs of the misery cord.

I looked at my cousin's farm, where he'd just
built his family a house of their own,
and I looked down into Fred's next house,
its clay walls of bluish maroon.

Just one man has broken the misery cord
and lived. He said once was enough.
A poem is an afterlife on earth:
Christ grant us the other half.

DECEMBER

Infant Among Cattle

Young parents, up at dawn, working. Their first child can't
be his own babysitter, so as they machine the orphaned milk
from their cows, he must sit plump on the dairy cement,
the back of his keyhole pants safetypinned to a stocking

that is tied to a bench leg. He studies a splotch of cream,
how the bubbles in it, too thick to break, work like
the coated and lucid gravels in the floor. On which he then dings
a steel thing, for the tingling in it and his fingers

till it skips beyond his tether. As the milkers front up
in their heel-less skiddy shoes, he hangs out aslant
on his static line, watching the breeching rope brace them
and their washed udders relieved of the bloodberry ticks

that pull off a stain, and show a calyx of kicking filaments.
By now the light stands up behind the trees like sheet iron.
It photographs the cowyard and dairy-and-bails in one vast
buttery shadow wheel on the trampled junction of paddocks

where the soil is itself a concrete, of dust and seedy stones
and manure crustings. When his father slings a bucketful
of wash water out the door, it wallops and skids
and is gulped down by a sudden maw like the cloth of a radio.

Out and on out, the earth tightens down on the earth
and squeezes heat up through the yellowing grass
like a surfaceless fluid, to pool on open country,
to drip from faces, and breed the insect gleams of midday.

Under the bench, crooning this without words to his rag dog,
he hears a vague trotting outside increase—and the bull
erupts, aghast, through the doorway, dribbling, clay in his curls,
a slit orange tongue working in and out under his belly—

and is repulsed, with buckets and screams and a shovel.
The little boy, swept up in his parents' distress, howls then
but not in fear of the bull, who seemed a sad apparition:
a huge prostrate man, bewildered by a pitiless urgency.

JANUARY

Variations on a Measure of Burns

When January is home to visit her folks
and official work is a public hoax,
soy sprouts dotting the serpentine strokes
    ploughs combed in the lacquered
hill soil that each afternoon's rainstorm soaks
    weave a green jacquard

and zucchini and wart squash and Queensland Blues
(not the dog, but the pumpkin) squeak together like shoes
in tractor trailers, and nectarines bruise
    from being awaited,
but the grizzled haze over mountain views
    looks faintly methylated

because Drought, who's in on every forced sale,
though he may have seen the farmers granted bail
this summer, has the continent in his entail.
    Even smashed, he's seen you:
that old man up a back road fumbling his mail
    gets letters from El Niño.

Disappointment, holiday and heatwave shilly-shally
round this snaky time of year. Stock prices plunge and rally
but the government's retreated for keeps from this valley:
    the flash brick erstwhile
Whitlam toilet block lacks its school, and stands orphaned
        on its gulley;
    the PO's a closed file.

We retain a public phone and some dirt main roads
on whose corners part-time squatters tip sprawling loads
of gravel for drunk drivers who for lifetimes and by codes
    like Whoa car! and hug-the-crown
miraculously get home to treat their families like toads
    or finish upside down

    in the dark, miles from town,
standing on my scalp with the rain's sparks falling upward,
    windscreen a collective noun,
delighted by the spinning tyre slowing above the cupboard
and the glare-path through inverted trees—myself as I could
have been, through brutal labour for a bare livelihood,

    myself on that quest
few families dare acknowledge, let alone go with you on,
    the hunger for the Rest
when mortgage world time politics, everything's on top of one
and the teenage girl you married is not months but decades
    gone:
I'm sorry for myself in his sideburns and cardigan.

    O he will like that,
murmurs his wife, wrestling farm accounts, steering above the
    rocks,
then bundling the children off to bed, switching off the box:
    Television makes you fat!
Our concern cuts away at once. Moorhen and flying fox
outside creak identical rusty keys in their vocal locks
    and the dark stands pat.

FEBRUARY

Feb

        Seedy drytime Feb,
        lightning between its teeth,
        all its plants pot-bound.

        Inside enamelled rims
        dams shrink their mirroring shields,
        baking the waterlilies.

Days stacked like clay pigeons
squeezed from dust and sweat.
Two cultures: sun and shade.

Days dazed with actuality
like a bottle shot
sniping fruit off twigs,

by afternoon, portentous
with whole cloud-Atlantics
that rain fifteen drops.

Beetroot and iron butter,
bread staled by the fan,
cold chook: that's lunch with Feb.

Weedy drymouth Feb, first cousin of scorched creek stones,
of barbed wire across gaunt gullies, bringer of soldered
death-freckles to the backs of farmers' hands. The mite-struck

foal rattles her itch on fence wires, like her mother,
and scraped hill pastures are grazed back to their charred
bulldozer stitchings. Dogs nip themselves under the tractor

of needy Feb, who waits for the raw eel-perfume
of the first real rain's pheromones, the magic rain-on-dust
sexual scent of Time itself, philtre of all native beings—

Lanky cornhusk Feb,
drilling the red-faced
battalions of tomatoes

through the grader's slots:
harvest out of bareness,
that semidesert mode.

Worn grasshopper month
suddenly void of children;
days tucking their tips in

with blackberry seeds to spit
and all of life root-bound;
stringy dryland Feb.

Masculeene, Cried the Bulls

Bang! it was autumn,
right on the first of the month,
cool overcast after scorchers
and next day it poured.

Four and a half inches
of rise in the dams, of wet in garden soil:
we know how long you were, rain,
four and a half deep inches.

As fresh green abolished
this summer's only white-blond month
the first autumnal scents
were ginger and belladonna

and as beds resumed their blankets
at the mopoke hour, bulls sang.
Among cattle, the more masculine
the higher the voice is pitched.

Our pumpkins took
first prize at Nabiac Show,
where a horse named Danielle
pirouetted, and posed on a tub,

and men raced through solid timber
backwards, with aimed steel strides,
and we met the Anglo-Nubian
tree-climbing goat, maker of,

and sheep of, the desert.
This was the weekend after clocks

jerked the sun an hour forward,
and all the time, leafage

of various winebottle colour
sprouted on the roses and lemon trees
and dew twinkled for longer
on the lengthening paddocks.

APRIL

The Idyll Wheel

And so we've come right round the sun
to April again. It's unique again
like each month, each year. Much less of summer
reached April this year. Yet grass burgeoned after Easter
and fenced cultivations rug up, blue and tan.

The sliding fit of month to season
sees more frogs bronze-backed now than green
and old fruit trees declare themselves
along creekbanks in russet and fawn
like cedars long ago spied from a mountain.

The seasons used to blur, or so we dream,
on the wheel of an idyll, before we came.
An idle wheel, we said, and lashed
the years to make them a driving wheel.
Idylls were idols, thefts of time.

But an idyll of land had brought us here
in ships from the far side of the year.
In the evening of our youth we'd stand
in good broad cloth, the spokes of one hand
on our belly, beneath oaks of a vast idea,

for *idyll* derives from *eidos*, form.
It too shapes cityscape and farm.

And the farms once made, they live by touches,
a stump burning, a scooped dam, new wire stitches
and unstated idylls had driving to and from.

So, into blue dimensionless as an ideal
with a Y-tipped prop our neighbour hoists the unreal
statures, flat and wet, of her whole family
for her glance and the warm sun to re-fill
above the pleats and rare flickers of their hill
where her old father tinily moves, keeping busy.
The idyll wheel is the working wheel.

INDEX OF TITLES

Abomination, The, 22
Absolutely Ordinary Rainbow,
   An, 29
Action, The, 117
Anthropomorphics, 173
Aqualung Shinto, 93
Art History: the Suburb of
   Surrealls, 219
Artery, The, 63
Aspects of Language and War on
   the Gloucester Road, 284
At Min-Min Camp, 265
At the Aquatic Carnival, 240
At Thunderbolt's Grave in Uralla,
   268
Away-bound Train, The, 7

Ballad of Jimmy Governor, The
   48
Ballad Trap, The, 33

Bats' Ultrasound, 260
Bent Water in the Tasmanian
   Highlands, 180
Birds in Their Title Work
   Freeholds of Straw, 59
Blood, 20
Boetian Count, The, 69
Boöpis, 74
Breach, The, 89
Broad Bean Sermon, The, 115
Buladelah-Taree Holiday Song
   Cycle, The, 141
Burning Truck, The, 3
Bush, The, 68
Butter Factory, The, 259

C19-20, The, 177
Canberra Remnant, The, 37
Canberra Suburbs' Infinite
   Extension, The, 96

Cardiff Commonwealth Arts
    Festival Poetry Conference
    1965, Recalled, The, 139
Chimes of Neverwhere, The, 209
China Pear Trees, The, 248
Commercial Hotel, The, 27
Commonwealth of Manu, The, 65
Company, 105
Conquest, The, 45
Cowyard Gates, 159
Craze Field, The, 164
Creeper Habit, 133
Cumulus, 228
Cycling in the Lake Country, 106

Death Words, 65
Dialectic of Dreams, The, 220
Discontent, Reading Conan
    Doyle, 85
Doorman, The, 172
Dream of Wearing Shorts Forever,
    The, 237
Driving Through Sawmill Towns,
    11
Driving to the Adelaide Festival
    1976 via the Murray Valley
    Highway, 140
Drugs of War, The, 246

Easter 1984, 232
Edge of the Forest, The, 118
Edgeless, The, 245
Elegy for Angus Macdonald of
    Cnoclinn, 155
Employment for the Castes in
    Abeyance, 137
Equanimity, 182
Escaping Out There, 102
Euchre Game, The, 120
Evening Alone at Bunyah, 13
Extract from a Verse Letter to
    Dennis Haskell, 280

Fastness, 254
Feb, 305
Federation Style on the Northern
    Rivers, 229
Fire Autumn, The, 34
First Essay on Interest, 169
Fishermen at South Head, The,
    171
Flight from Manhattan, The, 176
Flood Plains on the Coast Facing
    Asia, 224
Flowering Eucalypt in Autumn,
    208
Flying-fox Dreaming, The, 122
Folklore, 83
For a Jacobite Lady, 166
Forest Hit by Modern Use, The,
    184
Forty Acre Ethno, 298
Four Gaelic Poems, 151
Free Kirk Cemetery, Northern
    New South Wales, 151
Freshwater and Salt, 300
Fuel Stoppage on Gladesville
    Road Bridge in the Year 1980,
    174
Future, The, 158

Gallery, The, 134
Gōlōka, 76
Grandmother's Story, The, 277
Grassfire Stanzas, The, 167
Gum Forest, The, 153

Hall's Cattle, 72
Hayfork Point, 34
Hearing Impairment, 267
Helicopter View of Terrestrial
    Stars, A, 55
Homage to the Launching-place,
    168
Hypogeum, The, 203

Idyll Wheel: Cycle of a Year at Bunyah, New South Wales, April 1986–April 1987, The, 290
Idyll Wheel, The, 308
Ill Music, 19
Immigrant Voyage, 160
Immortal, An, 204
Incendiary Method, The, 28
Incorrigible Grace, 58
Infant Among Cattle, 303
Infra Red, 271
International Poetry Festivals Thing, The, 199
Inverse Ballad, 273

Joker as Told, 275
József, 81

Kiss of the Whip, 101
Kitchens, The, 294
Knuckle Garden, The, 84

Lachlan Macquarie's First Language, 120
Laconics: The Forty Acres, 132
Lake Surnames, The, 262
Lament for the Country Soldiers, 44
Late Snow in Edinburgh, 218
Leaf Spring, 291
Letters to the Winner, 247
Line, The, 279
Lips Move During Anointing, The, 88
Little Boy Impelling a Scooter, 201
Lotus Dam, 264
Louvres, 243

Machine Portraits with Pendant Spaceman, 195
Man with the Hoe, The, 282
Masculeene, Cried the Bulls, 307
Max Fabre's Yachts, 281
Mercurial, 299
Megaethon: 1850, 1906–29, The, 251
Midsummer Ice, 188
Midwinter Haircut, 297
Milk Lorry, The, 258
Misery Cord, The, 302
Mitchells, The, 121
Morse, 217
Mouthless Image of God in the Hunter-Colo Mountains, The, 212

Names of the Humble, The, 61
New Moreton Bay, The, 173
1980 in a Street of Federation Houses, 256
Nocturne, 263
Noonday Axeman, 5
Novilladas Democráticas, 71

On the Wreckage of a Hijacked Airliner, 102
Once in a Lifetime, Snow, 23

Physiognomy on the Savage Manning River, 233
Plainclothes Park, 85
Poetry and Religion, 272
Poley Bullock Couplets, 69
Police: Seven Voices, The, 84
Portrait of the Artist as a New World Driver, 104
Powerline Incarnation, The, 126
Princes' Land, The, 17

Public Figure, A, 277
Pure Food Act, The, 75

Quality of Sprawl, The, 186
Quintets for Robert Morley, 179

Rainwater Tank, 157
Recession of the Joneses, The, 178
Recourse to the Wilderness, 25
Relics of Sandy, 274
Retrospect of Humidity, A, 207
Returnees, The, 128
Roman Cage-cups, 260
Rostered Duty, 87

Sanskrit, 59
Satis Passio, 222
Second Essay on Interest: the
    Emu, 205
Self-portrait from a Photograph,
    202
Senryu, 33
Sergeant Forby Lectures the
    Cadets, 91
Shower, 185
Sidere Mens Eadem Mutato, 111
Skirl for Outsets, A, 152
Sleepout, The, 242
Smell of Coal Smoke, The, 211
SMLE, 50
Spring Hail, 9
Spurwing Plover, 131
Steel, The, 189
Stockman Songs, 67
Swarm, The, 151
Sydney and the Bush, 127
Sydney Highrise Variations, The,
    174

Tanka: The Coffee Shops, 134
Their Cities, Their Universities, 97
Thinking About Aboriginal Land
    Rights, I Visit the Farm I Will
    Not Inherit, 97
Three Interiors, 215
Three Poems in Memory of My
    Mother, Miriam Murray née
    Arnall, 188
Time Travel, 214
Toward the Imminent Days, 38
Troop Train Returning, 19
Tropical Window, 242

Variations on a Measure of Burns,
    304
View of Sydney, Australia, from
    Gladesville Road Bridge, 175
Vindaloo in Merthyr Tydfil, 55
Visiting Anzac in the Year of
    Metrication, 123
Vol Sprung from Heraldry, The,
    250

Walk with O'Connor, A, 31
Walking to the Cattle Place, 59
Weights, 188
When Bounty Is Down to
    Persimmons and Lemons, 292
Widower in the Country, The, 4
Working Men, 31
Writer in Residence, 276

Young Woman Visitor, The, 277

INDEX OF FIRST LINES

A car is also, 104

After the last gapped wire on a post, 153

After the war, and just after marriage and fatherhood, 247

A grog-primed overseer, who later died, 173

All day above the Japanese fleet, 93

All the air conditioners now slacken, 207

A long narrow woodland with channels, reentrants, ponds, 140

And entering on the only smooth road, 229

And so we've come right round the sun, 308

As we were rowing to the lakes, 128

At the hour I slept, 59

August, and black centres expand on the afternoon paddock, 167

A winter's day of wind, and no horizon, 31

Axe-fall, echo and silence. Noonday silence, 5

Bang! it was autumn, 307

Beanstalks, in any breeze, are a slack church parade, 115

Beasts, cattle, have words, neither minor nor many, 65

Beckoner of hotheads, brag-tester, lord of the demi-suicides, 204

Below the moveable gardens of this shopping centre, 203

Beside the odd gene, 274

Beyond the Divide, 19

Brisbane, night-gathered, far away, 263

Childhood sleeps in a verandah room, 242

CI: the detectives. After the age of belief, 85

Citizens live in peace and honour, 96

Coming out of reflections, 74

Dark stars that never fire, 271

Days of asphalt-blue and gold, 27

Dazzling blue eyes, 34

Dear Dennis, 280

Dream harbours Sin, and Innocence, and Magic, 220

Dried phlegm of lakes, 106

Eavesdropping rain, 37

Elites, levels, proletariat, 222

Empty rings when tapped give tongue, 157

Excavate, at a constant curving interval, 260

Farmer Cleve, gent., of the Hunter, 251

Fence beyond fence from breakfast, 61

Flashy wrists out of buttoned grass cuffs, feral whisky burning gravels, 180

Floodwater from remote rains has spread out, 245

Foiled hunters sulk homewards at dusk, 131

From the metal poppy, 185

Gelibolu, Chanakkale, 123

Going to Rubuntja, the cattle-train. Banging two trailers, 67

Grandfather's grandfather rode down from New England, 273

Hearing loss? Yes, loss is what we hear, 267

Hitching blur to a caged propeller, 224

How did the Oriental, 102

How many times did the Church prevent war, 209

Hungry that year, 28

I am a policeman, 89

I am listening for words the eldest, 254

I am older than my mother, 189

I am seeing this: two men are sitting on a pole, 121

I farmed in the land, 151

If this picture has survived, 202

I'll get up soon, and leave my bed unmade, 4

In Cardiff, off Saint Mary's Street, 101

I never heard such boasting, 277

In May, Mary's month, 292

In 1980, in a street of Federation houses, 256

In the afternoon, a blue storm walloped and split, 265

In the banana zone, in the poinciana tropics, 243

In the city of Cargo, 84

In the hanging gorges, 33

In the high cool country, 11

I saw from the road last time, our house, 159

Is it possible that hyper-, 179

I stand in a house of trees, and it is evening, 7

It began at dawn with fighter planes, 3

It is patience and stalks in the wide house of cattle, 63

It is possible the heights of this view are a museum, 176

I travel a road cut through time, 284

It's the opening of the surf season, 300

It was built of things that must not mix, 259

I was a translator at the Institute, 137

I was good at the Common Room game, 276

January, heat. Raw saplings stand like cattle, 50

John Brown, glowing far and down, 211

Just a few times in your life, you speak, 277

Just for a moment, 65

Just two hours after, 33

Leaves from the ancient forest gleam, 17

Left wing, right wing, 250

Little boy on a wet pavement, 201

Long before dawn, I rose by Paddy's Lantern, 22

Lorenzini's, Vadim's, 134

Lotus leaves, standing feet above the water, 264

Maudie, 69

Midmorning, September, and red tractors climb, 38

Misericord. The Misery Cord, 302

My cousin loved the violin, 19

My father, widowed, fifty-six years old, 13

My wife came out on the *Goya*, 160

Nests of golden porridge shattered in the silky-oak trees, 182

Night, as I go into the place of cattle, 75

Not a latch or lock could hold, 275

Not owning a cart, my father, 188

Not usury, but interest. The cup slowed in mid-raise, 169

Now that the west, 122

Now the milk lorry is a polished submarine, 258

Now the world has stopped. Dead middle of the year, 297

Old Poley, pin bullock. The round one has left me slack here, 69

Old Warwick, the husband, scratched his head, 91

On a stone wall, adrift from their hive, 151

On Bennelong Point, 133

On vinegar and sour fish sauce Rome's legions stemmed avalanches, 246

Opium and vitriol and a plug of twist, 279

Out of the Fifties, a time of picking your nose, 111

Outside the serious media, the violence of animals, 173

Out through a long bright window, 242

Phillip was a kindly, rational man, 45

Pig-crowds in successive, screaming pens, 20

Pleasure-craft of the sprung rhythms, bed, 168

Preindustrial haze. The white sky rim, 299

Proud heart, since the light of making lace, 166

Religions are poems. They concert, 272

Remember how I used, 188

Repeatedly out of grazed plateaux, the Dividing, 228

Saint Vincent de Paul, old friend, 58

Seedy drytime Feb, 305

Seeing the telegram go limp, 31

Sleeping-bagged in a duplex wing, 260

Snow on the day before Anzac, 218

So drunk he kept it at tens—and the bloody thing lost, 120

So we're sitting over our sick beloved engine, 174

Sprawl is the quality, 186

Stale pasture, midsummer, 134

Starting a dog, in the past-midnight suburbs, for a laugh, 212

Stopped, 88

That slim creek out of the sky, 208

"The boss at home, Missus?" A man couldn't tell suitors from buyers, 68

The bulldozer stands short as a boot on its heel-high ripple soles, 195

The Easter rains are late this year, 298

The edge of the forest, hard smoke beyond the paddocks, 118

The fancy rider sent his Texan boots, 71

The first night of my second voyage to Wales, 55

The forest, hit by modern use, 184

The Governor and the seer are talking at night in a room, 120

Their speech is a sense of place, 76

The king of honour, louder than of England, 44

The long-limbed hills recline high, 291

The man applying rules to keep me out, 172

The mansard roof of the Barrier Industrial Council's, 215

The men of my family danced a reel with sugar, 97

The New England Highway was formed, 268

The Nineteenth Century. The Twentieth Century, 177

The oldest tree in Europe's lost, 155

The people are eating dinner in that country north of Legge's Lake, 141

The power of three China pear trees, 248

There are rental houseboats down the lakes now, 262

There is nothing about it. Much science fiction is set there, 158

There's that other great arch eastward, with its hanging highways, 175

The sea smooths a page of its folio, 152

These lagoons, these watercourses, 164

The walls of the country this year, the forest escarpments, 34

The word goes round Repins, 29

The worldwide breath of Catching Up, 178

They have walked out as far as they can go on the prow of the continent, 171

Thinking about air conditioning's Willis Carrier, 282

Thinking my old old thought in the eye-stinging dark, 85

This deep in the year, in the frosts of then, 294

This is for spring and hail, that you may remember, 9

This is the hour the Crucified Bludger is fed, 87

Those conventions of the trade, 199

Three a.m., Tiger Bay. In the only, 139

To break the Judaeo-Christian mould was his caper, 277

To go home and wear shorts forever, 237

To revisit the spitfire world, 214

Towards the end of the long Australian peace, 25

Towers of swell fabric, 281

Tuckett. Bill Tuckett. Telegraph operator, Hall's Creek, 217

Turn slowly in fields, 55

Two racing boats seen from the harmonic railing, 240

Upasara, the heifer after first mating, 59

Upwind on Sandy creek, cooking, 72

Walking on that early shore, in our bodies, 233

Watching from the barn the seedlight and nearly-all-down, 97

Weathered blond as a grass tree, a huge Beatles haircut, 205

We dreamed very wide awake, 219

We have bought the Forty Acres, 132

We have spoken of the Action, 117

What are the sights of our town, 83

When I ran to snatch the wires off our roof, 126

When January is home to visit her folks, 304

When Sydney and the Bush first met, 127

When we saw human dignity, 232

Where two or three, 105

Winters at home brought wind, 23

With clutch-slip and tappet-noise, 102

You can send for my breakfast now, Governor, 48

Young parents, up at dawn, working. Their first child can't, 303

You ride on the world-horse once, 81

A Selected List of Titles Available from Minerva

While every effort is made to keep prices low, it is sometimes necessary to increase prices at short notice. Mandarin Paperbacks reserves the right to show new retail prices on covers which may differ from those previously advertised in the text or elsewhere.

The prices shown below were correct at the time of going to press.

☐	7493 9137 5	**On the Eve of Uncertain Tomorrows**	Neil Bissoondath	£5.99
☐	7493 9050 6	**Women In A River Landscape**	Heinrich Boll	£4.99
☐	7493 9921 X	**An Instant in the Wind**	Andre Brink	£5.99
☐	7493 9147 2	**Explosion in a Cathedral**	Alejo Carpentier	£5.99
☐	7493 9109 X	**Bodies of Water**	Michelle Cliff	£4.99
☐	7493 9060 3	**Century of the Wind**	Eduardo Galeano	£4.99
☐	7493 9080 8	**Balzacs Horse**	Gert Hofmann	£4.99
☐	7493 9093 X	**The Notebook**	Agota Kristof	£4.99
☐	7493 9174 X	**The Mirror Maker**	Primo Levi	£4.99
☐	7493 9143 X	**Parents Worry**	Gerard Reve	£4.99
☐	7493 9172 3	**Lives of the Saints**	Nino Ricci	£4.99
☐	7493 9003 4	**The Fall of the Imam**	Nawal El Saadawi	£4.99
☐	7493 9924 4	**Ake**	Wole Soyinka	£5.99
☐	7493 9139 1	**The Four Wise Men**	Michel Tournier	£5.99
☐	7493 9092 1	**Woman's Decameron**	Julia Voznesenskaya	£5.99

All these books are available at your bookshop or newsagent, or can be ordered direct from the publisher. Just tick the titles you want and fill in the form below.

Mandarin Paperbacks, Cash Sales Department, PO Box 11, Falmouth, Cornwall TR10 9EN.

Please send cheque or postal order, no currency, for purchase price quoted and allow the following for postage and packing:

UK including BFPO — £1.00 for the first book, 50p for the second and 30p for each additional book ordered to a maximum charge of £3.00.

Overseas including Eire — £2 for the first book, £1.00 for the second and 50p for each additional book thereafter.

NAME (Block letters) ....

ADDRESS ....

....

☐ I enclose my remittance for ....

☐ I wish to pay by Access/Visa Card Number

Expiry Date